The Diablo Diary

Joseph Belli

ISBN: 1516909445
ISBN 13: 9781516909445
Library of Congress Control Number: 2017902486
CreateSpace Independent Publishing Platform
North Charleston, South Carolina

Contents

Introduction

In *East of Eden*, John Steinbeck wrote, "The Salinas was only a part-time river...it was not a fine river at all, but it was the only one we had and so we boasted about it...you can boast about anything if it's all you have."

All I had was the Diablo Range. The Diablos have neither the grandeur nor the charismatic wildlife of the Rockies. They lack the majesty of the Sierra Nevada and the Bohemian chic of the Santa Cruz Mountains. Though millions watch the sun rise over its ridges and drive along its flanks on Highways 5 and 101, the range is practically anonymous. Ask someone to identify it, and you'll typically get an answer that's inaccurate (Mount Hamilton Range), vague (Coast Range), or most likely, a shoulder shrug. Technically it comprises California's Inner Coast Range south of San Francisco Bay, running from its namesake mountain in the north to the Paso Robles Highway in the south, nearly two hundred miles long and thirty or so miles wide. Lying east of the Santa Clara and Salinas Valleys, it forms the western boundary of the San Joaquin Valley. It has few inhabitants, and no one vacations there. Lacking lakes, rivers, towering peaks, with scant snowfall, no national forest, and relatively little public land, the mountains remain an afterthought. After crossing the range in 1776, Spanish explorer Juan Bautista de Anza christened them *Sierra del Chasco*—Mountains of the Joke. If the Salinas is only a part-time river, then the Diablo Range must seem like half-grown mountains. But they were the mountains I knew; they were all I had.

When I was three years old, my family moved from an east San Jose cul-de-sac to a home on six acres where the suburbs met those mountains. I grew up there and discovered nature, beginning modestly in the yard with katydids and salamanders before radiating outward to a half-feral orchard of deer and alligator lizards. Our family didn't camp or travel much. Instead, my curiosity was stoked by books, and I became fascinated with the American West: its prairies, deserts, forests, mountains, and especially its wildlife. I dreamed of such places in states like Montana, Arizona, Colorado, and New Mexico while growing up. When I was a teenager, my dad leased a ranch nearby, and suddenly thousands of acres were open for me to explore. True, they harbored no grizzlies, wolves, or bighorn sheep, but there were mountain lions, elk, and the remote possibility of a wayward California condor. I wanted to live on such a property. Aldo Leopold wrote, "There are those who can live without wild things, and those who cannot." I had become one of the latter.

But land is expensive, and a ranch like that was out of the question. I eventually came across a small parcel along Pacheco Pass, but years would pass before I could live there. In the meantime, I headed for the mountains as often as I could and kept a journal—the "diary" alluded to in the title of this book. I spent six years surveying ponds and streams at Henry W. Coe State Park for California red-legged frogs, which led me to pursue a degree in conservation biology at San Jose State University.

When at last I moved up into the mountains in 2005, I was finally where I wanted to be. Then something unusual happened: I developed an urge to write. Why, I'm not completely sure. Aside from several letters to the editor, I'd never written much of anything that I hadn't been assigned. But I had something to say, something about a sense of place. That place was the Diablo Range.

For me, nothing evokes a sense of place like the wild things that call it home. One of the cruel truths about developing an appreciation of nature is that you come face-to-face with the stark reality that so much is in peril. As I wrote, that cursed knowledge spilled all over the pages of this book.

In March 2006, I completed the first essay, "Stolen Beauty," which featured horned lizards and the threat posed by collecting. In telling the stories of animals, I often found myself confronting large-scale environmental problems. Thus, many essays are polemics, but they're not all anger and woe; there's appreciation, wonder, humor, and even a bit of hope. Some drifted away from the

Diablo Range, while later essays focused less on natural history than on the human element, cheery topics such as isolation and mortality.

Time has passed since I wrote many of the essays, and on some the information has become outdated. For example, the essay on California condors presents the number of condor deaths due to lead poisoning as of 2005, a fraction of what it is now. Likewise, the essay on the Panoche Valley solar farm reflects conditions as they were in 2013, and much has happened since then. I chose to leave the essays as they were originally written rather than rewrite them or insert footnotes.

When I started on the first essay, I had no plan to write anything other than a little piece on horned lizards. I certainly didn't intend to write a book. And while it may have begun as a catharsis—there's something satisfying about expressing yourself on paper—I always felt as if I were writing beyond myself, to an unknown audience. Before I finished the first essay, I found another topic. And another. I believed these were stories that needed to be told, even if the saga of San Carlos Creek, San Benito County's coyote control program, and Ishi's plight had been covered elsewhere. Similarly, there's no shortage of writings on condors, grizzly bears, or mountain lions, but I believed I had something novel and important to add. And outside research papers, no one was writing about Western gray squirrels, San Joaquin kit foxes, or California tiger salamanders. They deserved an audience, too.

I wanted each essay to be the best it could be, to hit it out of the park. Writing is an intensely disciplined and isolating task, and I ventured into some dark places to draw out what I needed to say. And although writing is a solitary chore, it is nothing if not a way of connecting. If these essays make you think, that's great. If they make you feel, that's even better. Thanks for reading.

Joseph Belli, Pacheco Pass, February, 2017

An Itch I Had to Scratch

Contracting a Wondrous Malady

IT WAS SPRING, 1972, and there was no better time to be a boy. While the nation at large was still reeling from the turbulence of the 1960s, the world beyond seemed remote. Even the Vietnam War seemed like an abstraction; it had been going on so long I couldn't remember a time of peace. More worrisome to me was a recent spate of murders in California, committed by the likes of the Manson Family and the Zodiac Killer, who for all anybody knew was still at large. Yet so much was good in the world, and all you needed to do to confirm that was turn on the radio. Don McLean's epic "American Pie" had just ended a lengthy run at the top of the charts; there was "Day after Day" by Badfinger, "Heart of Gold" by Neil Young, "A Horse with No Name" by America, and two gems by Elton John, "Tiny Dancer" and "Rocket Man." As spring yielded to summer, the airwaves pulsed with "Brandy" by Looking Glass, "Take It Easy" by the Eagles, "Layla," Clapton's masterpiece, "Tumbling Dice" by the Rolling Stones, and "The First Time Ever I Saw Your Face" by Roberta Flack. Back then, listening to the radio was one of life's two simple pleasures. The other was exploring outdoors.

Seven years earlier, my family had moved from an east San Jose cul-de-sac into a ranch-style house at the base of the foothills near Alum Rock Park. To the west were the suburbs of San Jose and the sprawling Santa Clara Valley; south lie the foothills of the Diablo Range—steep, grassy hillsides punctuated by remnant apricot orchards. North of us was a residential development, a white-collar neighborhood less posh than those on the west side of the valley overlooking Saratoga and Los Gatos, while in the east rose the Diablo Range, climbing two thousand feet above the valley floor.

Our home sat on six sloping acres. Surrounding the house was an orchard—not a commercial orchard but rather a labor of love fashioned by the man who built the house. He planted a variety of fruit trees, spaced at a generous distance, that were organic long before the term came in vogue, for they were never sprayed or fertilized. In fact, they weren't even watered. Those trees made do on rain.

That orchard, left in a state of benign neglect, was my sanctuary. In spring, I gorged on loquats; in summer I plucked honey-sweet apricots, plums, and white peaches, and in fall, tart tangerines and juicy oranges. Fruit, however, was always secondary to the other wonders in the orchard. Downed logs on the orchard's edge were home to both slender and arboreal salamanders during the damp winter. In summer, those same logs housed alligator lizards and fence lizards. Patches of milkweed grew in the summer, covered with orange and black milkweed bugs and monarch butterfly caterpillars. Flocks of quail scuttled back and forth between the brush at the bottom of the property and the trees surrounding the house. Ground squirrels and rabbits occupied the orchard's edge, while ring-necked pheasants hid in the tall grass. Hawks and vultures circled overhead by day, and at twilight, if you sat still, you could watch as deer made their way down the hillside. Often I would go out to see the sun set over the Santa Cruz Mountains or watch the full moon rise over the western flank of the Diablo Range.

The horizon over which that moon rose was a scene of sublime pastoral beauty, an open, undulant ridge featuring three rounded summits so symmetrical you'd swear they were polished. Atop the northernmost rose a weathered wooden fencepost. While I knew that somewhere beyond lie the Central Valley, Sierra Nevada, and the rest of the country, it was hard to imagine anything beyond that horizon, and if someone had told me that ridge was the end of the earth, I might well have believed him or her. By the time summer arrived, I had developed an itch I had to scratch. Our six-acre orchard was wonderful, but those hills were beckoning to me. I had to go and stand atop that ridge, touch the old fencepost, and see what lie beyond.

A group of friends who lived in the nearby residential development aided and abetted that venture. I was held in high regard because I had an orchard for a backyard, but while I may have lived on a choice piece of land, I had led a sheltered life. While I spent time in the orchard, they were off exploring the world beyond, the nooks and crannies of Alum Rock Park and the mountains surrounding it. They had not only been to the top of the ridge I so obsessed over, they were willing to take me there.

We had no day packs, sunscreen, trail mix, or even water bottles. We just opened the front door and started walking. Rather than follow roads, we took shortcuts, wandering through the spacious backyards of one homeowner after another. Passing beyond the residential area, we arrived at Crothers Road, a two-lane country road that was the end of the line as far as pavement was concerned. The next paved road was twenty rugged miles away, in San Antonio Valley. Crossing the road, we skirted carefully around an antiquated white farmhouse that had seen better days.

"Why are we crouching and whispering?" I asked.

"We gotta keep out of sight. We can't let Mean Man Moe see us."

"Who's Mean Man Moe?"

"The meanest sonofabitch in east San Jose. Last time I was up here, he brought out his pellet gun and shot me with rock salt!"

"You're so full of shit your eyes are brown!" refuted another member of the group.

"Full of shit, huh? Look at this…" Rolling up his pant leg, he revealed a blemish that according to him was a scar, a war wound he proudly displayed as testimony to his run-in with the old codger.

At length we came upon a barbed wire fence, which we crawled under. This was the property boundary, and we all breathed easier once we passed beyond the domain of Mean Man Moe. The top of the ridge was in plain view, though more distant than it appeared. Before the hour had passed, I was standing at the top, touching the very fence post I beheld so often. I was struck by the silence. I had never experienced such profound quiet before. I stared in awe at my surroundings. To the north lay the southern arm of San Francisco Bay and the spires of downtown San Francisco, fifty miles distant. To the west sat the broad expanse of the Santa Clara Valley, smothered with roads and buildings, yet wonderfully silent from my vantage point. To the southeast, the gleaming alabaster domes of Lick Observatory shone in the sunlight atop Mount Hamilton. That mountain had attained a mythical status in our minds, the kind of aura Mount Olympus exerted over the Greeks. Besides being the highest mountain in the Bay Area, it was also home to a sequestered community of astronomers who slept by day and observed comets, stars, planets, and maybe even UFOs at night. That it frequently bore a mantle of snow in winter while the rest of us endured the monotony of rain further explains why we held Mount Hamilton in such reverence.

Yet it was the land to the east that held the most mystery, for behind the ridge plunged a steep, wooded canyon, the Arroyo Aguague, more wild and rugged than anything I had seen in my young, sheltered life. I had scratched one itch, only to develop another.

Over time, those friendships melted away like snowflakes in sunlight, as adulthood scattered us far and wide. In 1995, I returned, moving into a small second residence on the property. Yet much had changed. The orchard, never assiduously tended, had lost many of its fruit trees. Oaks and elderberry took root, reclaiming a hillside from which they had been banished. The animal life had changed as well—the ground squirrels and cottontails were gone—so too were the pheasants, supplanted by wild turkeys. The quail and deer seemed as plentiful as ever, so I could take at least some consolation in that. But the orchard had lost its wonder, for a chain-link fence now stood around the perimeter, making it seem isolated from the mountains nearby.

Worse was the glut of recent development on the hillside to the south. Where once meadowlarks gurgled their flutelike songs, a series of trophy homes stood. They were oversize, gaudy, and landscaped with exotic plants. A dozen such monstrosities carpeted the hillside, facing west in lemminglike conformity, with a commanding view of Silicon Valley. Along with the houses came lights piercing the darkness and sounds: revving engines, barking dogs, stereo systems, and parties lasting into the wee hours. I didn't hold any personal malice toward those people, but I bristled at what those homes symbolized to me—the flaunting of wealth, a disregard of, and disconnect from, the surrounding land. How many of those homeowners, I wondered, loved the countryside surrounding their home?

My gut feeling is that those homes could have been built anywhere, as long as they had a view and were removed from the riffraff.

The transformation of that hillside troubled me, but it was more than just a "there goes the neighborhood" feeling that we experience when we return to a place from our past to find it altered. It left me confronting my childhood fallacy, the belief that I grew up in the country, when in truth the place I called home was merely a suburb. If what inspired me in my youth was an illusion, did that mean that the feelings and beliefs born out of that were illegitimate? How could a place that once held such importance now have no meaning? Did it change, or did I?

I was struggling with those questions one afternoon while driving up Crothers Road. As I drove, I realized something absent. When I was a boy, my friends and I were always outdoors. Today, things are different. I rarely notice kids playing in the street, and I never see them hiking the hillsides. Maybe parents these days are more restrictive. But I have a feeling that, with the advent of video games, personal computers, and cell phones, kids are choosing to remain indoors, and that worries me. Exploring outdoors is one of the best things about childhood. Missing out on that is bad both for kids and the environment.

I slowed down when I got to the old house where Mean Man Moe lived. I felt the urge to park the car and walk to the top of the ridge again, but I had long since dropped wanton trespassing from my repertoire of outdoor activities. I couldn't relive my childhood, but I wanted to hike that blessedly unchanged hillside with an adult's eyes. A quarter-century had passed, yet I still had an itch to scratch, a wondrous malady I contracted from a childhood outdoors. It's led me all over the Diablo Range in search of creatures great and small. How could I ever question something so good?

Searching for Dan'l Webster

Finding Irony Pursuing the California Red-Legged Frog

TOWARD THE END of the Civil War, an aspiring young writer named Samuel Clemens settled for a time just outside the gold mining town of Angel's Camp. During his stay in the Sierra Nevada foothills, Clemens penned a short story, "The Celebrated Jumping Frog of Calaveras County." The tale recalled an event that took place years earlier, recounted to Clemens by a local bartender. It featured a character named Jim Smiley, an inveterate gambler who had a frog named Dan'l Webster that he trained to jump, which he did with great prowess, so much so that Smiley was certain no frog could jump farther. Shortly thereafter a stranger arrived. The newcomer was unimpressed with Dan'l Webster and told Smiley that any ordinary frog could outjump his. Smiley could not believe his good fortune in coming across such a rube, and the two agreed to hold a contest, wagering on the outcome. The stranger, who did not have a frog, allowed Smiley to pick one for him, which he did after searching a nearby creek. But while Smiley was gone, the man pried open Dan'l Webster's mouth and filled it with shotgun pellets. When Smiley returned, the jumping contest started, but Dan'l Webster couldn't move, costing Smiley forty dollars.

That story is significant for two reasons. One is that it was the first published piece written by Clemens, who would soon rise to fame under the pen name Mark Twain. The second is that the frog in question must have been a California red-legged frog, for at the time no other frog in the state could jump like that. Jeremiah may have been a bullfrog but not Dan'l Webster; he was a red-leg.

The California red-legged frog (*Rana draytonii*) is the West's largest native frog. Striking creatures, they come in a variety of colors: chocolate brown, concrete gray, orange, and crimson. Dark blotches are also common, though not in any pattern, and some frogs are more blotched than others. Their namesake feature is a wash of salmon-red on the bottom of the thigh. They inhabit ponds, lakes, wetlands, marshes, creeks, and slow-flowing streams. Historically, they ranged from Northern California to Baja California, from the coast across the Central Valley and into the foothills of the Sierra Nevada. I mention the historical range because, like many amphibians, the California red-legged frog isn't found where it used to be anymore, having disappeared from about 75 percent of the waterways it formerly occupied. It may be gone from Southern California and is known from a meager handful of sites in the Sierra Nevada foothills. It has not been sighted in the Central Valley, where it must have been abundant in the once-glorious wetlands, since 1960. Its stronghold is the mountains along the coast, but remnant populations persist inland, including in the Diablo Range.

The decline of the California red-legged frog dates back to the Gold Rush, when hydraulic mining began degrading streams in the Sierra Nevada foothills. The draining of creeks and wetlands began shortly thereafter in the Central Valley, as the land was converted to agriculture. Like ducks and tule elk, red-legged frogs were decimated by market hunting, for frog legs were delicacies featured in restaurants in the burgeoning cities of Sacramento and San Francisco. With the red-legged frog population dwindling, people brought in bullfrogs from the Midwest and attempted to raise them for profit. Bullfrog farming, however, wasn't so simple. While tadpoles can be reared on algae, once transformed, they require live prey. Alas, there is no Purina Frog Chow. Large frogs also eat smaller ones, another obstacle to profits. As a consequence, would-be frog farmers set their charges free, and in short order they spread far and wide, with negative consequences for native amphibians. Large, fecund, and voracious, bullfrogs have a reputation for swallowing any live prey they can cram down their throats, including ducklings and mammals as large as young mink. Bullfrogs likely contributed to the decline of red-legged frogs not only by preying on them but also by outcompeting them for food. California was also inundated with nonnative fish, introduced to enhance sport fishing. This was also devastating to red-legged frogs, which then had another predator to deal with. As California's human population rose, frog habitat diminished as land was cleared and drained for development. Later, factors such as increased UV radiation and pesticides may have contributed to the decline of the California red-legged frog.

As a boy, I knew the red-legged frog only through field guides. Although it was present in the Diablo Range, I had never encountered it during my jaunts along either Penitencia Creek or Coyote Creek. In 1993, I was walking along a stream on Pacheco Pass when I noticed a frog jump into the water, where it dived and took refuge beneath a rock. Trapping it against the stone, I plucked it out of the depths. Because it lacked an eye stripe, I saw that it was not a Pacific chorus frog (*Pseudacris regilla*). I thought it might be a foothill yellow-legged frog (*Rana boylii*), but when I turned it over, I saw red rather than yellow on the bottom of its thighs. So this, I thought, was the famous California red-legged frog. To be honest, that particular creature did not make much of a first impression. It was smaller than I expected, and its appearance was nondescript. I would later learn that this was a juvenile that had yet to acquire the vivid color and impressive size of adults.

Later that year, I became a volunteer at Henry W. Coe State Park. Lying in the heart of the Diablo Range, Coe's extensive holdings supported an impressive assemblage of native flora and fauna. The park had recently acquired twelve thousand acres along its southern flank, and volunteers were enlisted to conduct a resource inventory. My study area contained three ponds, and I found red-legged frogs at two of them. When I informed the project coordinator, he was taken aback. While red-legged frogs were known to inhabit the park, their presence had been little documented. Someone suggested the park be surveyed for this species, which at the time was in the process of being listed under the Endangered Species Act. That planted a seed.

Several years later, I was back at the creek on Pacheco Pass. It was October, and the streambed was mostly bone-dry, yet here and there, small pools persisted. At the base of a culvert beneath the highway was a pool of water the size of a sandbox, with a mat of duckweed on its surface. Hidden and shaded by willows, it was the type of small, inconspicuous place you could pass by hundreds of times without noticing, a tiny gem of habitat amid the detritus left behind by addled road warriors.

I made my way toward the edge of the pool when something caught my eye. It was a large frog, five inches long, and it was orange! Its back was sprinkled with dark blotches, giving it a color much different from any I'd ever seen on a frog before. I was hooked.

Searching for things outdoors has appealed to me on a primal level since childhood, when I was forever peering under logs and stones to see what might be underneath. I loved creeks, with the abundance of life along the banks and in the water. Later, when I began hiking alone, I was usually out searching for some kind of critter. So, surveying ponds suited me well, even though I'd never undertaken anything like it before. Surveying ponds would also provide important data on habitat use and distribution of the park's aquatic amphibians.

What's the best way to survey the ponds of Coe Park? I planned to use a dip net to scoop up tadpoles and identify them. That task would need to be executed during a brief time frame, however. The optimal time to survey in Coe is from early spring to early summer. Before April, the eggs of several species may not have hatched. Start in June and both Western toads (*Bufo boreas*) and California tiger salamanders (*Ambystoma californiense*) may have already transformed and left the pond. Since the park contains over one hundred ponds, the project would take several years to complete.

Since some species bask along the shore, I also planned to walk the perimeter of each pond. I even pondered diving in deeper ponds like a freshwater Jacques Cousteau. That never materialized, for most ponds are either murky or rife with vegetation.

Long before I entered the water, though, there were bureaucratic hurdles to overcome. Using a net to capture tadpoles, however briefly, is considered a form of take, which is not allowed in a state park for native species, not allowed in California for a number of sensitive species, and not allowed by the federal government for species protected under the Endangered Species Act. As a consequence, I needed to apply for collecting permits from three different agencies: California Department of Parks and Recreation, California Department of Fish and Game, and the US Fish and Wildlife Service. I hoped to begin in spring of 2000. However, the permit approval process took nine months, and I didn't get out into the field until April, 2001.

One of the charms of Coe Park is that, despite its impressive size—roughly ninety thousand acres—no paved road pierces its interior. Its dirt roads are hold-overs from before the park was established and are little driven. Nowadays, they primarily serve mountain bikes. During the survey, the park allowed me to drive those roads, quite an advantage. Driving would enable me to spend more time surveying and less time walking from pond to pond, many of which are miles apart. Yet I was reluctant to drive; I worried about having car problems in the backcountry, and I didn't feel right driving past backpackers who were trying to distance themselves from civilization. I also believed that by walking, I would experience more than I ever could inside a vehicle. Some ponds, though, were twenty miles away, so I reached a compromise: I would hike to ponds within ten miles of trailheads; for more remote locations, I would drive to designated areas and walk from there.

I gave up on backpacking early on when I realized that the extra equip-ment and weight were more trouble than they were worth. I was already lugging field equipment; adding a sleeping bag, tent, and food made me feel like a pack animal. Meanwhile, the unwieldy minnow net, though not heavy, could not be disassembled. Although it was a godsend in the water, it was a six-foot-long alba-tross while hiking, for I had to hold it.

When I first envisioned the survey, I pictured myself brandishing my net in ponds teeming with life, surrounded by meadows of wildflowers undulat-ing in the breeze. In reality, I usually found myself toiling under less appealing conditions.

The first variable to go awry was the weather. Despite its reputation as a land lacking seasons and blessed with perpetual sunshine, California weather isn't quite so simple. While it's true that hardly any rain falls between May and October, early spring can be full of surprises. I surveyed in hailstorms with temperatures in the forties, and when you're in waist-deep water without waders with a stiff breeze blowing, the effects of the cold are magnified. Shrinkage is the least of your problems. On the other extreme were heat waves with triple-digit temperatures, absolutely miserable conditions to hike in.

As for the ponds, they varied greatly. Most were under an acre, though a few were considerably larger. Some were shallow and prone to drying early, sometimes before summer. Others were deeper and held water year round. Some were ringed with cattails, while many were covered with algae or pondweed. Operating a net through such vegetation was frustrating and physically demanding. While most ponds were easily located, I sometimes spent hours trying to find obscure ponds in remote sections of the park. Some days were spent on long sojourns to ponds that no longer exist. Some had their dams breached. Others had silted up. Documenting the demise of a pond was useful information, but it was still anticlimactic to walk miles to find that out.

Once I arrived at a pond, I began by slowly walking around the shore. This caused frogs to take to the water, and as they did, I could often identify them. If the water was clear, I might see tadpoles well enough to identify species. I used binoculars to scan mats of algae and pondweed on the surface, since turtles, bullfrogs, and red-legged frogs frequently basked there. Turtles were easy to recognize; their protruding heads resembled thumb-size periscopes. The two frog species were considerably more difficult. Basking frogs feature a pair of bulging eyes resting just above the surface, like pint-size alligators. To tell a basking bullfrog from a red-legged frog, the gods of lighting and distance would need to be on my side. For all their color variations, red-legged frogs don't come in shades of green. Thus, any green frog was a bullfrog. When colors were hard to detect, I tried looking at the frog's back. If I saw a fold of skin running down each side, it was a red-legged frog. The technical term for this is a dorsolateral fold, prominent in red-legged frogs but absent in bullfrogs. Field conditions often thwarted my ability to identify frogs. Sometimes, the glare of the sun rendered colors less discernible. The frogs themselves were often in no mood to cooperate. Notoriously skittish, they had a maddening habit of submerging just as I approached close enough for a good view. Getting a good look at the back was doubly difficult, since basking frogs are determined to face a would-be threat.

Bullfrogs can often be identified by sound. Bullfrogs are named for their loud bellow, which males emit during breeding season. When surprised on shore, they often squawk loudly as they leap into water, and that sound is enough to identify a bullfrog, for red-legged frogs leap silently. However, bullfrogs don't always vocalize when leaping, so I couldn't just assume that a frog jumping quietly was a red-legged frog.

After walking around the pond, I took to the water. Hiking boots and socks were removed and replaced with more appropriate footwear. At first, I used plastic sandals, but most ponds contained a thick, muddy bottom that adhered to those sandals as if they were suction cups. I avoided using waders for the same reason. As much as I valued the protection that sandals afforded, they were too much of a hindrance, so I opted to survey commando-style, barefooted. I would rue this decision many times when stepping on submerged pine cones, but my mobility was greatly enhanced. What I most feared was stepping on a giant water bug (*Lethocerus americanus*). These imposing insects, which can grow to a length of three inches, are capable of inflicting a very painful bite. Though I often saw them in the water and caught them in the net, I never did get bitten. By the end of each survey season, it looked as if something had taken hold of my feet. The mud and detritus did not wash off easily, making them resemble those of Howard Hughes in his later years. Eventually, I bought a pair of lightweight aquatic shoes that protected my feet without hampering my mobility.

Once in the water, I relied heavily on the net. For it to be most effective, it helped to be in water no more than waist deep. After each scoop, I lifted the net just above the water's surface, leaving the bottom submerged. Once I identified whatever amphibians were present, I inverted the net, releasing its contents.

The fine mesh netting was effective at containing all but the smallest organisms. Besides giant water bugs, there were nymphs of dragonflies and damselflies, as well as water boatmen and backswimmers. Some ponds contained an abundance of snails and various small, mysterious-looking arthropods. I occasionally caught leeches, and they sometimes caught me. Upon removing them, I was surprised by both the lack of sensation I felt and the copious amount of blood that flowed. I saw why they were used in medical practice; I'd give blood weekly if they used leeches rather than needles.

Amphibian larvae were the focus of my netting. There are six species of pond-breeding amphibians in the park. Larval salamanders and newts differ markedly from those of frogs and toads, for they hatch with all four limbs present. Two such species, the California newt (*Taricha torosa*) and the California tiger salamander, inhabit the park. Of the two, newts were by far the more common. Newt larvae were easily distinguished from tiger salamander larvae by the dark stripes down their back and their smaller size. Tiger salamander larvae were uncommon and restricted to the southwest section of the park. Their solid color and small eyes, which seemed entirely out of proportion to the size of their head, identified them. As they grow, they exceed four inches in length, becoming much larger than larval newts.

Of the four species of frogs and toads present, the most common was the Pacific chorus frog. Their tadpoles are easy to identify: when viewed from above, their eyes are situated along the outlines of the head, like a Dr. Seuss character. Less common were Western toad tadpoles. These were dark, almost black, and small. They often congregate in dense schools along the shore, forming teeming masses in the shallows.

The final two species, California red-legged frogs and bullfrogs, were harder to tell apart as tadpoles. Unfortunately, field guides were of little help. Several mentioned an iridescent, reddish wash on the abdomen of red-legged frog tadpoles, but this varies widely among individuals, so I didn't place much emphasis on that. For the sake of accuracy, I needed to tell the two apart, since red-legged frogs are fully protected while bullfrogs are an unwanted nonnative invasive. Early on I was struggling with this. I mentioned to a friend that I planned to contact a particular amphibian expert and ask for his help. I thought this was a pretty straightforward approach, but for my friend, who happened to know this biologist, it was fraught with peril.

"His time is valuable. Keep your questions short and to the point. And limit yourself to two questions."

Two questions, I thought. *If I rub a magic lamp, maybe I'll be granted a third.*

"One more thing. You didn't get his number from me."

At that point, I wondered whether or not I had made it clear that I was merely trying to contact a biologist, not conjure up an appointment with the Wizard of Oz.

In the end, I decided against approaching anyone who might view me as a nuisance, so I tried to answer my questions through field experience. Soon I came across a reliable trait: red-legged frog tadpoles show a faint, broken yellow line down each side of the back; bullfrog tadpoles don't.

Once I finished surveying a pond, which could take anywhere from fifteen minutes to several hours, I recorded my findings. I noted which species were present, estimated the size of the pond, how prone it was to drying, the amount of aquatic vegetation present, and the clarity of the water. I wondered if certain types of ponds were associated with particular species and if some species were more likely to be found with others. California tiger salamanders were more likely to inhabit murky water; bullfrogs were generally absent from ponds that dried regularly. Yet of all the patterns that emerged, the clearest was the negative correlation between fish and amphibians. If fish were present, amphibian larvae were almost always absent. Fish were originally stocked before the park was established, when the ponds were under private ownership. The park's policy is to allow fish populations to sustain themselves if they can. The park does not restock or transplant fish, which is encouraging, but they don't eradicate them, either. Of the more than one hundred ponds in the park, I found fish in twenty-one, including several that were thought to be fish-free, evidence that people had been illegally stocking fish. At first glance this may not seem like such a grave transgression, but were you to take a net into a pond full of fish, you would be shocked at the lack of amphibians. While I found tadpoles at some ponds where fish were present, they were few and far between. And even though adult frogs use such ponds as habitat, in terms of breeding sites, those ponds are population sinks, for fish consume both tadpoles and egg masses. More often than not, I failed to net a single tadpole at a pond containing fish, as beneficial to larval amphibians as chlorinated swimming pools.

By 2004, with three surveying seasons under my belt, I had surveyed most of ponds in the park. Ranger Barry Breckling suggested I broaden the study by exploring creeks, so I spent 2004 searching the park's streams.

Surveying creeks proved to be quite different from surveying ponds. Creek surveying was less systematic—I simply followed a stretch of creek and noted what I saw. Because the water in the streams was clear, there was no need to lug my cumbersome net, so at least one piece of equipment could be jettisoned during creek forays. That was a relief, for creek surveying was physically demanding.

Traveling to ponds, I was usually able to follow a trail most of the way. I had no such luxury when following creeks. Some narrowed through canyons too steep to walk around, leaving wading through the creek as the only alternative. There were fallen logs, boulders, and slick rocks to deal with. The most difficult creeks were those with steep descents. At times I spent more effort traveling through such terrain than in surveying.

Despite the clarity of creek water, amphibian identification was still problematic. A frog perched on the bank could be one of four species, each with a different status. All but one have the habit of diving to the bottom when alarmed and are adept at either taking refuge under stones or lying well-camouflaged against the substrate. If I failed to spot a frog before it entered the water, my chances of seeing it again were considerably lessened.

One day while surveying Coyote Creek, I surprised a frog sunning itself on the pebble-strewn bank. When it dived beneath a stone, I captured it. When I opened my hands, I was disappointed to find a juvenile bullfrog. Bullfrogs were not particularly common in the streams of the park, and this frog presented me with an ethical dilemma. While I firmly believe that bullfrogs should be eradicated for the good of native frogs, it's one thing to advocate eradication and another to implement it. My ethical crisis had less to do with taking the life of an animal than with causing undue suffering. While holding the squirming frog, I recalled John Goodman's character in the movie *O Brother Where Art Thou?*, the slick-talking, bible-peddling con artist who callously picked up a leopard frog and crushed the life out of it in his beefy, unrepentant hand. However I ended this creature's life, it would have to be done humanely. I spied a large boulder twenty feet away. If I hurled the frog toward it with all the force I could muster, it would surely perish painlessly. Or would it? Reluctantly, I let it go, but I took no pride in doing so.

For six years I surveyed the park and logged nearly a thousand miles on foot, and while this made the survey more time-consuming than it needed to be, I wouldn't have done it any other way. I encountered roadrunners, phainopeplas, poorwills, bald eagles, sharp-tailed snakes, horned lizards, gray foxes, tule elk, and mountain lions. I was treated to scenic vistas, stunning wildflowers, and tranquil silence broken only by the sound of the wind in the trees or the calls of birds. I learned the value of empirical observation honed by hours of fieldwork. Though it afforded me plenty of physical exercise, I appreciated the mental exercise I got from trying to understand and explain what I found, and I came to realize that the act of answering one question invariably spawned others.

For example, the most puzzling aspect of creek surveying was what I didn't see. Not once, in the many miles of streams I followed, did I see a red-legged frog tadpole. Their absence baffled me. I had always assumed that red-legged frogs bred in the park's streams. Why were they not present? It didn't appear as if toxins or pollutants were to blame, since the creeks showed a healthy diversity of life. Certainly, the presence of rainbow trout and Sacramento pikeminnows (*Ptychocheilus grandis*), both native predatory fish, could account for the lack of tadpoles in some locations, but those fish weren't found in all streams, and where they were absent, I still did not find red-legged frog tadpoles. Bullfrogs could also be ruled out, for they didn't have much of a presence in the park's streams.

The first explanation that came to me was this: red-legged frogs breed in winter and deposit egg masses shortly thereafter. However, during January, February, and March, creeks frequently swell in the wake of heavy rains. Perhaps at that time there is too much water, or more precisely, the water is too turbulent. Rushing waters could scour streams and destroy egg masses.

If red-legged frogs didn't breed in the creeks, where did they breed in the past? The park's ponds aren't natural features; they were constructed by ranchers relatively recently. Before then, did red-legged frogs breed in streams? If so, did they discover the ponds later and experience such success there that stream breeding fell by the wayside? Or does the truth lie elsewhere? Perhaps the red-legged frog originally inhabited the valley floor only and is a relative newcomer to the park. As ranchers constructed ponds, perhaps red-legged frogs used them as breeding sites and expanded their range into the mountains by colonizing ponds one by one. That, after all, is how bullfrogs invaded the ecosystem. There are ironies galore here: a native species expanded its range using artificial habitat (man-made ponds), just before losing the lion's share of its original habitat to development. Those ponds became a saving grace, for without them the frog would be gone from much of its already reduced range. Yet that new habitat was created without the least bit of thought attached to the fate of the red-legged frog; those ponds were constructed for cattle, the same plodding creatures that erode stream banks and degrade riparian areas.

Further irony: in Calaveras County, the annual frog-jumping contest held in Angel's Camp has become a spectacularly successful event, one the chamber of commerce latches on to like a wino to a bottle of port. Sections of sidewalk in the quaint, historic downtown section are inscribed with the names and distances of each year's champion, though it is unlikely any of those victorious frogs were of the red-legged variety. Calaveras County, so integral to the historical and cultural significance of the California red-legged frog, had lost its population by 1970. When the US Fish and Wildlife Service designated critical habitat for the frog, no land in Calaveras County was included. Some were disappointed with that decision, since it implied that the frog would not be restored to the region. Others, including some supporters of the frog jump, were relieved, for as an endangered species, the California red-legged frog had become a pariah. Because of that protection, the frog could not be captured, much less entered into any jumping contest, and plans to bring the California red-legged frog back to Calaveras County were met with opposition. Meanwhile, bullfrogs had become the darlings of frog-jump aficionados. Bullfrogs, being larger, can jump farther and have no regulatory protections. I sat through an entire competition, consuming several corn dogs in the process, and saw no other species. Yet without the California red-legged frog, Twain would have written no story, for bullfrogs had yet to be released in California during his time in Gold Country. Without that story, the main claim to fame for Calaveras County would not exist, and the tradition of the frog jump would never have started. It seems to me that Calaveras County owes a lot to the California red-legged frog; was it asking too much of the county to support its return? Apparently so.

Then one fall afternoon, two local children noticed some frogs in a pond on the family ranch. They captured one and showed it to their parents, who were puzzled. They contacted a herpetologist, who verified that the frogs were California red-legged frogs, not seen in those parts for over thirty years and presumed gone for good. Best of all, the family supported conservation efforts and pledged to maintain frog habitat on their property. One way or another, the California red-legged frog had returned to Calaveras County, if indeed it was ever truly gone. The story of the California red-legged frog is complex. I don't know if, in its ironies, it is worthy of Shakespeare, but I believe Mark Twain would have relished it thoroughly.

Stolen Beauty

The Curse Borne by the Horned Lizard

SOME THINGS NEVER cease to take your breath away, no matter how often you view them: a scenic vista, a striking painting, a stunning photograph. Hopefully, you have something in your life fitting that description. If you are truly blessed, you have found this attribute in another person. Not me. I have horned lizards.

Horned lizards are found exclusively in North America, where thirteen species inhabit the dry and semiarid lands stretching from Mexico to southern Canada. The United States harbors eight species, from the Pacific Coast to Missouri. While some areas can claim as many as four species, here in the Diablo Range, there exists only one, *Phrynosoma blainvillei*, the coast horned lizard. This species is unique among horned lizards for they, romantic devils, have been known to mate face-to-face. Or so I've heard.

What the coast horned lizard has in common with other horned lizards is its primary defense strategy. With rounded bodies and a waddling gait, horned lizards can't rely on speed like whiptails or scale trees in the manner of fence lizards. Unlike Western skinks, they don't have detachable blue tails to distract predators. They don't find refuge in holes in the ground, like side-blotched lizards, and lacking the formidable jaws of alligator lizards, they can't rely on biting their enemies. Horned lizards bet on camouflage.

This is not to say that horned lizards lack a plan B. They also hiss, bite, scurry away, and squirt blood out of their eyes. The latter tactic is not often used against people; it's estimated that blood squirting is used in only 5 percent of human/lizard interactions. Several intrepid souls whose curiosity I applaud have sampled the blood and report it to be tasteless. *Bon appetit.*

What's interesting is that horned lizards employ different strategies based on the predator they encounter. Horned lizards tend to run from rattlesnakes. Rattlers are slow and don't chase prey; they ambush, strike, and track down the victim later. Running from a rattler, then, is sound strategy. However, when approached by fast snakes like racers, they remain motionless, relying on camouflage.

Blood squirting they reserve primarily for members of the dog family, which react negatively to the taste of horned lizard blood. I've come across horned lizards dozens of times, yet the most dramatic response I've received has been a good hissing. I'm due for a squirt.

My first outdoor encounter with a horned lizard took place at Henry W. Coe State Park, during the inaugural Backcountry Weekend. There was a ceremony taking place, and a politician making a speech; I left the crowd and hiked up County Line Road, where I spied a horned lizard scurrying across the dirt. I scooped it up and gazed upon a creature resembling a miniature dinosaur, a tiny ankylosaurus, a relic from the Cretaceous. Large reddish spikes protruded from the back of its head; thorny scales ringed the perimeter of its earth-tone body, while its belly was a brilliant lemon yellow. The lizard didn't ruin the moment by biting or smearing excrement on my palm. No blood was shot my way. It just sat there, resigned to its fate. Before letting it go, I advised it to lay low for the weekend.

Several years ago I took my sons on a trip to the Southwest. Although the primary purpose of the trip was to soak up a part of the country we'd never visited before, a close second reason—for me, anyway—was a chance to search for lizards in the desert. Near Saint George, Utah, we saw a long-nosed leopard lizard, as well as a chuckwalla. In Zion National Park, we found collared lizards that rose and ran on their hind legs. We scoured gravel washes in Big Bend, where we came upon beautiful earless lizards. Outside Tucson, we explored Saguaro National Park and Buenos Aires National Wildlife Refuge, yet for all that searching, we didn't spot a single horned lizard. Shortly after we returned, they came along on a survey outing in Coe Park, where we found a horned lizard at the base of an ant colony. We had just spent days exploring three different deserts, home to as many as five different species of horned lizard but had come up empty. We returned home, walked half a mile, and—presto! There's a Chinese proverb in there somewhere, but I don't recall it.

It's not that easy to find coast horned lizards these days, and unfortunately, it's not due to camouflage. Of the eight species of horned lizards inhabiting the United States, none has lost more ground than the coast horned lizard. Urban and suburban developments have wiped out large swaths of habitat, while agricultural expansion has also played a large role in the lizard's decline. Besides habitat loss, coast horned lizards are threatened by an insidious foe that is but a fraction of their size: Argentine ants (*Iridomyrmex humilis*).

Argentine ants are native to South America. They found their way to the United States in the early twentieth century, though precisely how is unclear. Perhaps they arrived with coffee shipments or tropical plants imported for nurseries. However they came, once present they took a liking to California, settling in most everywhere people did. Their favorite haunts are suburbia, and they would almost certainly fly below the radar of most people were it not for their habit of invading homes. If you live in California, you're well acquainted with them. Unlike fire ants, there is no danger of being bitten by them. Their threat lies in their pervasiveness. If you should leave anything remotely edible lying around, heaven help you. You can call a pest control company, and they'll take your money to come out and spray, and the ants will disappear—for a while. But inevitably they'll return.

What does all this have to do with horned lizards? After all, horned lizards eat ants. Shouldn't more ants mean more lizards? Well, no, not in this case. Horned lizards, for some reason, find Argentine ants unpalatable. To make matters worse, Argentine ants, though small, are an aggressive lot, displacing the native ants that comprise so much of the coast horned lizard's diet. Though not federally protected, coast horned lizards are recognized in California as a Species of Special Concern.

In 1881, a store owner in Pasadena with a passion for taxidermy put several mounted horned lizards on display and promptly sold out. That man, William

Blakely, went on to establish a lucrative career in the curio business, becoming the horned lizard's arch nemesis. For almost forty years, Blakely paid gatherers for each horned lizard they brought him. One year, that total exceeded eight thousand. Blakely dispatched the lizards in a jar of chloroform before stuffing and mounting them. It was estimated that, before hanging up his scalpel for good, Blakely had sold in the neighborhood of 115,000. That's a disgustingly astonishing number of stuffed lizards. Most were coast horned lizards, the only species present in the Los Angeles basin. After his charges decimated the population around Pasadena, they had to travel farther abroad and, in doing so, collected desert horned lizards (*Phrynosoma platyrhinos*) in the Mojave Desert. This overexploitation was devastating to coast horned lizards in Southern California, even if urbanization would have eventually sealed their fate. In the 1930s, California banned the sale of stuffed horned lizards, though by then Blakely had "retired." As for live specimens, well, that was another matter.

There are a number of species whose existence in the wild has been jeopardized by collectors. Parrots and parakeets from Central and South America have had their wild populations decimated by the pet trade. In the United States, there are plants that have been driven to rarity through the overzealous efforts of collectors, though reptiles as a group seem to be most impacted. There is an entire menagerie of colorful snakes, unusual lizards, and at least one species of turtle in decline due to overcollecting. Yet if there were one creature that could serve as the poster child for this, horned lizards—with their universal appeal—would be it. They suffer the curse of charisma—too charming for their own good.

What makes the collection of horned lizards tragic is that they rarely last long in captivity. They require a steady supply of live prey and can be notoriously finicky. I suspect that most captive horned lizards die from starvation. The pet trade has adversely affected every one of the eight species of horned lizard in the United States. Coast horned lizards have been protected from collecting since 1981.

When I was a boy, a friend returning from a ranch east of Mount Hamilton brought me back a horned lizard. I remember preparing a terrarium. Then, details get a little fuzzy. After all, that was thirty years ago. In a feat of absentmindedness worthy of Inspector Clouseau, I somehow managed to lose the lizard inside the house. I never did find it. For weeks I felt there would be impending hell to pay when Mom found the lizard, dead or alive. But she never did. I'd like to think the little fellow did what it does best: remained hidden until it could safely make a dash for freedom. Once outdoors, I hope the lizard avoided a host of threats—scrub jays, cats, and automobiles—and was able to subsist on spiders, pillbugs, and earwigs in the suburban foothills east of San Jose. Not likely.

I have a further confession. I am a recovering petaholic. I had a predilection for acquiring pets, but not just any pets. Dogs, cats, goldfish, guinea pigs, noble beasts all, didn't excite me. My pets were wild things, and I had ample opportunity to indulge in that pursuit, growing up on six acres where the suburbs ended and the wildlands started. As if I needed further incentive, the property included an aviary, a holdover from the eccentric whims of the previous owner. That aviary was as spacious as a master bedroom and became home to quite a few furred and feathered creatures, while reptiles and amphibians were housed in terrariums.

Eventually, my passion for possessing wild things ceased. I can't trace it to any specific incident, but looking back I don't think it's a coincidence that as I got older and began venturing outdoors, my desire to capture wild creatures diminished. Maybe it was because I observed them in their settings. Captive animals lost their luster, becoming poor substitutes for those in the wild. A photograph became superior to a captive animal, and I came to realize that I could neither capture nor seize beauty. Perhaps it is that sentiment that drives people to make pets out of ocelots or mount trophy heads on walls. I understand the strong pull involved; I just can't buy into it anymore. My last pet was a tiger salamander I found while mowing the lawn. I can't see myself taking an animal from the wild again.

A horned lizard in its element, under a bright blue sky in some natural area, is a treasure. One languishing in a terrarium has had its beauty stolen, robbed by confinement, for only captivity can render it ordinary.

They Shall Take Up Serpents

A Snake for Everyone!

THERE'S AN ACCESS road off the main highway by my place, an undersize two-lane that long ago lost whatever median stripe it once had. It courses alongside a nameless seasonal stream, following the contours of the land, descending a gentle canyon in serpentine fashion. It's a beautiful pathway, shaded here and there by oaks. Years ago, this quaint ribbon of asphalt served as the highway over Pacheco Pass. At present, it's become obsolete, and the old highway is no longer a public road, belonging to and maintained by a small group of us living near the top of the pass. Winter storms bring rock slides and fallen trees, yet several neighbors have heavy equipment and do an admirable job clearing the road. Lately, however, I've noticed a more ignoble example of community service: someone is running over snakes, and it's hard to believe it isn't intentional. No one can drive that road in broad daylight and fail to notice a snake crossing the path.

Of all Earth's creatures, none are as feared, loathed, and misunderstood as snakes. Sharks and grizzly bears may frighten people but not as intensely as snakes do. Wolves are intensely detested but mainly by a small segment of the populace—livestock owners and big game hunters. Household pests—rats, mice, and cockroaches—are held in dim view, but they're seen as disgusting party crashers rather than objects of genuine fear. Spiders probably come closest to inspiring the same irrational fear, but even they are spared the wanton violence directed toward snakes. People squish spiders and poison them with Raid.

They wad them up in toilet paper and flush them on a journey to the afterlife. But all of these methods constitute a quick and painless death. Nobody tortures spiders, and once outside the confines of a home, no one goes out of their way to kill them. We seem to have an unspoken agreement with spiders that we do not extend to snakes: *just stay out of our buildings and we'll leave you alone.* And let's face it, for all the spider-hating going on in the world, there is no arachnid equivalent remotely resembling the sadistic American cultural artifact that is the rattlesnake roundup.

This animosity is not new, nor is it confined to the United States. Snakes figure prominently in the tales of many cultures, and rarely are they depicted in a flattering light. In Western civilization, snakes got off on the wrong foot in the Old Testament, when Eden was tarnished by a serpent introducing Original Sin. Medusa, one of the Gorgons of Greek myths, was so hideous that the mere sight of her turned mortals to stone. She featured a coiffure of writhing snakes. Saint Patrick was canonized for ridding Ireland of snakes, a feat more impressive had he performed it in India. Our language bristles with phrases illustrating our disdain for snakes: *speak with forked tongue, snake in the grass, snake oil salesman.*

Some people defy cultural bias and hold snakes in admiration, yet the fact remains that as a group, snakes constitute the most hated animals on Earth, Alice Cooper be damned. Why? Is it the fear of being bitten by something poisonous, or is there more to it than that?

Maybe snakes have characteristics that give people, for lack of a better term, the willies. Slithering, seamlessly floating along the surface of the ground, gives snakes an eerie, supernatural quality that scares the bejesus out of some. Meanwhile, the frequent flicking of a forked tongue lends a sinister aspect to the snake's character, and God forbid one should witness the grotesque contortions snakes undergo when swallowing prey.

The cross-cultural revulsion of snakes has some wondering if that fear is genetic. Monkeys and baboons react fearfully toward snakes, suggesting a deep-seated fear of snakes among primates.

I can't relate to any of those reasons. While not a snake fancier in the mold of the collector (no Burmese python lolls under a heat lamp in my house), I nevertheless find snakes alluring and not the least bit repugnant. And I'd like to believe that even the most fervent snake-hater would have a change of heart upon knowing them better.

There are roughly three dozen species of snakes inhabiting California, and half are found somewhere in the Diablo Range. Of those, I've had the pleasure of observing fifteen in the wild.

The snakes of the Diablo Range are remarkably diverse in size, color, habitat preference, prey, and activity patterns. There are snakes that take to water over rocks, snakes that inhabit forests, snakes that prefer moonlight to sunshine, snakes that climb trees, snakes that eat fish, snakes that eat slugs, snakes that are longer than you are tall, snakes that are as slender as a pencil and not much lengthier than one, snakes that are venomous, and snakes that wouldn't bite you if their very lives depended on it. In short, a snake for everyone!

The snakes I encounter most frequently are garter snakes, and the Diablo Range harbors four species. All enter water readily and often elude predators by swimming to safety. Three are very similar in appearance, and subtle clues are needed to tell them apart. One such clue lies in the chin shields, scales located on the underside of the throat. In order to examine chin shields, one must handle the snake. The first (and last) time I did this, the snake I was holding by the base of the head began writhing emphatically. Garter snakes often attempt to escape captors by smearing them with excrement. It was quite a challenge to hold this squirming reptile so that I could see the chin shields yet avoid being slimed. I thought I had done this; I certainly didn't *feel* any foreign substance on my skin. Just as I was feeling pretty good about myself, I sniffed my hands. They smelled like they had been in a place where fingers, as my aunt would say, don't belong. I spat on them, to no avail. I grabbed several fronds of sagebrush and slathered them all over my fingers and palms, in vain. I tried cleaning them in a pool of water in a nearby stream, but it was no use. From that day forward, I relied on other clues to identify garter snakes.

The largest snake in the area, the gopher snake, is also among the most common. These snakes can exceed six feet and kill their prey by constriction, as pythons do. Even though they lack a rattle, they are often mistaken for rattlesnakes. Both are large, thick-bodied, and have somewhat similar patterns and color. Gopher snakes often vibrate their tails when alarmed, perhaps an evolutionary adaptation, but this defense mechanism backfires when people confuse them with rattlers and kill them.

Constriction is by no means the only method by which snakes obtain food. Some chase their prey. Western racers (*Coluber constrictor*) and striped racers (*Masticophis lateralis*) are among the fastest snakes. Western racers are brownish/olive, while striped racers are dark brown with a thin, light stripe on each side. I've seen striped racers ten feet off the ground in the branches of buckeye trees, possibly searching for bird's eggs. Both species hunt with the head elevated above the ground, to allow them to spot prey easier.

Another snake similar to racers is the coachwhip. It favors dry, open areas and is occasionally encountered in the southern and eastern portions of the range. From Philip R. Brown's *A Field Guide to the Snakes of California* comes this description from an eighteenth century observer: "There be snakes made like a coachwhip…that will twist their head around a horse's leg and with their tayl lash a horse untill ye blood comes…"

Besides spelling atrocities, that account is folklore. Today, unfortunately, the San Joaquin coachwhip (*Masticophis flagellum ruddocki*) is in danger of becoming a fictional creature, for it has lost much of its habitat and its numbers are declining. My first sighting of one took place on a spring afternoon near the Tumey Hills. Driving the dirt road at the bottom of Jackass Pass, I glimpsed something on the road as I drove past. It was a snake, a long one, perhaps five feet from snout to tapered tail. There are but three snakes here capable of attaining such length, but this snake was too slender to have been a rattler or a gopher snake. I pulled over and approached the snake. I saw before me a striking creature: a whippet-thin serpent with the pinkish hue of weathered sandstone, the fastest snake in North America. Besides speed, coachwhips are endowed with a nasty temperament; though nonvenomous, they will strike readily and repeatedly. This one exhibited no such surly tendencies, for it remained still and placid as I took a series of photographs. I went back to the car to change lenses; when I returned, it was gone.

Unlike the coachwhip, the rubber boa (*Charina bottae*) is a denizen of cool forests, spending much time underground. It is solid brown, with a broad, blunt tail that has earned it the nickname of the two-headed snake. It is most active during mild or cool weather and is chiefly nocturnal and has so far eluded me.

Two other nocturnal snakes I have yet to come across are the longnose snake (*Rhinocheilus lecontei*) and the appropriately named night snake (*Hypsiglena torquata*). The former is a charming snake that looks as if it were composed out of beadwork. The night snake is small, rarely exceeding two and a half feet in length. It is also mildly venomous, though it lacks the prominent fangs found in rattlesnakes. The effect of its venom on humans is negligible, though, and the snake is reluctant to bite to begin with.

If there's such a thing as the most popular snake, it would doubtless be the common kingsnake (*Lampropeltis getula*). Its popularity stems from the fact that these snakes have been known to eat rattlesnakes, though being dietary generalists, it can hardly be said that they go out of their way to do so.

If there is one snake whose stunning beauty could sway the biases of snake-haters, that snake would surely be the California mountain kingsnake (*Lampropeltis zonata*). Found sporadically in the northern part of the range, this snake features a spectacular array of black, white, and red bands. Having seen them only in the pages of field guides, this reptile became my White Whale. I peppered those few poor souls I knew who had seen one with questions, demanding to know the location, month, time of day, and weather conditions surrounding their sightings. For a while, it seemed everyone was seeing them but me. One day while I was manning the visitor center at Coe Park, a middle-aged man entered. Before he uttered a word, I suspected he came from far away, beyond Nevada; this man had Europe written all over him. He was wearing a formal shirt, as if awaiting a job interview or a court appearance, the kind I could be married in, buried in, or both. His shorts were hitched up so high that his belt encircled his navel. His legs were, if possible, even paler than mine, a kind of translucence heretofore seen only in cave salamanders and nonfat milk. Atop his head rested a hat the likes of which I had last seen in black and white movies. Presently he spoke:

"I zaw znakes on ze trail…red und vite und black…"

"You saw a California mountain kingsnake?" I blurted.

"I zaw two of zem."

"You saw a pair together?" I queried, as my voice rose in skepticism.

"No. I zaw zem zeparately."

He was from Switzerland, and this was his first trip to California and his first hike here. I had lived here my entire life, hiked several thousand miles, and had never seen a single California mountain kingsnake, and this guy saw two on his first outing.

Several weeks later, I was exploring the Arroyo Hondo, Smith Creek Canyon. I followed Smith Creek from Mount Hamilton Road until its confluence with Isabel Creek. Though only four miles, it is a strenuous, slow-going affair. The canyon is rugged, with no roads or trails. There are boulders, fallen logs, and streamside vegetation to deal with, numerous creek crossings, and areas where the canyon is so tight that you have to wade in the middle of the waist-deep stream. The west side of the canyon is lush enough to support ferns and is heavily forested with live oak, madrone, and California laurel. The east side is markedly drier, featuring shrubs such as chamise, California sagebrush, and manzanita. From a distance, the terrain is beautiful, but in the canyon's heart—the belly of the beast—it's a pain in the ass to travel through.

It took me five hours to cover the four miles to Isabel Creek, and I saw a lot along the way: wood ducks and kingfishers, whose rattling calls reverberated throughout the canyon; Sacramento pikeminnows, the largest fish in the watershed; well-camouflaged sculpins; and wily native rainbow trout—no hatchery fish here.

While walking back, I lumbered over a boulder and witnessed, along the sandbar at my feet, my White Whale, interspersed with bands of red and black. Though I had seen numerous pictures, the real life incarnation was even more stunning. I imagined California mountain kingsnakes as rather small, but the one in front of me was three feet long and fairly wide-bodied, a gorgeous creature. I was able to take two pictures before the snake vanished beneath a boulder, leaving the scene emptier in its absence.

Ring-necked snakes (*Diadophis punctatus*) and sharp-tailed snakes (*Contia tenuis*) are diminutive snakes that prefer moist forests over dry areas, though I have seen ring-necked snakes in chaparral. The ring-necked snake has a habit of coiling and exposing a vivid salmon-colored underside to would-be captors. Sharp-tailed snakes are very small, topping out at eighteen inches in length and sometimes achieving full growth at a mere eight inches. My sole encounter with one occurred on a warm day in mid-April, at dusk. I was in Coe Park, walking back to my tent after a day of surveying. Stumbling along a dirt road, I noticed a tiny snake just ahead. It was smooth-skinned and solidly colored, like a newly minted penny, with a tail ending in a spiny tip. This snake was no more than ten inches long, with a head so preposterously tiny that not only would biting a human be out of the question, but procuring any type of vertebrate prey would seem impossible. Slugs comprise most of their diet.

Of course the snake that attracts the most attention is the rattlesnake, of which we have one variety, the Northern Pacific rattlesnake, *Crotalus viridis oreganus*. Though I've seen many, I have no exciting tales to tell—no stories of being bitten miles away from medical help, not even a wayward strike that was deftly avoided. I've been rattled at many times, always good for an adrenaline rush, but that's about it. Whenever that happens, I merely retreat from the snake and allow it to go about its business. Never once has one reacted aggressively.

A false assumption about snakes is that they love the heat of summer. I see snakes most frequently in spring, when temperatures are between sixty and eighty degrees. One reason for this is that spring is mating season, so snakes are out looking for love. Another is that spring marks the end of a lengthy period of winter torpor, during which they have not fed, so a spring snake is often seeking a meal. In summer, I sometimes see snakes in shady places, often lying still along the banks of streams in forested canyons. Out in the open, exposed to the heat, I don't ever recall seeing one. That makes sense when you consider that, as warm as the air is, ground temperatures can be significantly higher. Like telemarketers and Habanero peppers, a little heat can go a long way. Too much can kill you, especially if you're a rattlesnake. Take it from Jay Bruce.

A legendary bounty hunter, Bruce was the most proficient of a number of men employed by California to rid the state of mountain lions in the early 1900s. Endowed with a curious mind, Bruce questioned the prevailing notion that rattlesnakes thrived in hot weather. He tested this on hot summer days by removing rattlers from their shady resting spots and placing them in the middle of dirt roads, forcing them to endure direct sunlight. Their response was always the same: a desperate attempt to return to the safety of the shade as quickly as possible, just as you and I would react if plopped down barefoot on a blistering sand dune. But Bruce was, to be charitable, too precise to merely note that snakes disliked heat. He took temperature readings and used a watch to time how long it took for those snakes to convulse in agony and finally expire. That time was surprisingly short but not short enough, I suspect, for those unfortunate snakes. Kind of makes you wonder which of the two life forms was the cold-blooded one.

As his experimentation progressed, Bruce, the would-be scientist, wondered if snakes overheated to the point of convulsion could be revived by being splashed with cool water. Lo and behold, he found that overheated rattlers were instantaneously relieved following a dousing. Abracadabra. Lest you get the impression that Bruce was feeling a trifle guilty for his pseudo-experiments or was getting too emotionally close to his study subjects to permit objectivity, he assures readers that resuscitated snakes were summarily dispatched. Somehow, a Nobel Prize eluded him.

The most interesting rattlesnake yarn I can spin is one in which I was merely a third party. I was down in Poverty Flat one afternoon when out of the brush at my feet ran a woodrat. This was very odd, for woodrats are rarely out in broad daylight. As it scampered away, I could see that it was lame, for the left side of its body appeared to be paralyzed. It scrambled up a low-lying branch and proceeded to lie down. I watched it for several minutes, then noticed a small rattler about two feet long following the path of the woodrat. This could hardly be a coincidence. Snakebite would explain both the condition of the woodrat as well as its frantic dash in midday. Likewise, the snake was behaving accordingly by slowly tracking its victim, allowing time for the venom to take full effect. What I wondered was how could a small rattlesnake swallow a woodrat? With ultra-flexible jaws, snakes are capable of stuffing formidably large creatures down their throats. Large diamondback rattlesnakes are rumored to be able to swallow jackrabbits. Still, does a snake know when it has bitten off more than it can chew, when something is too large to get down? I couldn't imagine that snake swallowing that rat, but I lost track of the snake after it crossed the road, never to know if it was successful.

Several years ago I was out hiking along a grassy ridge, following a dirt road. It was a cool afternoon on Labor Day weekend, a precursor to fall. Something had been weighing on me, dragging me down, and as I often do, I headed outdoors. However, despite an azure sky laced with cottony clouds and the discovery of a fresh set of mountain lion tracks, I remained in a funk. While measuring the tracks, I glanced at the ground and saw a Western black-headed snake, *Tantilla planiceps*, a minuscule serpent that reaches the northern limit of its distribution here. Though not rare, they are nonetheless rarely seen, for this diminutive snake is one of the least-known reptiles in North America, and this was my first, and only, encounter with one. Its genus name, *Tantilla*, translates to "a small thing," for adults range from a mere five inches to fifteen inches. This wisp of a snake lying in front of me was about the length and width of the pen I held, with a beige color nearly identical to that of the soil. The minute black head was the size of the eraser on the top of a pencil. Supposedly, they feed on small insects. This docile snake endured my close observation without a hint of aggression. *How could anyone*, I thought, *even the most hard-hearted snake-hater, begrudge such an animal?*

The surprise encounter lifted my mood, and as I headed back I pondered the ironies of snake venom—that the cure is derived from the poison and that compounds in snake venom have helped treat a variety of human maladies. I thought, too, about the symbol of the medical profession, handed down to us from the Greeks in the time of Hippocrates, and I had to smile, for despite all the dark symbolism we have foisted upon them lo these many years, is not a snake, after all, the creature entwined around the Rod of Asclepius?

The Need for Speed

The Past Life of the Pronghorn

WE ALL CARRY with us the residue of past experience. It's part of the admission ticket to the carnival of life. Whether one is rich or poor, male or female, genius or doofus, matters not. This truism is cross-cultural, transcends languages, and is as valid today as it was when the first rock art was scrawled across the walls of a cave in what is now France. It joins death and surpasses taxes as being one of life's certainties. Whatever we are today was sculpted by that which happened before. Now this is not to say the past determines our future. It is merely an observation, often overlooked even by those seeking self-awareness. *To know the adult, you first must know the child.* Childhood, it seems, is especially important, the reservoir of a distant past exerting its influence on us. This has been on my mind lately, particularly when I think about pronghorn.

At the time of Lewis and Clark, the Great Plains were teeming with bison. As many as sixty million of those great, shaggy beasts once inhabited the continent, and alongside those vast herds were pronghorn. Unlike bison, which originally ranged east almost to the Atlantic, pronghorn were found only in the West, inhabiting open areas. Although the two shared much of their respective ranges, the pronghorn's extended into California.

Those two symbols of the wide-open West suffered similar fates. By 1900, bison were teetering on the precipice of extinction, their population dwindling to less than one thousand. Pronghorn fared only marginally better. By 1924, their population had dipped to around twenty thousand. In California, pronghorn eventually disappeared, except for a small population in the state's northeast corner on the edge of the Great Basin. It may be that the last pronghorn in the rest of the state persisted into the 1950s in western Fresno County, along the eastern edge of the Diablo Range.

Today, the outlook for pronghorn has brightened considerably. Their numbers have rebounded—as many as one million may grace the landscape, while in California attempts have been made to restore this iconic mammal to parts of its original range.

In the 1990s, the California Department of Fish and Game decided to reintroduce pronghorn, much as they did with tule elk during the 1970s. In the Diablo Range, several sites were selected. One was a large ranch north of Henry Coe State Park. That land wasn't ideal pronghorn habitat; it may not even have been marginal habitat, given its extensive oak forests, chaparral, and lack of level, open ground. The handful of pronghorn released there eventually made their way to Isabel Valley, one of the few parcels of flat land in the northern Diablo Range.

At three miles long and a mile and a half wide, Isabel Valley could hardly be described as a vast plain, but to those wandering pronghorn, it must have seemed like heaven. Aside from several ranch houses, Isabel Valley offers a glimpse into what much of California must have looked like prior to settlement: acres of oak savanna where bountiful crops of acorns nourished Native Americans and grizzlies. Its soil has revealed both archaeological and biological artifacts, for numerous arrowheads and several grizzly skulls were unearthed here. Through such hallowed ground flows Isabel Creek, meandering quietly through the valley, forming several miles of floodplain before entering a rugged canyon on its destination to Smith Creek.

The portal to that canyon lies within the ranch leased by my father. One afternoon I was exploring the canyon when I discovered mountain lion tracks along the banks of Isabel Creek. Hoping to make casts of them, I returned the next day with plaster. I set them, allowed them to dry, then headed back. I was walking through a stand of blue oaks when I spotted a deer a hundred yards away at the mouth of the canyon. Something about this deer, however, seemed unusual. Its coat was too light, and I couldn't see the black tail. On top of that, it appeared to move differently as it walked. After pulling binoculars out of my pack, I was astonished to see a pronghorn. I don't know if the animal was aware of me, for it never paused to look my way. Before I could retrieve my camera, it disappeared from view, heading toward the flood plain.

Though I desperately wanted to capture that pronghorn on film, attempting to follow on foot would be a fool's errand, for once I got beyond the mouth of the canyon, I would be out in the open and could easily be seen. My best bet lie in using my vehicle as a blind, driving down the dirt road skirting the edge of the floodplain. I hurried back to the car and cruised downhill. My plan unraveled, however, for the pronghorn spooked before I got to the flat. Looking down on the vale, I saw him sprint across the open field at a pace exceeding that of any creature I'd ever seen. That speed, along with an effortlessness that made it appear as if he were gliding, left me spellbound. I watched until the curvature of the road wrested him from sight. The two horses grazing in the flat were visibly excited, whinnying loudly long after the pronghorn had passed. I imagine they felt envious.

For me, the encounter was too brief. I wanted more: more wildness, more elegance, more of the inspiration that comes from seeing an animal that was once gone reappear, running free and unfettered. I could not bring myself to pursue that animal further; I had stressed him enough. I wanted him to come back, and though I would return many times, five years would pass before I would see a pronghorn there again.

Pronghorn are, to borrow from Bruce Springsteen, born to run. Four million years of evolution has produced an animal that covers ground more efficiently than any before or since. Increased lung capacity, a massive windpipe, an enlarged heart, and shock-absorbing bones are but several features enabling pronghorn to course over the landscape with ease. While not as fast as cheetahs, they are superior in their ability to maintain high speeds over distance. If Olympic events were held in the animal kingdom, pronghorn would be silver medalists in the one hundred and two hundred meters and gold medalists in every other race, including the marathon.

Pronghorn fawns are highly precocious, literally hitting the ground running. At five days old, they can outrun a person and, after several weeks, can best every other creature except their elders. Yet despite such accelerated development, fawns are vulnerable to predators during the early days of their lives. Prior to acquiring their superlative speed, fawns protect themselves by lying stock-still against the earth, relying on camouflage, motionlessness, and an absence of odor to avoid detection. Even so, predation rates are often high. Female pronghorn have adapted by giving birth to twins. If a pronghorn can survive past infancy, its chances of being taken by a predator lessen dramatically.

In historical times, the predator most equipped to prey on pronghorn was the wolf. Yet it's doubtful that wolves successfully hunted pronghorn very often. There were always larger, slower animals that were easier to run down. Today in Yellowstone, pronghorn are near the bottom of the list of species hunted by wolves. It's as if wolves realize that pronghorn are so swift that chasing them would be futile. Whether or not pronghorn can cover a mile in a minute is questionable. What is not debatable is that nothing runs as far and fast as pronghorn. The intriguing question is not how fast can they run, but why are they so much faster than they need to be? The answer lies hidden in the past.

Ten thousand years ago, an assemblage of large mammals that staggers the imagination inhabited North America. There were mammoths and mastodons, giant ground sloths weighing three tons, beavers the size of bears, and a multitude of grazing animals whose carcasses sustained a formidable array of predators, including dire wolves and giant short-faced bears, truly formidable beasts. Those bears dwarfed modern grizzlies, standing five and a half feet tall at the shoulder. Their long legs enabled them to run even faster than modern bears, which are surprisingly speedy in their own right, and unlike grizzlies, which eat a lot of plant food, short-faced bears were, judging from their fossilized teeth, highly carnivorous.

The cat family was also well represented. Cougars and jaguars shared the landscape with larger species, including saber-toothed cats, scimitar cats, and North American lions, similar to but even larger than today's African lion. Yet none of those prehistoric carnivores could approach pronghorn in swiftness afoot. To understand the pronghorn's need for speed, one must recall two other long-absent predators.

Pronghorn have inhabited North America for four million years. At least thirteen different species have been described, though today only one, *Antilocapra americana*, exists. For three million years, pronghorn were harassed by *Chasmoporthetes ossifragus*, the American hunting hyena, a long-limbed predator built, like pronghorn, for speed and endurance. But it was another creature that pushed pronghorn over the speed limit. From 2.5 million years ago until 20,000 years ago, twenty-five thousand centuries, pronghorn were pursued by cheetahs. Those eons of coexistence brought out the best in pronghorn, and they've been running ever since.

In June 2003, my father told me he'd seen a lone pronghorn while driving along the same floodplain where I had had my sighting five years earlier. The next afternoon, I drove up Mount Hamilton Road and descended the east side, turning just beyond the one-lane bridge hovering over the scattered pools of Isabel Creek. I slowly rounded a bend as the creek veered west, revealing a modest expanse of grassland above the banks of the drying creek bed. A quarter mile away, I noticed something in that open patch of ground that I would've taken for a tree stump had I not the familiarity with the area that hundreds of trips down that road fosters. Approaching closer I saw it was a pronghorn buck, reclining with his head elevated. I slowed the vehicle to a snail's pace until I reached a spot in the road closest to the buck, fifty yards away, before shutting off the engine. Rather than fleeing, he remained seated, a picture of serenity. I didn't dare jeopardize that by doing something as reckless as getting out of the car.

The late-afternoon light cast a golden hue on the grasses. Turkey vultures banked and dipped in the breeze. Bullock's orioles chattered atop blue oaks while the pronghorn sat, chewing its cud. I alternated between taking pictures and observing through binoculars. When he arose, I was struck by his slight build, a frame of an animal markedly smaller than a deer. When he moved, I saw a sinewy, muscular definition, all fast-twitch fiber and bone. He spent several minutes nibbling on ground cover before working his way up and over a small rise, out of sight. The clock in the car told me I had spent forty-five minutes there, but the timeless quality of the encounter rendered me incapable of guessing how long I spent in that state of willful oblivion.

I got out of the car, slithered under the barbed wire fence, crossed the creek bed, and walked out onto the grassy flat where the animal had been. I was searching for tracks, scat, a tuft of hair, something tangible to fortify the memory of observing this pronghorn, the rarest mammal in the Diablo Range. Driving back, I reached the summit of Mount Hamilton at sunset, yet all I could think about was pronghorn.

As of 2006, pronghorn were found in three widely separated locations in the Diablo Range. One was south of Livermore, at the northern end of the range. Another was in the low, grassy hills south of Pinnacles National Monument. The third was in Isabel Valley, which harbors a dozen or so animals. What concerns me about this low number is that the population has not grown. I keep hoping their numbers will increase and some eventually wander the short distance to San Antonio Valley, a larger block of land that should be to their liking. So far that hasn't happened. Perhaps the terrain between the two valleys is not open enough for them to risk venturing through. Maybe the habitat, though palatable, is not ideal. Not enough wide-open spaces, perhaps. That shouldn't pose a problem for the other two herds. Those locations seem like better pronghorn habitat, for they consist of rolling hills devoid of brush and trees. I hope they're doing well. Just knowing they're out there does me good.

Some of the best habitat in the range contains no pronghorn: the 150-mile stretch of barren foothills flanking the eastern edge of the range parallel to Highway 5. People who drive that stretch of highway describe it as one of the bleakest and dreariest in the state. Though I don't completely agree, I'll concede it can be a tedious drive, and perhaps the area could use a little revitalization. What better way to energize a landscape than by reintroducing pronghorn, with their grace, athleticism, and untamable wild spirit? While much of this area is privately owned, there are some sizable parcels of public land in the region—the lands surrounding San Luis Reservoir and the BLM holdings in the Panoche and Tumey hills. I don't know whether or not such reintroductions would be successful, but it's at least worth considering.

Pronghorn represent a kind of wildness and freedom unmatched by other hoofed animals. It's not merely their breathtaking speed; it's a wild essence, an unwillingness to become habituated. Unlike elk, you won't find them reclining on lawns surrounding Mammoth Hot Springs in Yellowstone. Nor will you see them resting alongside a hiking trail as mountain goats and bighorn sheep do at Glacier National Park. They won't allow you to approach closely for a photo, like moose in Grand Teton, nor will they casually walk along a road rife with automobiles, as bison do in Yellowstone. I'll concede that such habituation can have a magnetic pull on a person. I've certainly felt it. But that comes with a heavy price tag: not just the loss of wariness but the loss of the very wildness that defines each species. It's as if such creatures have lost something and have become diminished. Thank God for pronghorn and their wild spirit.

There's something gnawing at me. Maybe pronghorn will never be reestablished here. Maybe they can't be. Perhaps the land here is already too fragmented for something as wild as pronghorn. The obstacles to pronghorn reestablishment at times appear daunting. In addition to political and bureaucratic roadblocks, there are ecological hurdles to overcome. For instance, does the range, composed almost entirely of nonnative grasses, contain enough high-quality forage? Will the predation rate on newborns be excessive? Will fences impede movement and prevent dispersal? Something as simple as a barbed wire fence could prevent pronghorn from wandering, as is their wont. Pronghorn, for all their athleticism, don't handle fences well. A fence that deer bound over without a second thought might stop a pronghorn in its tracks. Pronghorn negotiate fences by ducking under them, and if there is not a sufficient distance between the bottom wire and the ground (eighteen inches is recommended) that unimposing fence might as well be the Grand Canyon. It's not that pronghorn can't jump, for they are capable of doing so. Occasionally, they will take a stab at leaping, though not always successfully. A few perish, getting caught on the highest strand of wire. But more often than not, they won't even try, for a fence is as much a psychological barrier as it is a physical one. For four million years, pronghorn have roamed wide-open spaces, relying on an extraordinary combination of speed and stamina. Those landscapes held few obstacles that required leaping over. The wooded habitat favored by deer is more complex, full of downed logs, uneven terrain, and other obstructions that place a premium on jumping ability. But pronghorn didn't evolve there. Pronghorn won't jump because they never had to. Barbed wire fences have been around for a little over a century, an amount of time that is insignificant when measured against their four-million-year presence in North America. As it was with speed, understanding pronghorn behavior entails peering into the past.

To know the adult you must first know the child. Early in life, I was fortunate to have had people who exposed me to the outdoors—nothing elaborate, simple things like picnics along Coyote Creek. I would explore, reveling in places without buildings, sidewalks, streets, or fences, a land of wild things that beckoned mightily to a young imagination. To this day, I still possess that zeal to explore, and I never feel more alive than when doing so.

My grandmother, in particular, used to indulge me. She would take me to the zoo or the Academy of Sciences in San Francisco, and we would always return with a book, invariably written for an older audience. I would consume those books, as much as a child reading what was written for adults could, and thus was instilled in me a love of reading and learning. Field guides with their range maps—tangible, visual representations a child could relate to and gravitate toward when the technical jargon of the text became confusing—especially fascinated me. It was in those field guides that I first learned the awful reality of extinction, that not only do individual animals die but entire species disappear. I remember feeling that there was something deeply and inherently wrong with that. How could people allow this to happen? You couldn't describe my grandmother as an environmentalist, outdoor lover, or avid reader. She had no philosophy to instill. She simply loved her grandchildren. She passed away in 2002. It was only later, after reflecting on both our lives, that I realized the profound influence she had on me.

The Song of the Phoenix

The Fall and Rise of the Tule Elk

SAN ANTONIO VALLEY lies halfway across the Diablo Range, in the northern section between San Jose and the Central Valley. As valleys go, it's not much, seven miles long and maybe one mile wide. The official name of the road running through the valley is Highway 130, but nobody calls it that. Depending where along the route you happen to be, it is known as Mount Hamilton Road, San Antonio Valley Road, or Mines Road. The road is a lifeline for the few residents of the area, the sole road linking them to the rest of civilization. For others, it's a scenic back road enjoyed on weekends. It is not for the squeamish; those afraid of heights or prone to carsickness would be wise to pass on this route. It is thin on amenities as well, for along its seventy-mile path, there are no gas stations, motels, or stores.

A drive through San Antonio Valley reveals scenes of old California. The valley yields impressive wildflower displays in spring, and blue oaks line the bucolic two-lane road. Gray pines, another drought-tolerant tree, dot the landscape, while chaparral cloaks the mountains rising east of the valley. The valley resembles Gold Country, sixty miles east. But if you were to drive the road at sunset in late summer, you might be fortunate enough to behold a scene that no longer plays itself out in the Sierra foothills: a herd of tule elk on the eve of the rut.

At the dawn of the mission era, vast herds of tule elk (*Cervus elaphus nannodes*) roamed the foothills and valleys of the state. Endemic to California, this subspecies grazed in profusion throughout the Central Valley and surrounding foothills, east to the Sierra and west to the coast. They shared much of this habitat with pronghorn, and wolves, mountain lions, and grizzlies preyed upon them. The Gold Rush had a devastating impact upon many creatures, especially tule elk. Prior to the rise of the livestock industry, wild game dominated the platters of settlers and miners. Market hunting became a full-time occupation for many, and this spelled doom for the once vast elk herds.

In addition to the devastation wrought by market hunting, agricultural expansion removed vital habitat, so much so that by the dawn of the twentieth century, tule elk were probably fewer in number in California than wolves, grizzlies, or condors. The last band of tule elk, no more than 150 animals, was concentrated in the southwestern corner of the San Joaquin Valley, on lands comprising part of the vast empire controlled by the Miller & Lux Land and Cattle Company. It would be hard to imagine a tougher situation: on the cusp of oblivion, with no laws protecting them, tule elk needed a miracle if they were going to avoid the fate of the passenger pigeon. But a miracle was exactly what they got, and from a most unlikely source.

Henry Miller was an immigrant from Germany who came to the United States as a boy with scarcely a dollar to his name. After settling in San Francisco following the Gold Rush, he opened a profitable butcher shop and over time parlayed that modest success into the largest ranching enterprise this country had ever seen. At their peak, his holdings included over one million acres, spread out over several states. Through hard work, attention to detail, thrift, shrewdness, and a certain amount of chicanery, Miller came to control a real estate empire that was the American equivalent of a kingdom.

So when it came to his attention that the last band of tule elk was roaming his land and occasionally raiding his alfalfa fields, Miller responded in an unpredictably remarkable fashion. He could have had the herd destroyed, for they were not protected at either the state or federal level. But for some reason, perhaps known only to him, he chose not to. Instead, he gave the herd to the federal government, which accepted them on the condition that Miller round up and corral the animals. Think what you may of Henry Miller—avaricious workaholic or personification of the American Dream, exploiter of nature or agent of progress.

The Diablo Diary

For that gesture, he is owed a debt of gratitude. That he did so in an era when the conservation ethic was in its infancy was all the more impressive.

In 1904, that last band of tule elk was rounded up, corralled, loaded onto wagons, and relocated to an enclosure in Sequoia National Park. That mission was not as simple as it sounds. The corral had to be fortified and reconfigured. Elk that couldn't be herded into it were pursued on horseback, roped, hog-tied, and transported by wagon while lying on their sides. Before mechanized transport and tranquilizer guns, there were few other alternatives. Such rough handling took a heavy toll. Some elk succumbed in the process, either from the stress of capture, lying immobile under an unrelenting sun, or being gored by a panic-stricken companion. At the corral, men sawed off antlers in the hopes of lessening injuries. The elk were unshackled and herded down a chute before being loaded onto a wagon. From there, it took several days to reach the enclosure along the Kaweah River. Yet the difficult work was yet to come. It's one thing to stave off extinction by rounding up the last of a species and taking them into captivity. It's another to restore a species. Reintroduction. Restoration. This is the language of redemption, of hope, of atonement for the ecological misdeeds of the past. While pulling a species back from extinction is noble and worthwhile, for a species to exist solely within the confines of captivity is a lamentable fate, relegating such creatures to the status of museum curios.

But reintroductions pose formidable challenges, the most basic of which is identifying and addressing the factors that brought about the species' decline. Failure to do so leaves little hope for restoration. For tule elk, the principle causes of their decline were market hunting and habitat loss. Fortunately, the market hunting era is long gone. However, habitat loss has rendered large chunks of formerly prime territory off-limits, for the vast grasslands that once covered the floor of the Central Valley have been reduced to a fraction of their original acreage. Another barrier to elk restoration lies not in the ecological realm but rather the societal one. Where will we allow them to exist? Conflicts are bound to arise when large animals repopulate the countryside. It's not hard to imagine elk wreaking havoc on vineyards and row crops and competing with livestock for forage. These are legitimate concerns, and if they are not adequately

43

addressed, future restoration efforts may be throttled more by political conditions than ecological ones.

Early restoration efforts were only marginally successful. Locating suitable reintroduction sites within historical habitat was difficult due to a paucity of public land. As a result, elk were released in Yosemite National Park and Owens Valley, areas they never occupied in the first place. The Yosemite herd struggled and fizzled out; the Owens Valley herd did better and persists to this day. Later efforts focused exclusively on lands within historical habitat.

For decades, tule elk remained in limbo. By 1970, sixty-six years after the initial roundup, there were only five hundred, with just three free-roaming populations. But change was in the wind, a good change that would finally propel tule elk from preserves out into their aboriginal habitat. The burgeoning conservation movement encouraged species restoration, as well as conservation easements and land stewardship. In the Diablo Range, ten thousand acres of land shifted to public ownership when the Grant ranch was sold to Santa Clara County to become Joseph D. Grant County Park. When neighboring landowners offered their property as a reintroduction site, elk were returned to the hills east of San Jose in 1978, following a centuries' absence. I remember seeing a lone bull grazing off to the side of Mount Hamilton Road, sporting a gaudy radio collar. And though at the time I was sure I would have plenty of opportunities to see tule elk in the future, twenty-two years would pass before I saw one while out on foot. For whatever reason, the elk did not find Grant Park to their liking. Most of the herd headed east, eventually settling in the Isabel and San Antonio Valleys.

In the meantime, the best place to observe tule elk was at San Luis National Wildlife Refuge. Located on the floor of the Central Valley just north of Los Banos, the refuge is one of a complex of preserves protecting nearly forty thousand acres of valley wetland and grassland habitat. The refuge contains a seven-hundred-acre enclosure surrounded by an imposing fence. A dirt road provides a pathway through which visitors can drive the perimeter of the enclosure. Several viewing platforms have been erected, since entering the confine is prohibited. The ideal number of elk inside is fifty. When the population rises above that, excess animals are rounded up and released at sites capable of maintaining free-roaming herds.

Those elk *seem* wild. They don't approach the fence in the presence of people, acting appropriately wary. They appear healthy. Yet I have to admit the whole experience was something less than inspirational. I needed to see them free, out on the land.

In the autumn of 2000, elk were sighted with increasing frequency on the ranch my father leased east of Mount Hamilton. Thus, I began spending time hiking the ridges of the ranch. Several November hikes yielded tracks and droppings but no sightings. As December approached, I zeroed in on Blumbago Canyon.

Blumbago is less a canyon than a hollow, a sliver of a valley flanked by a grassy rise to the east and the oak forest slope of Seeboy Ridge to the west. Access to the canyon is via an old Jeep trail that bears the foreboding moniker of Graveyard Road, so named for the pair of simple graves that lie alongside its path. The rustic burial site contains the remains of a pair of homesteaders, a husband and wife who passed away several years apart at the twilight of the nineteenth century.

It was while descending Graveyard Road, walking through a copse of blue oaks, that I noticed something large reclining in a hillside meadow two hundred feet away. As I looked closer, I saw it was a bull elk. With the wind in my face and the elk lying with its back toward me, I stood a chance of stalking close enough to take a good photo. I got down on all fours and made my way toward the elk. The first fifty feet of the stalk were easy, for oak trees were plentiful and concealment was not a problem. However, where the grove of oaks ended and the meadow began, the stalk became more challenging, for fifty yards of open ground stood between me and the bull. The sole source of cover in that distance was a fallen tree, a long-dead oak whose supine trunk provided a two-foot-tall barricade. If I could make it there undetected, I might be able to take an outstanding picture.

At this stage of the stalk, I had to be especially careful. I moved only when there was background noise—wind rustling through the trees, a plane passing overhead, or the raucous screeching of scrub jays. Otherwise, I would stay still against the earth. When I did move, I transported my camera by grasping the neck strap in my teeth, freeing both hands for crawling. In such fashion, it took forty-five minutes to cover the hundred-foot distance between the edge of the clearing and the fallen oak.

Arriving at the downed tree, I had a decision to make: do I stay behind the log and start taking pictures, or dare I edge closer? Advancing toward the bull risked jeopardizing all the time and effort spent so far in the stalk. Crawling about on all fours, I would be in no position to react in time to take a picture if the bull got wind of me and abruptly departed. I was also acutely aware that I had already come closer to this large wild animal than a person should. I decided to stay put. Slowly I rose and started snapping pictures.

With the first click of the camera, the bull turned his head, rose, and faced me. He stood motionless for an uncomfortably long time. Was he belligerent or merely curious? As I pondered this, the bull trotted off down the canyon. As I watched him recede into the distance, I marveled at how such a large and stately animal could roam free across the landscape, unencumbered by brand, ear tag, or bridle, property of no one, honoring neither fence nor corral. I took great solace in knowing that these mountains were still wild enough to allow such majestic animals to exist here. Though I had hiked this property many times, that encounter was enough to make me see the land in a different light. Something fundamental had changed, for the landscape now crackled with the electricity of possibilities because, against all odds, tule elk were back.

I judge an area largely by the species it harbors. Lands with a healthy array of wild creatures, especially if such animals are rare or large and wide ranging, are especially valued. A place becomes special if it provides a home for creatures such as condors, foothill yellow-legged frogs, grizzly bears, or wolverines. For all the human drama pulsing through cities and suburbs, I have always found such places lacking due to their inability to provide habitat for more than a handful of wildlife species, the majority of which are either habitat generalists or, worst of all, nonnative species. Even farmland, as aesthetically pleasing as it may be, and as preferable as it is to urban sprawl, fails to hold my interest long, for the list of wildlife possibilities has dwindled considerably, and I want to—I *need* to—surround myself with such potential.

For the past several years I've spent many August evenings driving the length of San Antonio Valley, hoping to observe tule elk during the rut. I arrive in the waning afternoon light, as shadows descend on the valley floor and the fading sun lights the slopes of Mount Stakes. Some evenings I see little. More often than not, however, I am rewarded with something memorable: young bulls locking their antlers in mock battle, a rite of passage as they approach breeding age—older males jealously guarding their harem, reigning in cows that seem hell-bent on straying. Once I watched in fascination as a bull and his harem ceased grazing and stood alert, fixing their collective stares on a coyote that trotted across the meadow. At twenty pounds, this coyote wouldn't dream of pursuing even the smallest animal in this herd; he posed no threat whatsoever. Yet his canine form elicited an instinctive response honed by countless generations of uneasy coexistence with wolves, which are now but a memory here.

It is the onset of a mild August evening. A waxing moon rises above the horizon, and the two-lane road is blessedly deserted. Rolling down the car window at a pullout, you at first hear nothing. Then, the faint stirring of a breeze caresses your ears as it passes through the branches of a gray pine, sounding almost liquid. A pair of mourning doves whistles past, heading toward a water trough for a final drink before retiring for the evening. A handful of yellow-billed magpies chatter among themselves as they fly across the valley en route to their evening roost. Then, in the distance, you hear it—a brief, measured wail, rising in pitch, the bugle of a bull tule elk. It is melancholy, eerie, and hauntingly beautiful. It is the song of the phoenix, rising timelessly in the late summer twilight.

Sciurus griseus, We Hardly Knew Thee

Mona Lisa and the Western Gray Squirrel

I USED TO see them. They weren't abundant; I wouldn't even say they were common. But they were here. They are *Sciurus griseus*, Western gray squirrels. Here would be the wooded canyons of the Diablo Range.

Much of the Diablo Range is dry and open, especially compared to the ranges to the west, the Santa Cruz Mountains and the Santa Lucias. Buttressed against the Pacific, those receive moisture-laden winter storms and summer fog, allowing forests of Douglas fir, redwood, and a variety of pines to blanket their slopes.

In contrast, with the exception of gray pines (*Pinus sabiniana*), conifers are rare in the Diablo Range. Yet there are forests. Behind the open ridges of the western front stand thick, closed-canopy woods descending unbroken to canyons and creek bottoms. This sizable chunk of forest habitat is one of the secrets of the Diablo range, hidden from view from the floor of the Santa Clara Valley. Those forests are comprised of trees such as coast live oak (*Quercus agrifolia*), California bay (*Umbellularia californica*), Pacific madrone (*Arbutus menziesii*), and black oak (*Quercus kelloggii*).

To enter such a forest is to venture into a world much different from the surrounding open environs. The dense canopy creates a realm of perpetual shade, where only occasional tendrils of sunlight reach the forest floor. Ferns are common, and bizarre fungi protrude from decaying wood, reminiscent of the rainforests of the Pacific Northwest.

Pathways are few. Jeep trails and dirt roads skirt the forests in favor of open ridges. Since the trees comprising the forest have little economic value, human intrusion into the forest has always been slight, and a variety of creatures that don't exist here in other habitats occupy such woods. There are birds such as brown creepers, so named for their habit of shinnying up and down tree trunks, and chestnut-backed chickadees, which forage in lively groups near the treetops. Flocks of band-tailed pigeons alight in trees, ready to depart in a flurry of strong wing beats. Raucous Steller's jays bring drama to the woods with a variety of vocalizations, talented mimics that they are. Beneath logs you might come across several species of salamanders, for ensatinas, slender salamanders, and arboreal salamanders all inhabit the forest.

Anyone wandering through the woods would be lucky to happen across a rubber boa, a rarely seen denizen of shady forests. An encounter with a Western gray squirrel would be even more improbable, for this species is inexplicably vanishing from a region it has occupied for eons.

Western gray squirrels inhabit the Pacific Coast from Washington to northern Baja California. Highly arboreal, they are restricted to woodlands, where they feed upon fungi, acorns, berries, and foliage. They cache acorns in the ground and retrieve them later, locating them by smell, and those they leave behind sometimes sprout to become oak trees, making Western gray squirrels agents of oak regeneration. They're found from sea level to around five thousand feet in the Sierra Nevada, where they are still common. They are absent from higher elevations, possibly because snow hampers their ability to detect stored food. Western gray squirrels are wary and intolerant of humans. My kind of critter.

Historical references to the Western gray squirrel in the Diablo Range are sparse. Black and white photos from the long-defunct resorts of Madrone Soda Springs and Gilroy Hot Springs reveal trappers with pelts hanging in front of cabins. Homesteaders hunted them as one of many game species relied upon for sustenance. Yet the squirrel outlasted the homesteaders, trappers, and game hunters and survived to see an era when the number of people living in the hills actually decreased. Trapping declined when the value of pelts plummeted, and hunters increasingly focused on larger targets such as deer, feral pigs, and turkeys.

When I began exploring, I occasionally saw gray squirrels. Several times I saw them scurrying across Mount Hamilton Road in a wooded stretch north of Hall's Valley. My last sighting had to be some time in the 1980s, though even this vague date is suspect, veiled in the forest of memory.

At about that time, I began noticing squirrel carcasses while driving through the tree-lined suburbs east of San Jose. At first I paid scant attention to such roadkill, figuring they were ground squirrels that had strayed too far from the fast-disappearing vacant lots. But as I paid closer attention to the rumpled remains, I could see that these weren't ground squirrels. Their brown coat lacked the grizzled patch of fur around the neck, and their undersides were orange. Soon I started seeing them running nimbly across telephone lines along Alum Rock Avenue, and I heard their raspy chattering at my parents' house, where they scampered about in the trees and plundered seed from bird feeders. No, these were definitely not ground squirrels, and they sure as hell weren't Western gray squirrels, either. They were Eastern fox squirrels, transplants from the East Coast that had been released in city parks several decades previously. Belonging to the same genus as Western gray squirrels, fox squirrels share much in common with them, but it was their differences that allowed fox squirrels to expand beyond city parks into the suburbs and beyond. One of those differences is their ability to thrive in areas with scattered trees, for they do not require the cloak of a dense forest. The other is a hefty tolerance for humanity.

By the 1990s, it dawned on me that the Western gray squirrel was disappearing from the area. Only rarely would I hear their rasping calls, and when I did, it was in places such as Robison Creek and Coon Creek, far from the forests of the west side. Those areas, toward the eastern part of the range, did contain some forest habitat, but not as much as the west side. In addition, the composition of tree species was different. Moisture-loving trees were absent, replaced by drought-hardy blue oak, interior live oak, and gray pine.

In June 2002, while hiking to Kingbird Pond, I heard the scolding chatter of a squirrel in a gray pine. Looking up, I saw a Western gray squirrel, the first I'd seen in almost twenty years. During the amphibian survey in Coe Park, I hiked almost a thousand miles, yet for all that hiking and time spent outdoors, that sighting was the lone encounter I had with a Western gray squirrel. This is all the more telling because tree squirrels are diurnal. I usually feel excited when I cross paths with a rarely seen animal, but this sighting left me subdued. A sense of foreboding came over me, as if in the branches of that ghost pine, I beheld a creature fast on its way to becoming a phantom.

What happened? What caused the precipitous decline of the Western gray squirrel in the Diablo Range? It wasn't habitat loss—the forests remain intact, with lots of acreage protected as park land. Hunting and trapping can't be blamed, since those activities have virtually ceased here, leaving behind an extant squirrel population. I don't know what caused the dramatic fall of the Western gray squirrel here, but I suspect that the arrival of the Eastern fox squirrel had something to do with it.

Soon after I stopped noticing gray squirrels, I began seeing fox squirrels. Having conquered the suburbs, they had advanced to the countryside, so much so that by 2005, they were found halfway across the range. And wherever they were found, it seems, gray squirrels were not. In any ecosystem, two species cannot occupy the same niche. Perhaps that is what is occurring. Maybe fox squirrels, despite being smaller, are more aggressive, able to drive out the natives. Or perhaps some disease, a pathogen percolating throughout the fox squirrel population, has spread to gray squirrels. Historically, the two were separated by over a thousand miles, and that isolation may have made gray squirrels vulnerable to diseases harbored by fox squirrels. It is highly speculative to advance such an idea without a stitch of evidence, but the rapid and near thorough disappearance of the Western gray squirrel here leads me to wonder if something beyond mere competition may be afoot.

As threats to biodiversity go, the second horseman of the apocalypse may be that posed by nonnative species, and while it may not be as large as the menace of habitat loss, it is more insidious. People have been unwittingly and haphazardly shuttling species around the globe for centuries. The earliest traveled as stowaways, hitching rides on vessels crossing the seas. That threat is more pernicious now due to the heady advances in transportation. Today, exotic species have many options for globetrotting. Modern ships facilitate species dispersal by releasing ballast water from port to port, resulting in a surge of exotic invasions along coastlines, bays, and estuaries. Vehicles spread the seeds of noxious weeds from one end of the country to the other via their tires, while airplanes, with their ability to bridge the gap between continents in a matter of hours, make it relatively easy for a disease or virus to establish itself in a new territory. As a result, we are in the midst of a biopollution crisis, one that has until recently gone unnoticed.

Unfortunately, it has not caught the public's eye in the same manner as habitat loss or overharvesting has. Clear-cut forests, oil-fouled bays, unchecked sprawl, overzealous whaling, and animal trafficking draw public ire for the damage they represent, as they should. But the invasive species issue has no image to sear onto the collective consciousness. How can it, when so few people can distinguish native species from foreign ones?

Pop quiz: which of the following species currently inhabiting the Diablo Range are not native: opossum, red fox, wild pig, bullfrog, bluegill, largemouth bass, wild turkey, house sparrow, starling, eucalyptus, tree of heaven, yellow star thistle, field mustard, poison oak? Answer: all but poison oak. If you scored one hundred on this impromptu test, congratulations, for I'll bet no more than one Californian in a hundred could match your score. If you didn't, don't fret. You have reason to be confused. Consider the tumbleweed, symbol of the American West. How many people realize that this plant is an alien, an impostor, a Eurasian transplant that, if called by its other name, Russian thistle, would never have been filmed blowing across the set of a John Wayne movie? Then again, John Wayne's real name was Marion Morrison, and he hailed from Iowa.

The exotic species crisis would be difficult enough to deal with if it was restricted to species that arrived accidentally, but unfortunately it is not. It also includes a number of species that were purposefully introduced, part of mankind's ceaseless urge to improve upon nature. Tamarisk was imported to the Southwest from Eurasia as a windbreak and ornamental plant. I'll admit that, in a confined setting, tamarisk in bloom has an attractive quality to it. However, its propensity for sucking precious water out of fragile desert riparian areas has devastated native plants, which tend to disappear with the arrival of the ever-spreading tamarisk. This plant is now a problem in the southern Diablo Range.

As troublesome as tamarisk is, at least it has no constituency challenging its removal. Unfortunately, the same cannot be said for several animal species. Just before 1900, red foxes were transplanted from the Midwest to the Central Valley in the hopes of adding another fur-bearing mammal to the region. The economic booster shot pinned on the tail of the red fox never quite materialized, and while fox trapping declined, the fox, unfortunately, did not. They spread to the coast and into the foothills, where they have a negative impact on ground-nesting birds. As they claim new territory, they have the potential to displace San Joaquin kit foxes, an endangered species. But efforts to eradicate them have faced staunch opposition from animal rights groups, which decry the lethal control deemed necessary to remove red foxes. It's a question of values, of the lives of individual animals over the health of ecological communities, and that conflict has driven a wedge between groups who have long been allies on many environmental issues.

Then there are species that were introduced for purely aesthetic reasons. By 1900, acclimatization societies arose in the United States. Composed primarily of immigrants from Western Europe, they sought to improve their new home by importing animals and plants from their native soil. Most of these attempted introductions failed miserably, for most species are not equipped to survive in a land where they did not evolve. But some succeeded, and the most notorious success story was that of the European starling.

In 1890, a drug manufacturer named Eugene Scheifflin released four dozen starlings in Central Park. History does not reveal what type of drugs Mr. Scheifflin produced nor to what extent he partook of his own concoctions. No accusations here; I'm just wondering if perhaps something other than eccentricity fueled his determination to let those damned birds go. His goal was to release every type of bird mentioned in the works of Shakespeare into Central Park. If only the bard had mentioned nightjars instead of starlings, the avian fauna of North America would be much better off today. As it turned out, those four dozen starlings took to this continent like a televangelist to a blank check, reaching the West Coast in fifty years and today nesting in every state except Hawaii. Their population is estimated at two hundred million, making them quite possibly the most numerous bird on the continent. Besides causing considerable agricultural damage, these aggressive, gregarious birds take over nesting sites and drive out native birds. The starling is a textbook example of why introducing species to areas outside their range is a phenomenally bad idea. No one can predict with certainty what consequences will arise in the aftermath of species introduction. It's hard to determine which species will become invasive and which won't, since none wrought ecological havoc in their native land. Certain traits might serve as warnings: adaptability, a generalized diet, and fecundity, among others. But the scientific study of invasive species cannot quite predict which species will over-run a landscape, let alone anticipate the many negative impacts associated with an invasion. That ability to run amok in new territory is what makes nonnative species so threatening, for once entrenched, they become virtually impossible to eradicate. Gaining a foothold in a new land, they achieve a type of species im-mortality enjoyed by few native organisms.

To be fair, I'd like to think that Mr. Scheifflin had no idea his small flock of starlings would transmogrify into the ecological monster they've become, and had he an inkling of this, he probably would've abandoned the whole idea and drowned his disappointment in a bottle of special elixir. Likewise, I want to believe that those responsible for releasing Eastern fox squirrels in the parks of California would have nixed the idea if they realized their actions might result in the disappearance of our native tree squirrel.

Yet there's another viewpoint that sees biodiversity differently. It's the line of thinking that argues, "So what if bullfrogs replace California red-legged frogs? They're larger, an upgrade. Why not red foxes instead of kit foxes? Kit foxes are drab compared to the handsomely colored red fox. And what's wrong with fox squirrels replacing Western gray squirrels? How can this constitute a biodiversity crisis? One creature goes; another takes its place. Out with the old, in with the new. No net loss. Don't you think you're overreacting with all this extinction gloom and doom? Aren't you being an elitist with that native versus nonnative drivel?"

To all of the above I say wrong, wrong, wrong. I for one don't want to wit-ness the species that have inhabited California for hundreds of thousands of years or longer disappear because of somebody else's idea of an "improved" version. I detest watching California become overrun with animals and plants from somewhere else. This isn't the South. We don't need bass and sunfish in our waterways or opossums in our woods. This isn't the Midwest; we could do without red foxes and bullfrogs. This isn't China, so the tree of heaven can go to hell. Those pining for the East Coast can go back and take your wild turkeys and fox squirrels with you. We have a fine assemblage of game animals here; there was no need whatsoever to release wild boar—*pigs*, for God's sake—into our woodlands.

Think of the *Mona Lisa*. Now imagine trying to improve it. Why not make her a blonde? How about replacing her demure smile with an ear-to-ear grin, flashing pearly white teeth? Maybe show a little cleavage as well. Would these, or any other changes, make for a better *Mona Lisa*? Of course not because if you alter the *Mona Lisa*, you no longer have the *Mona Lisa*. The Ramona Lisa, perhaps, or the Mona Leslie. But the *Mona Lisa* is lost, and although an alternative may hang in its place, it's not the same and certainly no improvement.

Here's an idea: anyone interested in releasing a plant or animal outside its range should first have to spend time observing the ecosystem they propose to alter. Look that red-legged frog in the eye. Marvel at the beauty of that wildflower. Follow the petite tracks of that kit fox. Take a good, long look at such things and then ask yourself which you'd like to replace with something from somewhere else. The more you acquaint yourself with a natural habitat, the more you will come to appreciate it and the less likely you will be to view an introduced species as an enhancement. When it comes to nonnative species, there are no improvements, just varying degrees of degradation. The introduction of opossums here was like adding rouge to the face of the *Mona Lisa*. Wild turkeys? Glossy lipstick. Red foxes? A nose ring. Wild pigs? A Mohawk hairdo.

A wild landscape, with its full complement of native flora and fauna, is like a work of art, eons in the making. To defile such an object would be unconscionable. It's time we began treating our wild places like the masterpieces they are.

Long before the state highway was constructed, prior to the placement of the stagecoach route, predating even the footpath trod by Native Americans,

Pacheco Pass has served as a pathway. Winds and fog from the Pacific funnel through, allowing closed-canopy forests to persist along the pass. My property includes some of that, a steep, north-facing slope, dark and rife with vegetation. One December afternoon, I descended the knoll where my home stands into that forested hillside. I entered a glade, through which filtered strands of brilliant sunshine. At the glade's edge was a small boulder, a promontory from which I planned to sit and observe.

As I took my seat, I glanced downhill to the base of a live oak, where I saw a Western gray squirrel. While I fumbled for my binoculars, the squirrel scrambled up the tree and vanished among the foliage. I peered into the treetops until dusk descended, but I saw the squirrel no more. The next day I returned, hoping the incident would repeat itself, but it did not. As the days passed, I returned dozens of times, watching and waiting, but I never again saw a squirrel. While I'm certain I saw a Western gray squirrel, I wanted a better look, if only to reassure myself that the animal, and the species, is still around. I keep hoping that maybe the situation is not so bleak, that there are still places in these mountains where the Western gray squirrel persists. So I will continue searching this slice of forest, hoping that providence, and Mona Lisa, will smile upon me.

Once There Were Bears

The Tragic Demise of the California Grizzly

ONCE THERE WERE bears. Here. In California. Yes, the state harbors a healthy population of black bears. But those are not the bears of which I speak. The bear to which I am referring is the Great Bear, the grizzly, *Ursus arctos*, icon of Western wilderness, the preeminent animal in North America.

Once there were bears. Here in the Diablo Range, a cursory look at place names reveals at least eighteen different geographical features named after grizzlies, far more than with any other creature. Within Henry W. Coe State Park, there are six such references, spanning three languages: Grizzly Creek, Bear Mountain, Bear Springs, and Grizzly Gulch—also *Canada de los Osos*, or Canyon of the Bears, and Orestimba Creek, *Ores* meaning bear in the dialect of the native Mutsun. The Great Bear is everywhere, yet it is nowhere to be found. And that is more than a shame; it is a tragedy.

Once there were bears. Not merely confined to the fastness of the High Sierra, grizzlies roamed throughout the state, thriving everywhere but the deserts. And how they did thrive! At the dawn of the Gold Rush, California was teeming with grizzlies, sporting the densest population on earth, more than in the salmon-rich inlets of coastal Alaska or the forests and meadows of what would become Yellowstone National Park. Lewis and Clark encountered grizzlies on their journey throughout the West, but with nothing approaching the frequency recorded by the Spaniards who colonized or the early Americans settlers. Early chroniclers reported seeing forty or fifty bears during the course of a day's travel, of observing dozens congregating around food sources such as a beached whale or valley oak.

The surfeit of bears in California staggers the imagination, for nowhere since have they existed in such abundance. Before the Gold Rush, ten thousand grizzlies may have roamed California. To put that into perspective, the entire grizzly population south of Canada is currently estimated at just over one thousand.

Grizzlies arrived in California over one hundred thousand years ago, after crossing the Bering Land Bridge, well before the arrival of the Paleoindians, the first human occupants of California and the ancestors of California's indigenous peoples. For the past ten thousand years, the California landscape was dominated by humans and grizzly bears, though not necessarily in that order.

The Native Americans inhabiting California did not belong to a single tribe; there were numerous small factions under several linguistic groups. In general, grizzlies and Native Americans managed a stable, if at times uneasy, coexistence. Both utilized many of the same food resources, in particular salmon and acorns. The close proximity of the two must have produced its share of conflict, for indigenous people regarded the bear with fear and reverence. Occasionally, they killed grizzlies, no mean feat for a people lacking firearms. Of the strategies employed, two in particular stand out. One involved constructing a pitfall trap with bait suspended from the limb of a tree. After falling into the trap, the bear was dispatched with spears or arrows. As sketchy as this method was, it paled in comparison to another involving pursuing a bear with bows and arrows. To accomplish this, five or six men fleet of foot were needed. Upon locating a bear, one of the men would approach it while the others hid behind trees or boulders some distance apart from one another. The first man would shoot the bear with an arrow, provoking the bear into chasing him. The man would then run toward the tree or rock where the next runner was stationed. Upon arriving, the second man would reveal himself, shoot another arrow into the bear, and the bear would take off after the new runner. This would go on, the bear receiving arrow wounds while encountering fresh runners. Eventually, the combination of wounds and exhaustion would finish off the bear, but for that to transpire, everything had to go right, and by all accounts that was the exception rather than the rule. I imagine some pretechnological equivalent of "Houston, we have a problem" was frequently uttered during such outings.

So, while Native Americans occasionally killed grizzlies, it was a dangerous undertaking. For their part, grizzlies seemed to show little interest in the affairs of California's native peoples. At the same time, they did not go out of their way to avoid them and didn't seem to fear their two-legged contemporaries. This would abruptly change with the arrival of the Spanish.

The Spanish colonization of California ushered in the mission era, a much-romanticized period when agriculture took root. Missions and pueblos were established along the coast from the San Francisco Bay region to San Diego, as a new and different culture arrived. Agriculture transformed the California landscape. Spaniards raised cattle for their hides and tallow, and vast herds proliferated in the mission lands. Horses were left to roam unattended, and cattle were often dispatched and skinned on the open range. Those carcasses nourished a multitude of scavengers, including grizzlies. Due to a surplus of livestock, drought and overgrazing jeopardized the holdings of the missions. During such times, excess horses were killed so that enough forage and water remained for cattle, which had greater economic value. Left out on the range, those carcasses provided a copious bounty for grizzlies. Cattle raised for food were housed in corrals near the missions and slaughtered on site. The remains of butchered stock were left there, once again providing a smorgasbord for bears. As a result, grizzlies acquired a taste for livestock, preying first on the herds of the missions, then later on those of the Mexican ranchos, and finally upon those of the American settlers who descended upon the state in droves following the discovery of gold in 1848. For these depredations, the grizzly would pay dearly. The habit of slaughtering and butchering livestock in settled areas led bears to associate humans with food. The worst transgression people can commit is to allow bears to make that connection. It's a recipe for disaster, sometimes for people but always for bears. Prior to the introduction of livestock, grizzlies were in all likelihood only occasional predators. Two carnivores better suited for hunting, wolves and mountain lions, were the primary predators in early California. With their keen sense of smell, grizzlies probably scavenged more often than they killed, and with an abundance of plant food, the omnivorous grizzly consumed more vegetation than meat. However, the easy pickings provided by the missions were too good to pass up, and the stage was set for a conflict that would eventually doom the California grizzly.

By bringing horses to California, the Spanish introduced an animal that would play a pivotal role in turning the tide against grizzlies. Horses enabled men to pursue grizzlies in ways unimaginable to the native peoples. Astride fleet, well-trained steeds, vaqueros subdued grizzlies with *reatas*. A team of riders would venture off in pursuit of a bear and vanquish it by lassoing its limbs and neck. Teamwork was essential, for to attempt to rope a bear alone was risky. A roped bear might sit on its haunches and use its forelimbs to draw in the astonished horse and rider in a tug of war. Unless the rider could sever the rope, he faced the grim prospect of dismounting and trying to escape on foot. This happened with enough frequency that vaqueros began greasing sections of rope beforehand.

Once subdued, one of several unpleasant fates awaited the bear. Sometimes the bear was tied to a tree, where, thus immobilized, it could be dispatched with impunity. Often bears were killed at the point of capture as horses pulled limbs in opposite directions. The thought of simply letting the bear go apparently never crossed the minds of those involved.

Unfortunately, the most enduring legacy of the grizzly in California was its starring role in battles against bulls. This tradition did not arise in California; it was imported from Spain, where European brown bears, the old-world twin of the grizzly, had long been pitted against bulls to satisfy an obsession with blood sports. In California, although impromptu bear and bull fights were occasionally staged on the open range, such spectacles were more frequently conducted in an outdoor arena. These battles were often held in conjunction with holidays, festivals, or *fiestas*. The other participant in this sanguinary affair, the bull, was a far cry from the placid creature that grazes contemporary hillsides. Today's bulls, despite their size, have had nearly all their wildness and aggression bred out of them. The bulls of the Spanish era were longhorns—hardier, wilder, ill-tempered, and more unpredictable than modern breeds.

If it was possible to turn those traditional bear and bull fights into even more disgusting examples of man's inhumanity toward animals, the post–Gold Rush settlers quite possibly succeeded. They lowered the bar by commercializing a tradition overflowing with sadism, charging admission, and placing wagers on the outcome. A victorious bear was sometimes forced to fight a second bull and even a third. There is at least one account whereby a bear was forced to fight two bulls simultaneously. To spice up the proceedings, bears were also pitted against other creatures such as mountain lions, donkeys, and on at least one occasion, an African lion. I found it interesting, and perhaps more than a little bit telling, that in all the accounts I've read of such battles, the bear was rarely the aggressor. When pitted against bulls, the two were often tethered together and frequently had to be goaded into fighting. Battle typically began with the bull on the attack, while the bear assumed a crouching position. A short fight usually went in favor of the bull. The more protracted the skirmish, the greater the advantage was to the bear. During the Spanish period, the bears usually won, while during the American era, most battles went to the bull. Perhaps as grizzlies became scarce, smaller bears, maybe even black bears, were used. Not everyone approved of this sorry spectacle. After years of public outcry, the state legislature took steps to outlaw such fights, initially by barring them on the Sabbath. Obviously, something about this tawdry practice was deemed to be offensive to the Creator. I would hope that it involved more than a disapproval of wagering. Over time, additional laws were passed, but the sad fact is that bear and bull fights ended because the grizzly became increasingly rare.

The Gold Rush marked the beginning of the end for the California grizzly. Gone were the sprawling ranchos providing an unprecedented windfall of carrion. In their place were smaller farms and ranches where cattle were raised not for hides or tallow but for meat. The days of skinned carcasses lying about the open range were over. The herds of semiwild horses periodically shot and left to the bears also vanished. American settlers practiced animal husbandry on a smaller scale. Unfortunately, grizzlies had by then accumulated several generations' worth of experience feasting on livestock, and with carrion greatly diminished, they turned to depredation. In response, a legion of bear hunters arose, and they were highly effective despite the shortcomings of their weaponry. Prior to the invention of the repeating rifle, bear hunters armed themselves with single shot muzzle-loading rifles or pistols. The wise hunter carried both, allowing him a second shot. An even safer strategy was to hunt with several similarly armed companions. Because those rifles lacked the power of modern artillery, hunters had to fire at an uncomfortably close distance if the bear was to be taken with one well-placed shot. Hunters often fired from within fifty yards. An otherwise placid grizzly can be ferocious when wounded, and many men were maimed or killed while hunting bears. This aggression on the part of wounded bears, rooted though it was in self-defense, only served to increase the enmity with which settlers viewed grizzlies.

Yet firearms were but one of several weapons in the arsenal of men against bears. Massive steel-jawed traps were set to incapacitate bears, which could then be shot with little fear of retaliation. In forests, log cabin traps were constructed. During the 1870s, repeating rifles emerged, giving hunters a further advantage. The least risky and most effective weapon was strychnine, a poison applied to bait and used heavily in ranching areas. This may have been the *coup de grace* for the California grizzly. As early as 1870, grizzlies were becoming scarce, disappearing first from the settled valleys and lowlands. They disappeared in earnest during the 1880s, and as the twentieth century dawned, they persisted only in the mountains of Southern California and the southern Sierra Nevada. It has long been supposed that the last grizzly in California was shot in 1922 just north of Sequoia National Park in a small valley called Horse Corral Meadow. However, it is likely that at least one more bear held on. In 1924, workers in Sequoia National Park reported seeing a large grizzly in the vicinity of Moro Rock. Another sighting occurred later in the year near the headwaters of Cliff Creek, a half-dozen miles east. However, no grizzlies were reported thereafter in the region, and although reports trickled in from various parts of the state until the 1940s, it could be that this bear truly was the last California grizzly. If it was, I'm glad it defied the odds and died a natural death. I'm happy that it did not convulse in agony after swallowing bait laced with strychnine. It's pleasing to know that this bear did not end up as a hide covering someone's living room floor or a head mounted in surly repose on the walls of some mountain cabin. Most of all, I am grateful that no one could claim credit for killing the last California grizzly and thus milk that dubious accomplishment for some twisted form of social status.

With the California grizzly relegated to oblivion, what are we to make of him today? There are many accounts of California grizzlies, though the veracity of some can be called into question. It is testimony to the cultural importance of the bear that so many references to it exist, for it was surely the most prominent animal in California, both on the landscape and in the psyche of the people who dwelled in its midst. In sharp contrast stands the paucity of museum specimens and scientific literature devoted to the California grizzly. For all the bears that met their fate at the hands of man, a paltry few skeletons, skulls, or hides remain preserved. Photographs exist, but all depict captive bears or bears that had been slain. Unfortunately, there are no pictures of wild California grizzlies, nor are there any scientific studies.

That grizzlies were once abundant in California is well documented, but more telling than references to a large population were accounts of large numbers of bears seen together. One witness in the Salinas Valley described a dozen grizzlies gathered beneath a large oak, feasting upon acorns, shaking overhanging limbs to get more to fall. Such social behavior is unusual, its closest equivalent being the grizzlies gathered along salmon runs in Alaska. Assuming these sizable congregations were the result of a bountiful food supply, it may have been that the home ranges of California grizzlies were smaller than those of contemporary bears and that the carrying capacity of the land allowed more grizzlies to occupy a given area.

Historical accounts of California grizzlies had them attaining prodigious size. Slain bears were often said to surpass one thousand pounds, and there are even reports of bears exceeding a ton. Certainly, the propensity for exaggeration is great, but even allowing for a healthy dose of truth-stretching, it's likely that California grizzlies were larger than those in the Rockies. This size difference may be attributable to an abundance of food rich in fats and carbohydrates. With a substantial year-round food supply anchored by acorns and healthy salmon runs, grizzlies in California may have attained sizes exceeding those of grizzlies anywhere outside of coastal Alaska.

Though classified as carnivores, grizzlies are highly omnivorous. In fact, their dentition suggests a plant-oriented diet. Their molars are broad, like ours, designed for plant material, unlike the sharper shearing molars possessed by the cat and dog families. Their long claws, roundly feared as lethal weapons, are used primarily for digging the roots and tubers of plants. Of course, grizzlies also eat meat, feasting on creatures varying in size from ants to beached whales.

Grizzlies have the ability to adapt to changing circumstances. California grizzlies became more nocturnal over time, transforming from a creature that did not fear humans into one that took great measures to avoid people. Such adaptability suggests a high level of intelligence. Individual grizzlies vary widely in temperament and personality. Part of this complexity reveals itself in a tendency to indulge in play. Both Storer and Tevis (*The California Grizzly*) and Snyder (*Bear in Mind*) relate a fascinating story from the pre–Gold Rush era that took place on a ranch in Southern California. The husband was out tending stock while the wife was at the ranch house with their young son. She left the boy unattended while she washed clothes a short distance away. Upon her return she was horrified to discover a grizzly frolicking with the boy. This went on for quite some time, for the boy's mother was hesitant to interfere lest her presence anger the bear. The bear eventually ambled off, leaving the boy unmolested. Perhaps this story is a tall tale, but accounts of grizzlies sliding down snow-covered slopes and footage of a grizzly and a wolf engaged in what for all the world looks like play serve as reminders that there is more to the grizzly than meets the eye.

Still, ferocity captures our attention. The historical record is replete with accounts of bear attacks, but to understand these, it's important to consider the context. Grizzlies are most likely to attack when wounded, surprised at close range (particularly a female with cubs), or disturbed at a food source. To bears, these conditions all represent threats; subsequent attacks are in self-defense. It is ironic that the grizzly, long branded as a ferocious man-eater, has fear at the base of its aggression. This is by far the most misunderstood aspect of the grizzly, ingrained deeply in our collective perception. Its former scientific name says it all: *Ursus horribilis*, the horrible bear.

Settlers were both surprised and indignant when grizzlies turned upon those who had wounded them. This was something animals just did not do; mankind finally encountered a creature that would not limp away to expire but would literally fight for its life. No creature they had encountered retaliated like the grizzly. Yet if such pluck evinced grudging admiration, it also raised the level of animosity between man and bear. The balance of the blame in these skirmishes lies squarely in the camp of the bear hunters, who, after all, were the aggressors. Time and time again, newspaper accounts tell of men shooting bears at uncomfortably close distances, usually with woefully inadequate weaponry. Frequently, this blunder was compounded by trailing wounded bears into thickets, which is as foolhardy an act of bravado as I can imagine. Stories abound of wounded grizzlies maiming men, and bears were demonized as bloodthirsty killers, but when all the sensationalism is stripped away, grizzlies are actually peaceful unless provoked. For all the hair-raising accounts of bear attacks in early California, examples of grizzlies stalking and preying upon people are nowhere to be found.

More than perhaps any other wild beast, bears have played a prominent role in human culture. This is especially true in the Northern Hemisphere. In the West, the grizzly has assumed a cultural significance exceeding that of any other animal, and tales of legendary grizzlies abound throughout the region. Bears serve as symbols, representing a type of strength, courage, and independence that we can only aspire to. The grizzly takes center stage on what is, for my money, the finest flag of them all, the California flag. We have taken much from bears, and this has been greatly to their detriment. As sources of entertainment, bears have been abused for centuries, and if you believe that we've outgrown the barbarity of the old bear and bull fights, think again. Though no longer pitted in life-or-death struggles, bears throughout the globe provide "entertainment" as they perform stunts and "dance" for us. While at first blush this may seem benign, delving deeper into the dancing bear phenomenon reveals a culture of appalling abuse. Dancing bears are obtained as cubs, in a process that often involves killing the mother. Once captive, cubs must endure having their septum pierced to allow the passage of a chain or rope. The rope is affixed to a leash, which the trainer tugs to force the bear onto its hind legs. The ensuing "dance" is no expression of exuberance; cubs "dance" to alleviate pain. While grizzlies have not been subjected to this particular brand of inhumane treatment, their old world counterpart, the European brown bear, has, and this deplorable practice still takes place in Eastern Europe and Asia.

During their heyday, California grizzlies were exploited for entertainment in roadhouse zoos and menageries. The most famous of these was that of Grizzly Adams, frontiersman turned showman. Even if you extend the benefit of the doubt to the proprietors of such exhibits and believe that the animals are treated well, is there not something profoundly disrespectful about displaying such noble creatures for no motive other than profit?

Sadly, the exploitation of bears is not limited to entertainment. Bears, or more accurately their body parts, are used to cure a wide variety of ailments in traditional Eastern medicine. Again, grizzlies do not suffer the brunt of this carnage, but occasionally they're poached to fuel the demand for gallbladders. Contained inside the gallbladder is bile, and bear bile is believed to cure a variety of maladies. Several decades ago, bear "farms" were established throughout China and Southeast Asia, where captive bears could be milked for bile. The idea was to procure a steady supply from captive bears, since their wild cohorts were getting harder and harder to come by. Besides, a wild bear could provide bile just once; captive bears could, like cows, be milked over and over. What with all this talk of dancing, farms, and milking, you'd think there was one hell of a hoedown going on. Unfortunately, those terms are euphemisms. In a typical bear farm, bears live out the bulk of their miserable lives caged in pens that are scarcely larger than they are. Years of confinement in such cramped quarters result in deformities and impaired internal organs. Bears are held in such fashion all for the ease and safety of the "farmers," who can thus extract bile without fear of injury. As for the bears, well, that's the way it goes. Although some bear farms claim to be more humane than others because they allow larger living areas, the mere notion of a "humane" bear farm strikes me as oxymoronic. The wretched conditions and the painful milking process preempt any use of the term.

The most frustrating aspect of the bear medicine trade is that alternatives exist, such as herbal remedies and synthetic drugs. Convincing people to use them, however, is another matter. I swear to Bob Dole I would put up with a lifetime's worth of asinine Viagra commercials in which old goats giddily resurrect their libidos if it meant that bears would no longer have to suffer or lose their lives for no greater purpose than to allow some middle-aged man to pitch a tent. Yes, indeed, restoring male virility is one of the alleged curative powers of bear medicine. Find a rare animal threatened by poaching, and I'll bet dollars to doughnuts that aphrodisiacal qualities are spurring the demand. A stiff prick has no conscience—there's a proverb you won't easily find in a collection of venerable pearls of wisdom, but it's as true as anything ever uttered by Confucius or Aesop. I weep for my gender.

The last. How many times has that forlorn adjective been applied in conjunction with the grizzly? In some areas, the last wolf has attained legendary status, and I suppose some Easterners have stories of the last mountain lion. In California, good luck finding a reference to the last pronghorn, elk, or condor in a given area. But the grizzly was different. Every community, it seems, has a legend surrounding the last grizzly. Such was the influence the Great Bear had upon us.

I began searching for stories of the grizzly's last stand in the Diablo Range when I was a teenager. I questioned several old-timers, men who were born around the turn of the century and had lived in the hills, asking if they had seen bears in their youth. All responded similarly: they had never encountered bears but knew of others—fathers, uncles, older brothers—who did. I was hoping to speak with someone who had come across grizzlies along the same paths I walk. At the time it was of great importance to me, although I could not explain why. What I knew full well was that time was of the essence, that the window of opportunity for hearing first-hand tales of California grizzlies would soon close forever. And it did.

Having failed to find anyone who remembered grizzlies in the Diablo Range, I searched historical references. The writings of Sada Coe tell of the last grizzly in the region, which she claimed resided in what is now Henry W. Coe State Park until 1910. The journals of William Brewer contained in the epic tome, *Up and Down California*, were particularly revealing. Working for the United States Geological Survey, he was a member of a survey party traveling throughout the state from 1861–4. Brewer's detailed accounts of flora and fauna were insightful, and he devoted several chapters to his adventures in the Diablo Range. He writes of seeing grizzlies, or grizzly sign, at several locations. On the slopes of Mount Oso, he describes large patches of ground raked by the claws of bears digging for roots and bulbs. In Del Puerto Canyon, numerous tracks were discovered in their camp following an overnight stay. Along Pacheco Pass, two members of the party were exploring a canyon when they happened upon a bear with cubs. To their great relief, the bears beat a hasty retreat. Though the exact location wasn't specified, there is a slim possibility that it may have taken place on property I now call my own.

But of all the accounts I read, the one that resonated most is an article featuring Adam Hubbard, a homesteader who settled in the mountains east of Mount Hamilton. Among his travails was an encounter with a grizzly. Hubbard was headed toward a corral where he had lost some colts to a mountain lion. While traveling through brush, he surprised a grizzly, which left him seriously injured. He survived this ordeal and lived to the age of eighty-five. The Hubbard ranch was eventually sold, and the current owners have leased it to my father for over twenty years. During that time, I've devoted many days to exploring that property and have come to know its canyons, creeks, and ridges well. I have thought often of Hubbard's encounter, trying to determine where it took place. It soon occurred to me that to better understand the California grizzly, I had to expand my search beyond the written record and back onto the land.

Aspen trees are renowned for their dazzling displays of fall color. But that's not what brought me here, to a grove in Yellowstone National Park, in midsummer. Aspens have another feature I find fascinating. Their smooth, bone-white bark, when punctured, produces black scar tissue that stands in stark contrast to the rest of the trunk. While this leaves them vulnerable to imbeciles who carve their initials on tree trunks, it also reveals the activities of animals. The tree beside me shows the clamberings of a bear cub, a succession of claw marks ascending the trunk, like footprints in mud. Aspens record stories, suspending a moment in time that can be read years later. As I returned to California, the question that ran through my mind was "Can a tree tell a story that occurred over a century ago?"

Aspens are cold-tolerant trees and cannot exist in mild climes such as the Diablo Range. The nearest aspens are found in the Sierra Nevada, and while a close relative of aspens lines the borders of streams throughout the range, the bark of the Fremont cottonwood (*Populus fremontii*) is coarse and lacks the ability to preserve markings. There is, however, another type of tree that could function in the Diablo Range much as aspens do in the Rockies: manzanitas. Though technically shrubs, some assume treelike form and exceed fifteen feet in height. Thickets of manzanitas are common throughout the Diablo Range and were popular with grizzlies. As bedding areas, their cover provided relief from the scorching summer sun, while their fruit provided a plentiful food source. Manzanita, after all, is Spanish for "little apple." More importantly, manzanitas possess a reddish-brown bark that is as smooth as polished stone. While running my fingers down the trunk of a large manzanita, I was struck by an idea that straddled the chasm between brilliance and lunacy. If marks left by grizzlies remain visible on aspens, might they not also be preserved on manzanitas? I spent several afternoons exploring this possibility in a ten-acre thicket on the ranch formerly owned by Adam Hubbard, scouring the trunks of dozens of large manzanitas. Some bore the markings of antler rubs. Others depicted the scratch marks of bobcats. Girdled low around several were cakings of dried mud, the rubbings of wild pigs. Yet nothing I saw resembled the markings of a grizzly. I dejectedly pondered that my notion was less genius than absurdity. Several conditions would have to be met in order for grizzly sign to remain visible on bark for over a century. One is that, like aspens, manzanita bark would need to possess properties allowing perforations to remain visible for a long while. It may be that manzanitas heal quickly and thoroughly. Another involves life span. My knowledge of manzanitas lies toward the shallow end of the pool, for I have no inkling how long they live. One would have to survive for at least a century and a half in order to display grizzly sign. It may be that the manzanitas I examined simply weren't old enough, while those that were had passed from the scene, like the bear itself.

Once there were bears. If I was asked to encapsulate all the ills that have befallen the California landscape using just one sentence, those four words would be my response. When California lost the grizzly, the Golden State was forever blemished, its gold fading to pyrite in a matter of decades. A one-hundred-thousand-year tenure on the land produced a creature more uniquely Californian than any artifact of our brief and harried culture. When the grizzly vanished, California lost part of its soul, its wild heart. California may have the fifth-largest economy in the world, it may be the hub of the motion picture and television industry, the epicenter of the high-tech universe, and it may have a benevolent climate, but none of that alters the shameful fact that the creature adorning the state flag was exterminated. When you kill off your symbols, something is amiss. Such a culture can hardly aspire to greatness. There are over five hundred place names throughout the state referring to bears; I doubt any were inspired by black bears. When that last grizzly expired, those names became hollow. To get an idea of just how far we have fallen from grace, consider this: some ecologists assert that feral hogs—swine, for God's sake—have assumed the role once held by the mighty grizzly in our degraded ecosystems. These creatures of a lesser God were released in California around the time the grizzly disappeared and are about as awe-inspiring as the prize in a Cracker Jack box. Anybody suggest putting a pig on the state flag? I didn't think so.

I don't remember when I first learned that grizzlies once roamed California, only being astonished that such a magnificent creature once dwelled here. As a boy, I sought out old-timers, but all I got was tantalizing secondhand knowledge—the location of a tree under which a bear had been shot or that of a canyon where they were frequently sighted. I searched for century-old scars on manzanitas, to no avail. One delirious afternoon, I was examining Native American house pits above Isabel Creek when I was overcome with the feeling that something lay buried just below the surface. I returned with a shovel and a pickax, dug down into that hard Diablo ground until blisters formed and sweat poured off my face. Of course I found nothing. I don't even know what I was expecting to find. Maybe a bear claw necklace or some such amulet. I would've been happy with a mandible, even a lowly molar, any tangible evidence that something of the Great Bear remained, that it was not gone forever. After striking out again, it was time to pay a visit to Monarch.

In 1889, newspaper magnate William Randolph Hearst decided he wanted a grizzly bear. Not a cute cub or modest-size female—he wanted a big, hulking bruin. His intent was not to bring attention to the plight of the grizzly, which by that time had vanished from most of the state. Hearst was strictly interested in self-promotion or, more precisely, promoting the *San Francisco Examiner*, of which he was the publisher. The *Examiner* proclaimed itself to be "the monarch of the dailies," and in keeping with that theme, Hearst dispatched a reporter with extensive outdoor experience to capture a grizzly to serve as a living symbol of the paper.

Alan Kelly trekked down to the mountains surrounding Santa Barbara and Los Angeles in the spring of 1889, but as summer came and went he still had not procured a bear. Accustomed to getting what he wanted when he wanted it, Hearst was impatient and close to firing him when Kelly received word that a large grizzly had been captured in a log cabin trap in the San Gabriel Mountains. Kelly purchased the bear, and Mr. Hearst finally got his wish. The bear was transported to San Francisco, where he was dubbed "Monarch" and put on display before a curious public. Monarch adapted to life in captivity, which was fortunate, for his capture was no short publicity stunt; Monarch spent the rest of his life in a cage in Golden Gate Park. By 1911 Monarch had grown old and decrepit and was euthanized after twenty-two years in exile, quite possibly the last captive California grizzly. Handlers recalled that he was intelligent, with a distinct personality. Upon his death, he was weighed, and he tipped the scales at over eleven hundred pounds. Shortly thereafter he was stuffed and put on display at the California Academy of Sciences in San Francisco.

On the day I came to pay homage, the academy was bustling. I found Monarch preserved in a glass case, a representation as stark and spartan as that of a creature preserved in formaldehyde. In life Monarch was a dark grizzly, but exposure has rendered his pelage light brown. He was also ridiculously overstuffed, as if filled with helium. I remained at the exhibit for half an hour, yet during that time, no one else came by to linger for even a moment at this extraordinary creature. While I appreciated the solitude, it bothered me that nobody was paying attention to what was, in my opinion, the most meaningful exhibit in the entire collection. The Great Bear deserves to be remembered. Actually, it deserves much more.

Several years ago, I was leafing through a book when I set eyes upon the most compelling picture I have ever seen, the kind that sears itself into your consciousness, piercing your dreams while you sleep and invading your thoughts when awake. In the middle of the picture stood a stately oak and, beneath it, a contingent of grizzlies. The photo, lamentably, was not authentic but rather a digitally enhanced creation, yet its impact upon me could not have been more real. It evoked a visceral reaction, a pang of loss, of something sacred and hallowed lying just beyond my experience. It clarified why I spent so much time searching for a creature that had vanished long before I was born. I love the Diablo Range with the kind of hard-earned emotion that can only come from decades of familiarity with the land. I've seen its great creatures, from mountain lions to golden eagles; in recent years, I have marveled at the return of elk, pronghorn, and condors. Yet there was always something lacking, some element of missing grandeur that would revive the glory that was once present. It is all too easy to forget that wild places are more than a collection of the physical features—mountains, rivers, canyons—of which they are comprised. They are all that and then some: the wondrous assemblage of wild creatures and plants dwelling therein. Every time a species disappears from a landscape, that place loses something and becomes lessened. Without the animals, living landscapes become reduced to mere scenery. Our society has done a fine job of protecting scenery—witness the multitude of ice and rock wilderness areas—but has performed less admirably in saving living landscapes. We preserved the wonders of Yosemite Valley, yet its namesake (Yosemite is a Native American term for grizzly bear) received no such consideration.

While our nation was developing its national park system, the grizzly was disappearing from California. The grizzly didn't vanish due to habitat loss; it was exterminated. Some scoffed at the notion that the plentiful grizzly could ever vanish. As they passed from the scene in locale after locale, it was always assumed they were present in the next patch of wild country. By the time anyone noticed, it was too late. The bear was no more. Had the bear been able to hold on longer, when an environmental consciousness arose, perhaps people would have realized what they were losing and demanded its protection much as they did for sea otters and condors. But that's asking a lot of the bear, when we've already asked so much. It's time we give something back.

We can start by protecting them in the few remaining areas where they still exist. Within a decade after California lost its grizzlies, those in Oregon, Utah, and Arizona were killed off. New Mexico soon followed suit. Colorado, with a remnant population in the San Juan Mountains, held on to its grizzlies for decades—rumors of their existence in the state persist to this day—no thanks to the state's wildlife agency, which would just as soon see the grizzly gone for good. Washington lost all its grizzlies with the exception of a pitifully small number inhabiting North Cascades National Park along the Canadian border. Bears are nearly as scarce in Idaho, despite the presence of thousands of square miles of suitable habitat. Idaho grizzlies are restricted to the area around Yellowstone and the panhandle at the northern end of the state. In the continental United States, grizzlies persist in reasonable numbers only in the vicinity of Glacier and Yellowstone National Parks. The sanctuary provided by those tracts of land allowed the Great Bear to remain part of our nation's natural heritage in the lower forty-eight. That, and the protection under the Endangered Species Act, has helped to reverse the downhill trajectory the grizzly population has experienced since the days of the pioneers. Bear populations have started to rebound, and while that's good news, the fact remains that outside the boundaries of national parks, threats to grizzly habitats remain largely unabated. Subdivisions, mining, road construction, clear-cutting, and other habitat-altering practices continue to threaten the long-term viability of the grizzly, for despite the size of those parks, neither is large enough to sustain an isolated population of bears over the long haul. Moreover, the population increase may not be cause for celebration just yet. As grizzly numbers approach population goals set forth by the US Fish and Wildlife Service, the likelihood of removing the bear from the protection of the Endangered Species Act increases. While this sounds like good news, delisting the grizzly now could be disastrous. The focus on population goals over assessments of habitat viability may be a mistake. To truly recover the grizzly, its fragmented population needs to be connected. There has for some time now been a plan in place to do just that.

A reintroduction proposal for the Selway/Bitterroot region, containing the nation's largest wilderness outside Alaska, aimed to release twenty-five grizzlies there over a five-year period. Grizzlies have been absent there since the 1940s. If all goes well, that population could climb to several hundred in fifty to one hundred years. That population would link the population in Yellowstone with that in the Northern Continental Divide, providing additional genetic vigor. By the end of 2000, this plan was ready to be implemented, but then George W. Bush became president. One of the first things he did upon taking office was to shelve the proposal, at the request of Idaho governor Dirk Kempthorne. During his tenure, Kempthorne drank deeply from the well of ignorance as he assailed reintroduction efforts, citing public safety. His fearmongering led me to wonder if perhaps at some point he attempted to jump the Snake River Canyon—*sans* motorcycle. Kempthorne's successor, Butch Otter, may be even less enthusiastic about the prospect of grizzly reintroduction, if that's possible. Judging by his stance on wolf management (if eradication can be deemed management), Idahoans who value their natural heritage would be better served with a real otter as governor. As for Kempthorne, he has since been *promoted* to Secretary of the Interior. The fate of grizzly reintroduction now rests in his hands. Sigh.

Though the plan is nixed for the time being, the day may come when a more environmentally friendly administration occupies the White House and the proposal becomes a reality. If we can accomplish that—to recover the grizzly where it still persists—then perhaps we can dare imagine the only truly good and just ending to the saga of the California grizzly, which is no ending at all, but a resurrection. Prevailing wisdom holds that there is no room left in California for the grizzly. The remaining wild areas may be too insubstantial and fragmented to support them. Perhaps that's true, but is it not possible that with a greater abundance of food, California's wild places might be able to support higher densities of grizzlies than comparable tracts in the Rockies, so that a population might sustain itself in a smaller area? Call it wishful thinking, but I believe that grizzlies could once again exist in California, though not in the numbers they once did nor in all the places they occupied. The major obstacle is tolerance. Coexisting with grizzlies requires people to change, perhaps more behavior modification than most are willing to undertake. The reality is that grizzlies will continue to exist if and where we want them to, and if we can't commit to restoring them to a vital linkage corridor in the wilderness of Idaho, it's hard to see them being reintroduced to California. Nevertheless, I hold on to the dream that someday, somehow, the grizzly will return, and a wrong will have been set right. I want to live to see that day.

Gazing south from my balcony, I see the pinnacle spire of Cathedral Peak separated from Mariposa Peak by a swale that looks as if it had been sculpted. The panorama contains no buildings. After nightfall, the land is blessedly dark, save for the light of the moon. The scene before me looks as it must have a thousand years ago. Mountain lions still prowl the canyons, elk graze the ridges, and the occasional condor soars over skies it last graced over a century ago. It is as if the mountains themselves are reawakening after a long, dreary slumber. Yet all is not well, for whichever remote, dusty trail I walk, I see no tracks larger than my own. The magnificent beast whose name still haunts the land remains achingly absent, and California, once the kingdom of the grizzly, seems empty, its glory gone. Once there were bears. Now there are none.

February 2007

A Forest, One Tree
at a Time

An Ode to the Valley Oak

CLOSE YOUR EYES and imagine a picture of California. What did you come up with? The Golden Gate Bridge or H-O-L-L-Y-W-O-O-D spelled in blocky, white letters on a chaparral-covered hillside? If you're cynical, perhaps you envisioned commuter traffic progressing at a snail's pace or a kingdom of suburban culs-de-sac with street names that bastardize the Spanish language.

Now think of natural areas. Maybe the rugged beauty of Big Sur, the granite-spired peaks of the High Sierra, or the grandeur of Yosemite Valley best represent California to you. Me, I see a series of undulating hills, dotted with that most magnificent tree, the valley oak (*Quercus lobata*).

Oaks have long been associated with human culture, especially in Europe. They provided the lumber for dwellings and the ships that ventured forth onto the open seas, including those that reached the New World.

In North America, oaks are found from coast to coast. All but the coldest states contain at least one species, and California features eighteen. No culture before or since has relied upon a tree for sustenance as did the native Californians upon oaks. Acorns constituted the primary food source for as much as 75 percent of the indigenous population. As a source of fats, carbohydrates, proteins, and vitamins, acorns compare favorably to modern grains such as wheat and corn. Harvested in fall, acorns were stored in granaries. While they could be roasted and eaten whole, they were typically pounded into flour, which could then be used in soups, mush, or baked into loaves of bread, which could be stored for months. Early ethnographers attributed the robust health and longevity of native Californians to this acorn-based diet, and John Muir himself swore by the favorable qualities of acorn bread.

Oaks are the most prominent trees in the Diablo Range. Scrub oak (*Quercus berberidifolia*), Tucker oak (*Quercus john-tuckeri*), and leather oak (*Quercus durata*) are found in the southern and eastern parts of the range, the last on serpentine soils. Live oaks, so labeled because they retain their leaves year round, are represented by three species, the coast (*Quercus agrifolia*), interior (*Quercus wislizenii*), and canyon live oak (*Quercus chyrsoleps*). The foliage of live oaks is considerably denser than that of deciduous oaks, resulting in a heavily shaded understory. The deciduous black oak (*Quercus kelloggii*), with large, pointed leaves, is found in the northwest portion of the range, where higher rainfall levels permit it to grow. Its fall color displays are the most striking of any tree in the region. Blue oaks (*Quercus douglasii*) are the most abundant oaks in the Diablo Range, equally at home in valleys or steep slopes. They are the most heat and drought tolerant oak, able to persist where other oaks cannot. They are closely related to valley oaks, and the two species are genetically similar enough that they often hybridize. Yet despite similarities to the blue oak, the valley oak stands alone.

Valley oaks stand alone, not just metaphorically but as a presence across the landscape. Unlike most tree species, valley oaks often grow at a considerable distance apart, typically in flat or rolling terrain. Such places drew the admiration of many early travelers. To describe the floor of the Santa Clara Valley as a parklike setting today would be unimaginable, yet early chroniclers described it in such glowing terms. Others viewed California's oak groves as superior to any they had witnessed elsewhere. Those early diarists were fortunate, for they beheld many venerable, awe-inspiring trees that are today in short supply. Regrettably, most of those were felled long ago.

Valley oaks grow best in the fertile soils of inland valleys, lands highly valued for agriculture. Many acres were lost as oaks were toppled to accommodate row crops, orchards, and vineyards. Those same lowlands were also coveted for residential development, and were cleared to slake the thirst of urban sprawl. Occasionally you can still see a remnant valley oak located in the midst of even a thoroughly developed area.

The city of Milpitas lies languorously west of the Diablo range, shoehorned inside a wedge of the Santa Clara Valley, one of a number of indistinguishable cities in the megalopolis that is the Bay Area. Whatever small-town charm it once possessed was bartered long ago in exchange for "progress," a swelling sea of tract housing and revenue-producing industrial sites. In its current incarnation as a bland nether land of chain restaurants, megamalls, and suburban houses, it is hardly unique. Milpitas has within its borders a number of business parks, an oxymoron for the ages, for there is nothing even remotely parklike about them, neither in the natural nor the recreational sense. The "park" I reluctantly drag myself to for employment is a twenty-acre patch of scorched earth, a dreary colony of concrete buildings more drab than a Siberian winter. The only plants exist on meager strips of landscaping, where nonnative shrubs, tan bark, and a sorry excuse of a tree species from the Southern Hemisphere pale miserably compared to what once covered that soil.

Just beyond the boundary of the "park" sits a narrow no-man's land, a vacant buffer a hundred yards wide. Its chief feature is a series of transmission towers strung out for miles in the distance. Through the center of this runs the neutered remnant of Berryessa Creek. In its present condition, the creek has been straitjacketed and channelized so that it resembles an oversize irrigation ditch. This furrow is unnaturally deep to keep the creek from rising above its designated path and flooding something as valuable as a parking lot. The trees that once lined its banks used to provide a natural form of flood control, but they have long since been removed. No place for willows, cottonwoods, or sycamores here. The only trees left are a pair of regal valley oaks. Thousands of cars whizz past those trees daily, and I wonder if any of those motorists even notice them.

I don't know why there's been reluctance to plant native trees in our cities. Those lining our sidewalks and providing shade in urban parks usually come from some other part of the world. Equally vapid examples are found in housing tracts and shopping centers, where banal eucalyptus trees and pregrown palms are erected like statues honoring immediate gratification. These insta-trees contribute nothing in the way of atmosphere, cheapening their surroundings into *faux* versions of Acapulco, Morocco, or Melbourne. To add insult to injury, palms are often used as roost sites by nonnative pigeons, famous for leaving behind shit-spackled sidewalks. For all the valley oak habitat that has been usurped in the name of growth, the least we could do is honor the oak by planting it in our cities and suburbs.

With their penchant for growing at well-spaced distances, valley oaks are more likely to be viewed as individual trees rather than as a forest. Some have even received names, such as the Charter Oak and the Peter Lebec Oak. Spend enough time in the presence of valley oaks and you may conclude that, like snowflakes, no two are exactly alike. Some grow straight and tall, others spread considerably with crowns wider than high. Some possess cumbersome limbs that veer downward, touching the earth. Such individual variation contributes mightily to the charm of the valley oak. Some people are fortunate to have a valley oak growing in their yard. I think it is hardly a coincidence that many of the old farm houses still standing in the area are graced with the presence of an ancient valley oak, imbuing onto the property a kind of character that cannot be purchased. Those who built those houses must have known this, and I'd like to think they valued those trees for more than just shade. There's something therapeutic about lying under a magnificent oak, watching clouds scuttle across the sky while listening to the wind in the branches.

Valley oaks provide habitat for a multitude of creatures. Woodrats, raccoons, and a host of mammals dwell in their cavities, while deer and elk recline in their shade during the heat of the day. Fallen limbs are home to a number of ground-dwelling creatures, from salamanders to scorpions. Many bird species nest in valley oaks, and a greater number still alight on their branches to roost or glean insects.

Longevity is another admirable valley oak attribute, for the oldest may live over half a millennium. Think about that: there may be valley oaks standing that sprouted before Columbus set sail. My property contains perhaps three dozen valley oaks, the largest of which is probably over two hundred years old. As I sit beneath its branches, I wonder what it may have witnessed.

It may have emerged as a seedling in the middle of the eighteenth century, before the Spanish missions, when California's hillsides were cloaked in native bunch grasses rather than the alien grasses that have since taken over. The tree would've been a sapling when, across the continent, the Declaration of Independence was signed. In its youth, the tree doubtless saw the passage of many Native Americans, for a nearby stream was used for leaching acorns and a boulder containing bedrock mortars sits aside its banks. Tule elk may have scraped the velvet off their antlers against the tree's trunk, while pronghorn might have grazed on forbs in the meadow nearby. Certainly the tree knew well the California grizzly, with which it shared the landscape for nearly a century and a half. Grizzlies may have raked their claws against its furrowed bark and relished the acorns that dropped during the fall. It may have served as a roost site for California condors, drawn to Whisky Flat by the carrion provided by deer, antelope, elk, and later cattle.

That oak must have seen its share of human history, located near the historic route over Pacheco Pass. Initially a travel corridor for Native Americans, the pass was traversed by Spaniards, Mexicans, and later Americans on horseback and stagecoach. Nearby, a pair of minaret-like rock outcrops is rumored to have provided a lair for bandits such Joaquin Murietta and Tiburcio Vasquez, who might have rested under the shade of this tree. Other travelers may have also, including John Muir and Grizzly Adams, who crossed the pass with a pair of captive grizzlies. Although it sprouted at a time predating property ownership, the land on which this tree stands has at one time or other been the property of several prominent citizens. Don Francisco Pacheco, for whom the pass was named, held title to the vast Mexican land grant covering the area. Later, cattle baron Henry Miller acquired the land as part of his extensive holdings. I wouldn't be surprised if Henry took a leak at the base of the tree, for everything he touched seemed to prosper.

As the tree approaches the halfway point in its life, it has witnessed many changes. It has seen Pacheco Pass grow from footpath to horse trail to stagecoach route to two-lane road to a four-lane highway. It remembers when nothing larger than a condor or more powerful than a golden eagle sailed across the sky, though by now it must be used to all sorts of airplanes and the occasional helicopter buzzing above. Even more recent has been the intrusion of a gravel road and power poles delivering electricity to my home. And if the oak considers them eyesores, I certainly understand.

This oak has observed many things, but one it has yet to see is a successor. For the hundreds of thousands of acorns it has deposited, not one has managed to develop into a sapling. On the surface, this may not seem so worrisome. After all, the tree should be around for a couple more centuries, plenty of time in which to replenish itself. If its biological clock is ticking, it is doing so only faintly. But look beyond onto Whisky Flat, and you'll see a larger problem. There are perhaps a hundred valley oaks spread throughout the flat, and though they vary in appearance, they're all over a century old, yet nowhere in their midst is there so much as a single sapling. Like inhabitants of a sequestered monastery, they appear destined to live out their long lives without producing any heirs. That troubles me.

Oak regeneration has only recently emerged as an issue, even though it was first mentioned nearly a century ago. There are several reasons why this has been overlooked. California still contains impressive tracts of oak woodlands, and it may be hard to believe that a threat exists in the midst of such abundance. However, regeneration is not a big concern for many oak species. The problem is most pronounced among a handful, none more than valley oaks. It's also worth noting that while most people are familiar with oaks in a general sense, far fewer recognize them at the species level. Claiming that valley oaks are in jeopardy carries less meaning, since most people don't distinguish them from other oaks.

It is also easier to galvanize opposition to something that is killing trees than to bring attention to the less obvious plight of poor regeneration. If a disease was afflicting valley oaks, an alarm would have sounded long ago. Similarly, if logging threatened valley oaks, the public outcry would be substantial. Compared to more tangible threats, a subtle obstacle to the future of the valley oak is hard to grasp, harder still since there may not be a single explanation for the poor reproductive state of the species.

The question of why valley oaks are failing to replenish themselves has yet to be conclusively answered, but several theories exist. One holds that oak seedlings never get a chance to establish themselves due to the thick carpet of nonnative grasses lying below valley oaks. When the Spaniards arrived in California, they brought not only livestock with them but also the grasses upon which they fed. Much of this was inadvertent, as seeds were transported along with shipments of grain and hay. Upon taking hold in the benevolent California climate, those Eurasian grasses were able to out-compete native bunch grasses. Their competitive edge lies in their ability to sprout, grow during the rainy season, and go to seed before dying in summer, leaving the next generation in place. Valley oak seedlings may be unable to compete with those water-hogging alien grasses, and wither soon after sprouting.

Others see grazing as the main culprit. Seedling oaks may be consumed long before they have a chance to grow, and many acres of valley oak savanna have been grazed for over two hundred years. However, native ungulates such as tule elk and deer also dine on seedling oaks, and those species have coexisted alongside valley oaks for tens of thousands of years. In addition, gophers often consume the roots of young oaks, killing them as thoroughly as the larger grazing mammals. The overgrazing hypothesis is complicated by the effects of several types of native mammals with which valley oaks have long been associated.

Both explanations seem plausible. I've seen little evidence of valley oak regeneration in grazed land. Yet I have also observed areas closed to grazing that seem to be doing no better. On the surface this may favor the alien grass theory. However, the overgrazing hypothesis began to carry weight after I began noticing saplings in roadside embankments. Drive up Mount Hamilton road or East Dunne Avenue on the way to Henry W. Coe State Park and you'll see a number of young valley oaks growing between the road and barbed wire fences, a strip of no-man's land off limits to cattle and rarely frequented by deer. As is often the case with ecological questions, there may be more than one factor contributing to the lack of valley oak recruitment.

There are approximately eighty-five thousand acres of valley oak woodland remaining, and while that sounds like a lot, it is actually very little when you compare it to historical estimates and when you consider that valley oaks are a California endemic, found nowhere else, their range stretching from Los Angeles County to Shasta County. Further, only a portion of that acreage is protected. The rest is at risk, threatened by development and agricultural expansion, especially vineyards. Though never prized as a source of lumber, valley oaks are still occasionally felled for firewood, which to me is as sacrilegious as burning a grand piano.

The valley oak is to California what the American chestnut was to the vast hardwood forests of the East: the tree that defined the landscape. Chestnuts, unfortunately, were obliterated by blight from Eurasia. The valley oak has withstood habitat loss and has avoided the threat of the chainsaw and pathogens. It lives for centuries, standing sentinel over a changing world. How ironic it is that even in places where they are fully protected, their future is uncertain. In order to see valley oaks into the future, their propagation dilemma must be solved. Otherwise, we risk witnessing the death of a forest, one tree at a time.

April 2007

Flower Child

Toward a Blossoming Awareness of Things Sessile

I'LL ADMIT TO having a smug bias favoring animals over plants as I was growing up. How fascinating could any living thing be if it never moved or displayed even the slightest sense of self-awareness? With that mind-set, I relegated botany to the attic of my natural history studies, where it shared ample space with geology. Likewise, I had difficulty understanding why so many people took up gardening. I could see the enthusiasm if those efforts produced something edible. But flowers? I couldn't see flowers adding anything unless they attracted butterflies or hummingbirds. I'd overhear people at Orchard Supply lamenting that we could put a man on the moon yet failed to produce a deer repellent to protect the roses lining the driveway. While my teenage mind fretted over the threat of nuclear annihilation, those folks seemed more concerned with whether or not snapdragons should be planted in full sunlight.

At about that time, a new fad gripped the culture, as people adorned their homes with potted plants. During the 1980s, they were everywhere. This phenomenon catered not only to the trendy but also to the lazy, when plastic plants became available for those too lethargic to water and too persnickety to allow soil inside their domicile. *What's next?* I thought. *Porcelain parrots? Bas-relief bulldogs? An entire line of shit-free, danderless pets?* I trace the whole movement back to the seventies, when there arose the dubious notion that plants could feel pain. The basis for all this, if I recall correctly, was a series of pseudoscientific experiments whereby various instruments were attached to plants to measure responses to certain stimuli. Plants supposedly exhibited strong reactions when branches were hacked off. They responded favorably to classical music but negatively to rock music. This was a time when people paid attention to biorhythms, and if you're going to place stock in that absurdity, the idea that plants endure their condition in mute, stoic agony suddenly seemed plausible. After all this, I grew leery of my botanical brethren, viewing them as precursors to the New Age movement, a quirky but otherwise benign group, much like nudists.

My tepid interest in plants goes back to childhood. Growing up on a six-acre property, I was exposed more often to wildlife than native plants. The previous landowner was an eccentric man who dotted the property with a number of ornamental plantings, including an orchard featuring a variety of fruit trees. The only native plants were several oaks and some milkweed, which I treasured as a host plant for monarch butterflies. The orchard was tilled annually, and because it was, whatever wildflowers that once graced its contours were long gone. Throughout my teenage years, I was only dimly aware of the presence of wildflowers. At that point in life, the only plant I had any interest at all in identifying was poison oak.

Yet slowly my attitude changed. Involvement with the Coe Park volunteer program brought me in contact with wildflower enthusiasts for the first time. At first, their tendencies—referring to plants by their scientific names, keying flowers out—did little to dispel my notion that these people were cut from a different cloth. But in time, I found myself walking the hillsides in spring, noticing for the first time the displays of California buttercups (*Ranunculus californicus*) and popcorn flowers (*Plagiobothrys nothofulvus*). My attention was diverted, however briefly, to include plants in bloom. I was becoming a flower child.

Regrettably, the profusion of wildflower meadows that once existed throughout California is now greatly reduced. In the 1860s, John Muir claimed that he could walk across the Central Valley in spring with wildflowers beneath every step. However, the conversion of the valley to agriculture soon decimated those wildflower fields. Occasionally, California poppies (*Eschscholzia californica*) and lupines line roadways, but the vast majority of roadside wildflowers are nonnatives such as wild mustard. Fortunately, bountiful displays of native wildflowers still exist in the hills, and the Diablo Range possesses some of California's finest examples.

When it comes to wildflowers, the most stunning fields occur in unexpected places. Rather than in the lush forests of the Northwest or the moisture-rich meadows of the East, the arid West puts on the continent's finest shows. In fact, it is in the deserts where the most spectacular blooms are found. Yet while those desert displays are magnificent, they are highly variable. While the Mojave may be awash in color one year, it may be as dry as a paper bag the next. For consistency, the Diablo Range ranks second to none.

As a boy, I dreamed of owning a vast property like Ted Turner's Gray Ranch in New Mexico, which I would maintain as a wildlife sanctuary. As it turned out, I had just enough money to put a down payment on fifty-five acres along Pacheco Pass. While it was a far cry from my childhood vision, I was nonetheless able to start a worthwhile project: cataloguing the native species present—mammals, reptiles, amphibians, and birds. As an afterthought, I included wildflowers, figuring I might find a couple of dozen.

If there's an advantage to owning fifty-five acres over fifty-five thousand, it is that one will become much more familiar with a smaller parcel. Working on less acreage forced me to notice the little things. One March morning, I was walking along the edge of the property when I spotted a strange-looking flower. My knowledge of botany is slim but enough to realize that this was a flower I had never seen. It was small—just six or eight inches tall—and its blossom drooped inconspicuously. It reminded me of a globe lily (*Calochortus albus*), but its petals weren't white but a muted color, like checker lilies (*Fritillaria affinis*). However, I had only seen checker lilies in forests, and this area was sloping grassland. As I often do when encountering a flower for the first time, I sniffed it. I was instantly struck by a powerfully fetid smell that memory told me I was familiar with but couldn't pinpoint. That reeking little flower was the worst blossom I had ever smelled, its aroma ranker than that of the cheesiest horndog cologne, more noxious than the cheapest "my specialty is Happy Endings" perfume of a desperate divorcee. I could not place that odor, so I sniffed again. Finally, it hit me: carrion. This unassuming flower emitted the odor of rotting flesh, the last thing I expected. This plant was indeed related to the checker lily. *Fritillaria agrestis* is its scientific name, but its common name, stinkbells, is highly appropriate.

If only all wildflower identification was so easy. I always smugly believed that flower identification was child's play compared to identifying wildlife, since animals usually do everything they can to evade observers. I've counted scale rows on snakes, measured tail lengths in mice, and looked for minutia such as eye rings, wing bars, and notched tails on small, drab-colored birds that never seem to sit still. Identifying flowers? Simple. Note the color, count the petals, look it up in the field guide, easy as pie.

That pie, however, turned out to be of the humble variety, for I found wildflower identification more difficult than anything I had experienced with wildlife. The first wave of culture shock hit when I purchased a field guide. Accustomed to Stebbins's *Field Guide to Western Reptiles and Amphibians* and Sibley's *Guide to Birds*, I was dismayed to find flower guides with no illustrations, just a collection of photographs that often did nothing to draw attention to the pertinent features of each plant. Worse was the challenge of translating botanical terms into something my brain could comprehend. Stipules, racemes, calyxes, stigmas, pedicels, pappuses—what the hell were all those things? I vaguely remembered pistils, stamens, and ovaries from high school biology. I couldn't have daydreamed through all those other terms. Could I have? As a result I spent more time probing the glossary than any other section of the book, and more often than not, the definition that was provided did not suffice, since it usually referenced yet another unfamiliar plant part. Thus, in order to determine what a perianth is, I first needed to find out what a calyx is and what a corolla is. I felt like a dog chasing its tail, and more than once, I became so sidetracked pursuing multiple definitions that I lost track of what I intended to look up in the first place. I desperately needed one of those Idiot's Guides that proliferate throughout Barnes and Noble. In my tortured mind, I saw all those plant people gathering together, snickering. *"No, Mr. Belli, there are no Idiot's Guides to plants. Idiots don't try to identify plants. If you want Idiot's Guides and books with lots of pictures to do your thinking for you, we suggest you return to the animal section from whence you came ..."*

When I first began tallying wildflowers on my property, I figured I'd find maybe two dozen species. So far, I've counted seventy-eight. A local expert believes there may be over one hundred. As with animal tracking, it's amazing what you see when you slow down and look at the ground. There are flowers such as California poppies that grow only in the full glory of sunshine, folding their petals on overcast days and at the approach of nightfall. In contrast, there are flowers such as evening primroses and soap plant (*Chlorogalum pomeridianum*) that unfurl their blossoms under the cover of darkness. In forests, a completely different cast of characters is present. Hound's tongue (*Cynoglossum grande*), with its lavish leaves and dainty violet flowers, and Chinese houses (*Collinsia heterophylla*) thrive in the shade of oaks. While one would expect to find wildflowers along watercourses, it may come as a surprise that quite a few species occupy chaparral. The white-blossomed zygadene lily (*Zigadenus fremontii*) and the beet-red Indian warrior (*Pedicularis densiflora*) thrive in such areas. Even rock outcrops and talus slopes contain treasures such as Lindley's blazing star (*Mentzelia lindleyi*).

Examine the blossom of a large flower such as mule ears (*Wyethia helenioides*) and you may find a world unto itself, populated by a variety of insects—butterflies, beetles, and native, stingless bees. Once, while admiring a yellow mariposa lily (*Calochortus luteus*), I was amazed to watch as one of the anthers crawled up to the top of the nearest petal. It was not an anther at all, of course, but rather a tiny, supremely camouflaged crab spider, its entire body lemon yellow.

The beguiling qualities of wildflowers extend even to native thistles. While its nonnative relatives are noxious, invasive weeds that grow in thick stands of worthlessness, the Venus thistle (*Cirsium proteanum*), bless its soul, spreads itself out, sending forth brilliant, blood-red flower heads.

In the Diablo Range, there are often entirely different assemblages of wildflower species on opposite sides of the same hill. North-facing slopes are more wooded, shadier, moister, and cooler than south-facing slopes, and rare is the flower frequenting both. Recently, as I was walking across a north-facing slope on my property, I noticed a splash of color coming from a small clearing, provided by several plants with sickle-shaped leaves at the base, a bare, upright stem, and ten or so striking lavender flowers jutting out like colorful miniature trumpets. I had never seen such a flower before, even though I had walked this game trail many times. The plant turned out to be peninsula onion (*Allium peninsulare*), and while not rare, it is nonetheless uncommon. Growing as they do, without the aid of fertilizers, frequent watering, and other displays of tender loving care, those simple wild onions awe me more than by the most carefully cultivated orchid.

As compelling as individual flowers are, it is as fields that wildflowers resonate most. I wouldn't doubt that the act of beholding a field of wildflowers has a therapeutic effect. John Muir was asked what he would do if he had but one day to spend in Yosemite; he simply replied that he would sit down and cry. Well, if I had but one day to spend in the Diablo Range, I'd seek out a wildflower field. I'll reserve the crying for a terminally frustrating baseball team.

Many wildflowers produce impressive displays: brilliant orange California poppies, purple owl's clover (*Castilleja exserta*), several species of linanthus in shades of white and pink, miniature lupine (*Lupinus bicolor*) covering the ground with a light blue carpet, and lemon-yellow cream cups (*Platystemon californicus*). My favorite, though, are goldfields (*Lasthenia californica*). As individual plants, these tiny flowers standing just inches above the earth would hardly warrant a footnote. However, they grow in thick masses covering large patches of open ground. The result is a staggering splash of color, as if gold had been poured across a hillside. Several spots on my property contain modest goldfield displays. I anticipate their arrival each spring, and I would not trade those ephemeral wildflower patches for the most carefully tended rose garden or lavishly nurtured flower bed, despite the fact that goldfields bloom for only several weeks each year. Walk that same ground in August, and it will seem beyond belief that anything ever blossomed there. Amid a parched sea of dead grass, it seems inconceivable that wildflowers will ever return, but they always do.

I take no small amount of solace in that. Wildflowers are about as sure a bet as there is, at least among the good things in life. How rare is it that something so good disappears yet returns time and time again? Golden opportunities vanish, while friendships wither under the strains of time and distance. Change is good, chimes the new mantra, and though this is sometimes true, it is not always so, and there's something to be thankful for in the reliability of those few good things that stay the same.

So, seek out those wildflowers. Not for my sake, not even for the sake of the flowers, but for your own. Capture their beauty with a camera or sketch pad.

Admire their intricacies with a hand lens. Guide book in hand, head outdoors and discover new species—new not to science but those you have never seen, or more likely never noticed, before. Devote your garden to native plants. Become a flower child. Just remember: tie-dye underwear is optional and beware of poison oak.

Of Mice and Man

Shades of Gray in a Black and White World

I TRIED TO do it right. Lord knows, I tried. I'm referring to building a home and living in the country while attempting to minimize the damage to other life forms inhabiting that same patch of planet Earth. Within that philosophy was a set of ideals that took on the importance of vows: no trees would be cut, I would conserve space by building up instead of out, and I would install a gas fireplace rather than burn wood. You get the picture. For years, the property had been part of a cattle lease, and while I wasn't crazy about the grazing deal, I hate barbed wire fences and wasn't about to erect one just to exclude cows. Having no creeks or riparian areas, I saw no pressing need to keep cattle out. Besides, the lessee was a responsible land steward. He avoided overgrazing and saw no need to control predators or ground squirrels. So, I allowed the land to be grazed.

The presence of cattle bore a hidden cost, however, so a fence around the house and a cattle guard across the driveway became necessities. Cattle have no qualms about approaching buildings, and despite their general dim-wittedness, they retain a sense of curiosity. They pressed their moist nostrils, God knows why, up against sliding glass doors, peering inside with vacant stares. They scattered copious patties across the driveway. They rubbed their hides against white pillars, staining them brown, while their bovine bladders allowed them to take prodigious leaks on the concrete patio. With my patio reeking of ammonia for weeks after the urine had dried, I swore those cows must have grazed in a field of asparagus. Keeping them out became a must. Hence, the fence. I didn't want a fence; the cost of fencing a half-acre area as well as the installation of a cattle

guard ran into the thousands. This figure would have been lower had I opted for barbed wire, but I didn't want the perimeter of my home resembling a
minimum-security prison, and I wanted wildlife to roam as freely as possible
across the landscape without the hazard of the wire that tamed the West. So, I
settled for a white vinyl fence. My quaint notion of a life where I could walk out
my front door and into the great outdoors had been breached.

With cattle on the property, I saw no need to add any other livestock. No
horses, goats, hogs, chickens, sheep, emus, or alpacas. I don't want to set up a
conflict with carnivores, be they weasels, foxes, raptors, bobcats, coyotes, or
mountain lions. I don't even have a pet. Dogs, though loyal companions, are
territorial and would only serve to scare away wildlife. Cats, though lacking the
assertive territoriality of dogs, have a powerful instinct that doesn't mesh well
with wildlife: the urge to hunt. Though cats score points for being blessedly
quiet (most of the time), they quickly lose whatever cachet they may have earned
by plopping down a veritable Noah's Ark of tiny critters on the doorstep: birds
of all kinds, rodents, shrews, lizards, you name it. Keeping a cat outdoors in the
country is like hiring a hit man with a seven-day work week.

Once upon a time, I envisioned a modest vegetable garden—some zucchini,
maybe some tomatoes, too—as well as several apricot trees. Alas, I learned early
on that nothing green is safe here, especially in summer. Before any trees were
purchased, before any seed was planted, friends presented me with a house-
warming gift, a pair of foot-tall succulents in a flowerpot, fleshy and spineless.
They fared well through the winter and spring, surviving an unusual March
snowstorm that dumped six inches of powder on them, but with the onset of
summer, they were living on borrowed time. As the grasses and forbs withered,
ground squirrels turned their attention to those succulents and, in the course of
an afternoon, had gobbled both down to the roots. I saw that between the deer,
rabbits, and squirrels, having a garden would put me at war, so I decided not to.

Instead, I chose to take on nonnative species, particularly plants. Since
eliminating all alien plants from my property was never a realistic goal—that
genie was out of the bottle long ago—I focused on the most noxious: thistles,
poison hemlock (*Conium maculatum*), and hedge parsley (*Torilis nodosa*), an absolute
shit stain of a plant that produces rice grain–size burrlike seed heads that affix

themselves to shoelaces and fabric in staggering quantities, sticking with the tenacity of Velcro. My goal was to eliminate them first from the area around the house and move outward later, using a machete. Although they were established here well before my arrival, I also believed that the construction of the road and the disturbance to the ground that occurred during the building of my home helped them proliferate. So my attempts at control were undertaken in part as atonement for my own habitat disruption.

As for nonnative animals, the most potentially troublesome, wild pigs, only rarely wandered onto my property, perhaps due to nearby control efforts. Likewise, opossums and wild turkeys were not commonly sighted, and I've seen no sign of red foxes, either. Starlings became established several years ago, soon after barns and utility lines appeared. House sparrows (*Passer domesticus*) have also arrived and have begun nesting on the sides of the house, filling the air with the same drab, monosyllabic song that rings out from every shopping center from sea to shining sea. They gotta go.

As for native species, my policy was live and let live. Without a garden, I saw no need to control squirrels. I'll leave that to the experts, who work for free— coyotes, bobcats, weasels, and a variety of raptors. Snakes, of course, are held in high regard, even rattlers.

My integrity wavers, however, as we descend the ladder of the animal kingdom. Native or not, mosquitos, though not common, are slapped with impunity, and ticks are dispatched with a vengeance. Inside the house, flies live on borrowed time. And while most spiders are uneasily tolerated, webs are not, and if a spider perishes during the course of web obliteration, *que sera, sera*. There is a zero-tolerance policy for black widows, given their habit of constructing their haphazardly strung webs in little-used portions of houses and garages. Yes, the aforementioned species caused my integrity to waver but still, I believe, remain intact. It was the humble deer mouse (*Peromyscus maniculatus*) that caused it to collapse.

The genus *Peromyscus* represents the most abundant and widespread group of mammals in North America. At least one of the sixteen species comprising the genus is found in all of the lower forty-eight states. In the Diablo Range, four species occur: *Peromyscus maniculatus*, the North American deer mouse; *P. californicus*, the California mouse; *P. truei*, the pinyon mouse; and *P. boylii*, the brush mouse. Deer mice are large-eyed, nocturnal, and highly adaptable. In a cautionary understatement, one text succinctly noted they are known for entering cabins.

My first inkling that mice were present came late in the building process, just before the flooring was installed. In the fine, chalky dust, I noticed minuscule rodent tracks. I figured someone must have left a door open overnight, and since I doubted house mice (*Mus musculus*) were present in a rural area, I didn't think the intrusion would amount to much. After all, what would a wild mouse see in an unnatural environment? I couldn't have been more wrong.

Several days after moving in, I was surprised to spot a mouse scurrying against the wall in the kitchen. I cornered it, captured it, and examined it under the light. This was no house mouse, the bane of urbanites everywhere. It had large, dark eyes, handsome brownish fur, and a long furred tail. Grabbing a field guide, I declared that, judging by the length of the tail, ears, and hind feet, this creature was *Peromyscus maniculatus*, a North American deer mouse. I let it go outside, figuring I'd rid my house of a freeloader.

Alas, there is never just one mouse. Shortly thereafter I saw signs: trails of droppings along the sides of walls and in corners. I also started seeing mice just after sunset, like clockwork. Taking extra precaution to secure my food, I assumed they'd leave once they failed to find anything to eat. But while I did an admirable job of securing my food, I did a less than stellar job denying them theirs. I realized this when I opened the cabinet below the sink and found my garbage thoroughly ransacked, with the perpetrator still at the scene of the crime. How the hell did it invade a closed cabinet? Peering under the sink, I noticed a quarter-inch space surrounding the pipes. I could've sooner believed that mice were capable of shape-shifting than squeezing through such tight quarters.

The preternatural capabilities of deer mice confounded me. They climbed imposing shelves for the sole purpose, it seemed, of gnawing on book bindings and magazine covers. They peed, incontinent little bastards, on piano keys. When chased, they disappeared into crevices so small I hadn't even known they existed. They gnawed wires, in one case shorting a fuse box in my dryer that cost $200 to fix.

They shredded towels and toilet paper to use as material for nests, which they constructed beneath couches and bookcases. Their most impressive feat, however, was climbing. One summer evening, I was awakened shortly after midnight by a sound coming from the closet. At first I thought it was the wind blowing through the window, but I had closed the windows earlier, after a chilly coastal fog spread in. I heard again the jangling of clothes hangers, and my adrenaline spiked. I'm the last person to believe in ghosts. This house had just been constructed; if any bastard spirit is going to haunt it, it'll be mine. I wondered incredulously if someone was hiding in the dark recesses of the closet. Heart pounding, baseball bat in hand, I tiptoed in the dark toward the closet, flipped the light switch, and there he was: a tiny vagabond, atop the highest shelf. He had climbed to the top by way of my clothing.

As impressive as that was, it paled in comparison to another act of legerdemain. My earliest attempt at rodent control involved live-trapping. One evening I was in no mood to drive out toward the main road and release mice one at a time. Instead, I decided to place them in a plastic bucket and release them all when I left for work in the morning. I kept the bucket outside on the deck. Ten minutes after catching the first mouse, I caught another. However, when I went to transfer my captive to the bucket, I found it empty. Maybe an owl had made off with it. I placed the new mouse into the bucket, returned indoors, and ten minutes later had trapped a third. Preparing to dump this newest mouse into the bucket, I was confounded, for once again it was empty. This time, I kept the porch light on and, watching from the kitchen window, witnessed the mouse scale the side of a plastic bucket. This was no ordinary kitchen bucket, either; it was a large painter's bucket, eighteen inches high, with sides as smooth as glass. Or so I thought. Actually, a thin layer of dried paint provided enough of a toehold to allow mice to escape as readily as a person climbing a ladder.

Several sympathetic souls offered advice. They suggested setting out poison, rodenticides with God-awful names like Rat-Prufe and Mice-B-Gon. I had no intention of using such an arsenal. It wasn't that I doubted they would work; my fear was that they would work all too well. I couldn't condone the agony such poisoning entailed. If I must kill something, I'll do it humanely, with a minimum of pain. Poisons are too sanitary—out of sight, out of mind doesn't mean a painless death. In addition, I didn't want cases of secondary poisoning to occur further up the food chain. I didn't want to risk poisoning a weasel, bobcat, owl, or any other predator that happened to swallow a poisoned mouse. Finally, I could never in good conscience purchase a product the very name of which blatantly dismisses the English language with intentional misspellings. I know the rationale behind such hijinks is an age-old advertising ploy designed to catch the eye of consumers. However, with so many market-driven misspellings out there, I'm afraid that in a generation or two, will becum a nayshun uv morrons.

My first attempt at rodent control involved a couple of gizmos that plug into electrical outlets and emit a sound barely audible to human ears but supposedly nerve-wracking to mice. So irritating is that sound—I'm imagining a nonstop barrage of eighties techno-pop—that mice purportedly vacate the premises upon hearing it. Did they work? Hell no. I might as well have played Wang Chung, Culture Club, and Men Without Hats at full blast for all the good those devices did.

Next was trapping. I purchased several live-catch plastic traps, barely larger than the mice themselves. Having recently squandered money on worthless ultrasonic devices, I doubted such small, close-ended traps would work, but they actually performed very well. For a while, during the heady days of that first summer, it looked as if those traps were just what the doctor ordered. It became a nighttime ritual, beginning just after sunset. I'd catch one mouse, then another, and so on, often over half a dozen per night. Upon hearing the loud clank as the trap struck the tile floor, I would retrieve the trap, take it outside, and let the mouse go.

But those halcyon days did not last long. It was all well and good when I caught mice at eight, nine, or ten at night before going to bed. It was not so good when I caught them after midnight. Being a light sleeper, I was awakened dozens of times in the wee hours by the springing of the trap. Leaving mice in the trap all night was not a pleasurable experience, either for me or the mice. They moved relentlessly, causing the trap to pitch back and forth, striking the tile with a reverberation that was the sonic equivalent of water torture. Once I was awakened by that, falling back to sleep was a pipe dream.

After a month of catching mice on a nightly basis, I got concerned. How many mice could there possibly be? I had trapped and removed nearly a hundred, with no sign of abatement. All along, others insisted that I was catching the same mice over and over. I had labored under the illusion that my home was impregnably sealed. Once again, deer mice had proven me wrong.

The next step was to contact a handyman to seal the openings. This he did with petroleum-based foam that hardened after spraying and was impervious to the gnawing of rodents. He sealed many areas, but evidently he didn't get them all, for mice remained present. My trapping efforts also became more laborious, for no longer could I simply release mice outside the front door with any sense of accomplishment. I needed to set them free a mile down the road, a distance that would ensure no return visits. Live trapping became slow and tedious, and the frustration of living with mice was mounting. Then came the Incident.

I was reclining on the couch, and as I was resting, I heard mice scuffling nearby. I assumed they were frolicking behind the couch. A minute or so later, I heard them again, this time surprisingly close. I furtively lifted the seat cushion and immediately slammed it down in horror. Beneath it lie a writhing, squirming mass of mice, at least ten huddled together in a grotesque free-for-all. In a fit of delirious genius, I devised a plan to rid myself of the whole mess. I eased the sofa, ever so gently, toward the sliding glass door. I planned to move the whole damned thing outside, upend it, and scatter that unholy deer mouse commune into the daylight and the realm of red-tailed hawks. There was only one problem. In my self-congratulatory haste, I neglected to measure the dimensions of the sofa and the door. Great was my chagrin when I realized the sofa would not fit past the door unless tilted. The moment I did this, the mice abandoned ship, scurrying back to the safety and comfort of the house. That did it. If I hadn't realized it before, I was in the midst of a full-blown infestation. What weighed on me was the notion that I was tempting fate.

Deer mice have been identified as the principal vector of hantavirus pulmonary syndrome, a rare but virulent affliction known mostly from the Southwest. The mortality rate for those unfortunate enough to contract the virus approaches 50 percent; death comes quickly, usually within several weeks. Hantavirus makes chronic illnesses like malaria, Lyme disease, and syphilis look tame in comparison; even HIV appears more benign. Between 1990 and 2000, twenty-nine cases of hantavirus were recorded in California. Fourteen resulted in death. Hantavirus is spread to humans when microbes present in the urine and feces of infected mice are inhaled, say, in the act of dusting or sweeping. If I've vacuumed one trail of mouse droppings, I've vacuumed hundreds. I was engaging in high-risk behavior, and sooner or later, the odds might catch up to me. On top of that, hantavirus had been detected in several vacant trailers in Coe Park ten miles from my home. Made me rethink the whole dusting and sweeping thing.

I finally broke down and called an exterminator service, one that specialized in nontoxic solutions. The representative told me the best way to get rid of mice was the old-fashioned mousetrap. Reluctantly, I began setting them. Those wooden traps worked but not as well as I had hoped. Sometimes they sprung without catching anything, but that was the least of their deficiencies. Worse, they simply were not as humane as they were cracked up to be. While most of the time a mouse was killed instantly upon springing the trap, such was not always the case. On more than one occasion, a mouse was caught by a limb, and in that situation, the only humane alternative was to put it out of its misery, something I loathed but felt compelled to do. I was frustrated with those traps, but I was also frustrated with myself. Eventually I found a better mousetrap, a plastic model resembling a broad clothespin. Those did a better job of humanely killing their captives. They were highly efficient, and in time the infestation was greatly reduced. I haven't seen a mouse in weeks. But even as my frustration with traps subsided, my internal angst remained.

I had come to this place and vowed to live in a way that caused the least disruption to native wildlife. It seemed straightforward, so black and white. Yet reality is almost always some shade of gray.

It was folly to assume that constructing a home and living on the property would have no effect on the surrounding natural community. Good intentions can't negate the impact visited upon the landscape. Whether I liked it or not, what I did here was going to hurt some species and benefit others. It was my goal to limit the presence of exotic species and minimize the damage I did to the natives. Yet even this simple credo had complications. The stucco siding of the house provided nesting sites for cliff swallows, a native migrant that arrives here to nest in spring and returns to Central and South America in late summer.

However, their gourd-shaped nests of dried mud attracted house sparrows, an invasive species more commonly found in cities, and the sparrows soon usurped some of the swallow nests. Ergo, I now have a sparrow problem.

I never envisioned a scenario in which I would wage war on a native species, even on a small scale, and when I did, I felt I compromised my principles. Oh, I rationalized it over and over. I reminded myself that deer mice are not only common, but abundant, and that my extermination efforts would have absolutely no effect upon the population. In fact, I told myself my house had allowed the local population to increase unnaturally, as it provided a sizable sanctuary, offering food, shelter, and relief from predators. I argued that killing surplus mice would restore conditions similar to those that existed before the house was built. And of course there was always the tiny but potentially disastrous threat of hantavirus. Yet no matter how I rationalized my actions, I was left with the lingering feeling that I could have handled it better.

It also forced me to confront the notion of how to take a life. And while it's easy to espouse humane modes, things become complicated once such measures are put into practice. Is there an iron-clad method for humanely ending the life of something capable of feeling pain? I used to think so. Now, I'm not so sure. Whether it's trapping mice, slaughtering livestock, or carrying out a capital punishment sentence, we tell ourselves over and over that we conduct such activities as humanely as possible. But there are no guarantees, and the orderly black and white world we construct in our minds often turns to be inconveniently gray.

May 2007

The Years of the Cat

The Mystery and the History of the Mountain Lion

THE LARGE, DARK eyes still held the viscous gaze the animal had during its brief life. It hadn't been dead long; it died during the night, sometime between midnight and dawn, for I had not noticed its carcass upon my return from the all-too-rare social occasion as the clock approached twelve. Lying on the side of the dirt road in the canyon below my house, the young deer appeared to have been struck by a vehicle. The road, however, is secured by a locked gate, used only by my neighbor and me, and it is very unusual for either of us to be behind the wheel at such a late hour.

Next I wondered if this was the work of a poacher. Yet as I approached the body in the predawn light, I saw that this deer had not been shot. Newly emerging grasses revealed a path where the body had been dragged. A jumble of stones at the bottom of the embankment told the tale of two bodies tumbling over the twelve-foot ledge. A boulder stained red with fresh blood provided mute testimony to the drama that had played out here just hours before, the blood having yet to attain the purplish-black hue that drying and exposure produces. I searched for tracks in the dirt, but the soil was compacted, and although it was the eve of December, no rain had fallen recently. A short distance from the carcass, the rumen remained intact. The clinical precision with which the entrails were removed struck me. Yet this was not the work of a surgeon. Rather, this was graphic testimony that my property is at least occasionally visited by *Puma concolor.*

Mountain lions have the most extensive distribution of any mammal in the hemisphere, from northern British Columbia to Patagonia. Yet despite that extensive range, there is much about these animals that remains unknown. One of the most pressing mysteries is where, exactly, do they exist? Reports of sightings trickle in from the Northeast, the Midwest, and Appalachia, yet the only known population east of the Mississippi dwells in south Florida, where the beleaguered Florida panther, an isolated subspecies, clings to a fraction of its former habitat.

Another question: How many are there? It's notoriously difficult to conduct censuses on mountain lions, and state wildlife agencies can do little more than guess at the size of populations. When I was a boy, there was considerable debate as to whether or not mountain lions even roamed the Diablo Range. They were bountied throughout California until 1963, and that took a toll on the population. I remember being shown a cast of a track at a rustic cottage near my childhood home, yet no one I knew had ever seen a mountain lion. I was well into adulthood and had come across tracks many times before I caught my first glimpse of this elusive animal.

Arroyo Aguague is a seasonal stream that empties into Penitencia Creek in Alum Rock Park east of San Jose. Its headwaters originate in Grant County Park, a ten-thousand-acre refuge that was once a prominent cattle ranch. One March afternoon, I descended the headwaters, looking for amphibians. The upper reaches of the stream are heavily forested, and even on sunny days, the canyon remains cloaked in shade. The creek turned out to be a disappointment, for it was barely trickling, and if amphibians were present, I didn't see any. As I followed the creek around a bend, I paused beside a moss-draped boulder. Peering out from behind the rock, I saw fifty feet ahead of me something with a solid, tawny color and a lengthy, black-tipped tail. As it continued toward me, I realized I was in a delicate situation. Standing at the bottom of a canyon, I did not have gravity on my side, and the uneven footing among the rocks and downed logs made self-defense challenging in the extremely unlikely event that the cat should act aggressively. I remained as still and silent as possible. I tried to recollect everything I had ever read about lion encounters, and I wondered whether or not I should make some noise. Would that scare it off or, at close quarters, provoke it? On the other hand, if I remained still, the cat would be at my side in moments. Try as I might, I couldn't recall hearing of anyone surprising a cougar, and I didn't know what to do. Before I could decide, the cat crossed the stream, ambled up the side of the canyon, and vanished. I climbed out of the canyon on the opposite side. Upon reaching level ground, I paused to admire the maroon bloom of a giant trillium, and as I did so, I noticed my right leg shaking uncontrollably.

Mountain lions were formerly found from coast to coast, but they suffered persecution early on, for colonists established the first bounty on the species in the 1600s. Such bounties, along with an expanding human population that cleared the wilderness and decimated populations of elk and deer, the lion's chief prey, combined to banish the animal from the East by 1900, save for a small, isolated population in the swamps of south Florida.

Out West, settlers launched predator extermination campaigns with unsurpassed intensity. In the course of winning the West, the federal government was enlisted to wage war against a menagerie of sharp-toothed and taloned creatures that were even remotely suspected of being injurious to livestock or game. Extra effort was expended in ridding the land of its apex predators. The big three—grizzly bears, gray wolves, and mountain lions—were targeted with a vengeance, so much so that by the middle of the twentieth century, wolves had been eliminated and grizzlies held on only in the sanctuaries of Yellowstone and Glacier National Park. Only the mountain lion remained with anything near its original range intact. How did it avoid the fate of the wolf and the grizzly?

Two of the major weapons in the war against predators, leghold traps and poison, were less effective against mountain lions. Baited traps or meat tainted with strychnine were less tempting to cougars, which don't often scavenge. A poisoned carcass might kill several bears or a pack of wolves yet be of little interest to a mountain lion. In fact, the hounds used to track and tree mountain lions were much more likely to eat poisoned meat. Mountain lions might have emerged completely unscathed were it not for a quirk in their evolutionary history.

Mountain lions are athletic, yet those talents have trade-offs: despite their speed, they can't run for long. They're ambush hunters, relying on stealth and explosiveness rather than endurance. When the tables are turned—when the hunter becomes the hunted—cougars forsake speed for agility, taking refuge in treetops.

That mountain lions should flee from anything may seem surprising. After all, they're the top of the food chain. But this wasn't always so. During the Pleistocene, a formidable array of larger predators shared the landscape with mountain lions, including two species of wolves, dire wolves and gray wolves. Both existed in packs and probably stole carcasses from mountain lions. This rivalry was lopsided, for as solitary animals, cougars stood little chance of fending off a wolf pack. Because they lacked the stamina of wolves, running was an ill-advised strategy. The best strategy for coping with wolves was to climb. For eons, yelping canines chased mountain lions up into the safe haven of branches. It didn't matter whether the protagonists were dire wolves (which have been extinct for over eight thousand years), gray wolves, or more recently, hounds. Instinct compels them to climb. Mountain lions, so difficult to poison or trap, are vulnerable to a pack of dogs. Armed with this knowledge, those who sought to eradicate the cougar finally had a potent strategy.

In 1907, California established a bounty on mountain lions, hiring hunters to eradicate them. The state fish and game commission launched a public-relations campaign, exhorting hunters, ranchers, and outdoor enthusiasts to do their part by killing them whenever possible, all in the name of making California safe for livestock and deer. Even the federal government got into the act, employing hunters to gun down cougars in California's national parks. The annihilation campaign was highly successful, so much so that by 1930, they had become rare in Southern California. Mike Davis, in his book *Ecology of Fear*, notes that cougar control efforts in the Mount Hamilton area in 1934–6 resulted in an irruption of deer in 1940, when deer spilled over onto the floor of the Santa Clara Valley, invading the fruit orchards that were once the basis of the local economy.

The bounty system persisted until 1963, when it was discontinued less out of concern for the state's diminished cougar population, which was probably at an all-time low, than the decision that it was no longer fiscally worthwhile. During its fifty-six-year tenure, the bounty claimed over twelve thousand mountain lions, yet the job was left unfinished. Hunting with hounds may have been effective, but it had drawbacks. If hounds fail to come across fresh scent, the chance of encountering a lion is virtually zero. As cougars became scarce, fresh scent became harder to locate, and the success rate dropped. In addition, there were plenty of rugged mountains and steep canyons that were very difficult to access, and cougars held on in such enclaves.

The 1963 termination of the bounty, though a step in the right direction, did not in itself constitute much in the way of protection for mountain lions; it just removed the government from the lion-killing business. Despite evidence that the population was severely reduced, lions were still classified as vermin and could be killed with impunity. It was a damning indictment of the department of fish and game that nonnative, ecologically disruptive feral hogs were given more protection than the state's top predator.

In 1969, mountain lions finally received a degree of protection when the state upgraded their status to that of a game mammal. Though today it may seem odd to view that as an improvement, that's precisely what it was then. As a game mammal, lions could no longer be shot at any time of year and in any number. There would be seasons and quotas, and so for the first time, the state acknowledged some value to mountain lions, even if that value was found in providing recreation for trophy hunters. Game-mammal classification was a step forward from the preceding policy of extermination and apathy. The game-mammal designation also implied an obligation to uncover certain truths about mountain lions in California. After all, if you're going to establish hunting zones and harvest quotas, then you need to know where they exist, how many there are, and how many can be hunted annually while still maintaining a viable population.

For such a prominent animal, it's surprising how little we actually know about mountain lions. It was not until the 1960s that studies shed some light on cougar ecology. Studying a population of large, solitary, far-ranging animals requires covering a sobering amount of land: thousands of square miles, much of it rugged. What's also needed, in the case of the cougar, is a blend of old methods—the use of hounds—with newer ones such as radio telemetry and GPS, essential in plotting the locations and movements of animals.

The first groundbreaking study of mountain lions was conducted in the mountains of central Idaho in the 1960s. That study depicted them as creatures requiring large tracts of land, occurring sparsely throughout the landscape. Male territories did not overlap, though the territories of one or more females were frequently contained within the borders of a male. It is perhaps no coincidence that in the wake of this study, several states, including California, upgraded cougars from unprotected vermin to game mammal. Today, only Texas still classifies them as vermin.

Several studies conducted in the 1970s and 1980s were undertaken in California, including one in the Diablo Range. That study provided an interesting contrast to the results from Idaho. The major difference was in population density. Diablo Range lions, in addition to having smaller home ranges, were more numerous than those in Idaho. The term "numerous," however, is relative. Over a ten-year period, three population-density estimates were offered, with the highest being 1.9 to 2.7 adult lions per one hundred square kilometers. That translates to between twelve and fifteen cougars roaming ninety-thousand-acre Henry W. Coe State Park. That may not seem like many. Still, the Diablo Range population remains among the densest yet recorded for mountain lions.

Such high numbers suggest a large prey base. The Diablo Range, with its ample cover and forage, constitutes prime deer habitat. Scat samples of Diablo Range lions revealed, not surprisingly, that deer comprised the bulk of their diet, while feral hogs came in a distant second. Few other species were noted. Interestingly, cattle were barely detected in the diet, despite the presence of a large cattle ranch in the study area. Sheep, however, were taken with gusto, and twice lions were dispatched after wreaking havoc in a small corral.

As in Idaho, male home ranges frequently included those of one or more females, yet ranges of male lions sometimes overlapped as well. This may be a result of a denser prey base, and it is noteworthy for showing differences between populations. Not everything in nature is set in stone, and it shouldn't be surprising that a creature with such a wide distribution exhibits behavioral flexibility. Ranges of individual lions shifted over time, expanding and contracting in response to those of neighboring lions. Diablo Range lions, rather than wandering randomly, tended to travel along ridgetops and creek bottoms.

Females bore an average of two kittens per litter, and the young remained with their mothers for eighteen to twenty-four months before dispersing. It was unusual for both kittens to survive that long, for more often than not, only one lived to see adulthood. Despite a lofty perch atop the food chain, it's a rough life. The violent life of an ambush predator carries with it no small risk; injuries are common in the course of bringing down prey. If the wounds are severe, the cat may die from those injuries or perish of starvation if it is unable to hunt. Add to this the possibility, particularly for males, of getting killed in a battle with another male, and perhaps it is not surprising that cougars, even where they are protected from hunting, often lead short lives. Few live as long as ten years.

The sport hunting era in California was brief, consisting of just two seasons. In 1971, the state legislature passed a moratorium on cougar hunting. In less than a decade, mountain lions had gone full circle, from being vermin that the state paid to exterminate to an animal receiving full protection.

In 1990, Proposition 117 was placed on the ballot. The initiative elevated the status of mountain lions to that of specially protected mammal and outlawed sport hunting. And while Proposition 117 protected cougars from hunting, it allowed them to be killed if they posed a threat to lives or property (such as livestock) through depredation permits. The proposition passed handily, and so California became the first, and so far only, Western state to ban mountain lion hunting.

For all the mystery swirling around mountain lions, the most controversial is the danger they pose. Years ago the consensus was that cougars were extremely wary and went out of their way to avoid mankind and so posed no threat to people. In a general sense, that's true but not absolutely. Though few and far between, there are records of attacks on people dating as far back as the 1600s, when a Pennsylvania colonist was killed. California recorded its first fatal attack in 1890. A 1909 attack that claimed the lives of two victims occurred in the Diablo Range east of Morgan Hill, though the incident contained extenuating circumstances— the cat was rabid, and the victims perished from the disease rather than from wounds inflicted by the cougar. So while mountain lion attacks were rare, they were not without precedent.

In 1986, two separate attacks occurred in Orange County, the first docu- mented in California since the rabid cat of 1909. Both victims were children, and while one suffered minor injuries, the other was mauled severely. Attacks occurred with increasing frequency in subsequent years, culminating in 1994, when two women were killed, one in Northern California and the other in Southern California, the state's first such fatalities in eighty-five years. In the aftermath of those attacks, there arose a call for the return of hunting to reinstill fear in the hearts of an animal that, to some, had lost its fear of humans and was now regarding people as prey. In the minds of some, Proposition 117 symbolized a breakdown of law and order, and the recent attacks served as a sobering reminder of the consequences of a lax, permissive California culture. For lion hunters in other states, California's decision to ban hunting never sat well, and they were among the first to exploit the safety issue as a justification for lion hunting. Over and over, they echoed a dire warning: *look at what happened in California.*

Let's take a good look at that. California hired bounty hunters for fifty-six years, hoping to eradicate mountain lions. When the program ended, anyone could still kill as many as they wished, for lions received no protection. That phase lasted seven years. Then, for the following two years, they were classified as game mammals, and hunting was regulated. Since then, mountain lions have been protected, yet a number of lions have been killed in defense of lives or property through the issuance of depredation permits.

California's lion population surely plummeted during the bounty era. The decades since have seen a rebounded population that would be difficult to quantify. Pro-hunt forces contend the population is not only too large but has become aggressive due to the hunting ban and cite the increased attacks as proof.

Granted, cougar numbers have risen since the cessation of hunting, as have attacks. But before conceding that hunting lessens the likelihood of further attacks, or that cougars in California have lost their fear of people, several points need to be considered. Of the eleven contiguous Western states, California is the largest, and on that basis alone would be expected to have more attacks than a state such as Utah. Not only is California larger, it contains more cougar habitat. Much of the West, in spite of its relatively sparse human population, does not provide the type of high-quality lion habitat California does. The Southwest, the Columbia Plateau, and the Great Basin, despite their wide-open spaces, contain less prey and in turn support fewer lions over a given area than California. And while the Rockies and the Cascades provide good lion habitat, neither surpasses that found in California.

Yet while the cougar population in California has increased in recent decades, the deluge of people has dwarfed it. Since 1963, California has added nearly twenty million people to its collection, more than doubling in size. Cram thirty million more people into Montana, twenty-five million more into Idaho, and twenty million more into Colorado to give those states a population density similar to that of California and then we can compare attack rates.

The longer I pored over the data surrounding mountain lion attacks in California, the more I became convinced the cougar "problem" is not nearly as alarming as it's made out to be. As tragic as the 1994 fatalities were, California has had only one since. If lions are truly becoming bolder, I would have expected many more. Consider all the people who live in lion habitat, as well as the vast number who recreate seasonally in cougar country. There are thousands of lakes, campgrounds, and cabins throughout the state situated smack-dab in the realm of the cougar, and numerous county, state, and national parks with trails galore in prime lion habitat, yet for all this shared acreage and human activity, cougar attacks, though no longer unheard of, are still extremely rare occurrences. There are nearly ten million people in the central coast/San Francisco Bay Area, yet the region has not experienced a cougar fatality since the rabies deaths of 1909. In the Diablo Range, Pinnacles National Monument receives over two hundred and fifty thousand visitors annually, and Henry W. Coe State Park draws over fifty thousand people per year, yet neither has ever experienced an attack, despite being situated in an area where the cougar population is about as large as it can be. If California cougars have become more aggressive in the last thirty-five years, I'm not seeing it.

I spent the spring and summer of 2004 surveying the streams of Henry W. Coe State Park, and occasionally I would happen upon a stark reminder that I was in lion country. In the Coon Creek watershed one afternoon, I came across two sets of lion tracks, both fresh, probably deposited the night before. It was during such moments that I realized I had been violating several safety precautions. I was traveling alone, along a canyon bottom (where I could be easily ambushed from above), and worst of all, I was constantly bending down, providing a tempting target. Mountain lions typically attack the back side of their victims, particularly the neck, and mine was often exposed. While I realized the extremely low risk, I must admit I was tempted to stack the odds even more in my favor by adopting a tactic used by villagers in India, who have taken to wearing masks on the back of their head to discourage tigers. I was considering a mask along the lines of Jack Nicholson's Joker in the movie *Batman* when I came across one even more grotesque: an ungodly Alfred E. Newman/George W. Bush composite, replete with "What, me worry?" thought bubble. That was a little too much. I can't speak for cougars, but it scared the hell out of me. It never made it out into the field.

Toward the end of the dry season, the tadpole search was coming up empty in the pools of Coyote Creek. My last hope was Pacheco Falls Canyon, a series of cascading waterfalls, a tight slickrock gorge of steep, weathered stone, impassable without climbing gear. By the end of summer, the falls had ceased flowing, and what water remained was restricted to a series of deep, lucid pools that eons of erosion had sculpted out of stone. It was in these pools that I hoped finally to find red-legged frog tadpoles.

Arriving at the top of the gorge, I made the easy descent to the first of those pools. The water was deep, crystal clear, and inviting, but held no tadpoles. I lingered along the smooth stone perimeter of the pool while I contemplated dropping down to the next pool, a much more difficult endeavor. As I approached the edge of the dry waterfall, a deep growl and the sound of splashing water from the pool below, hidden from view by the stone overhang, startled me. This was no small critter; whatever made that noise was big, and while there are four large animals roaming the park, three are hoofed, and no hoofed animal this side of a mountain goat could reach the pool where that sound was coming from. Besides, I was familiar with the sounds made by deer, elk, and wild pigs, and this was different. Slightly unnerved but brimming with curiosity, I walked toward the edge of the overhang. I shouted in the hope of startling the cougar into fleeing down the canyon, where I could get a good look. After several seconds of my own caterwauling, a brief bout of silence ensued. I kept my eyes on the canyon, expecting the cougar to bolt in that direction. Instead, to my surprise, the cat, which had remained silent during my solo, resumed growling, and the splashing footfalls I heard, rather than signaling a retreat, seemed to get louder as if the cat were heading toward me. That was the last thing I expected. I distinctly remember the metallic taste of adrenaline—the flavor of fear—in my mouth as I backed away. The cat never ascended the gorge.

There's a consensus today that California's mountain lion population is the highest it's been in over a century. Circumstances have changed since lion hunting was abolished in 1972. Back then, cougars were scarce and attacks on people were unheard of. Perhaps it's time to rethink cougar management. Maybe the time is ripe for a scientifically based hunting season. But I just can't support that. Here's why.

Hunting proponents argue that mountain lions need to be hunted to maintain a sense of fear in the population and reduce the likelihood of attacks on humans. On the surface, this sounds plausible, but is it valid? Every other Western state allows lion hunting, yet attacks have occurred in nearly all of them, despite those states having smaller human populations and, in all likelihood, fewer cougars than California. One would expect that Texas, with its Wild West management credo, would be attack-free. With the most lax cougar hunting laws in the land, where hunting is limited by neither season nor bag limit, Texans must have surely rendered their cats timid by now. Yet this is not so, for cougar attacks have occurred there. On the other end of the spectrum lies Florida, with its endangered subpopulation of cougars eking out an existence in the swamps. Those cats have been protected even longer than California's, yet there has never been an attack involving Florida panthers.

But the most convincing rebuttal to the "hunting induces fear" theory is the case of Vancouver Island, which has incredibly accounted for nearly *half* of all attacks recorded in North America, a staggering percentage when you consider that the island's human population is tiny compared to California's. Clearly, something is at work there, compelling cougars to become unusually aggressive, but it certainly isn't protection, for lion hunting has a long history on the island and continues to this day.

I've also wondered how hunting evokes fear throughout a population of solitary, wide-ranging creatures such as mountain lions. Perhaps the unpleasant experience of being chased by baying hounds would give a cougar a traumatic experience it won't soon forget, but the goal of lion hunting isn't hazing but killing the animal. Dead animals don't learn lessons, nor is there a pack or group to witness the event and associate it with humans. The only type of hunting that might educate cougars would be a catch-and-release format whereby lions are chased, treed, and maybe fired upon with rubber bullets but left otherwise unscathed. I don't hear much support for that.

When lion hunting proponents invoked public safety in support of their position, shamelessly exploiting the 1994 fatalities, whatever sympathies I had with their cause evaporated. In linking lion hunting to public safety, they stepped squarely into a trap they themselves set. With their zero tolerance for cougar attacks, it would be all too easy to travel down that path a little further. Specifically, why stop at sport hunting? If mountain lions are so menacing, why not revive the bounty system and revive the extermination policy? Of course lion hunters didn't mention that; they wanted to play both sides of the fence.

Another blunder was their insistence that lions enjoyed complete protection by law. They were reluctant to admit, however, that Proposition 117 allows exceptions for problem lions. The state of California typically kills between one hundred and two hundred mountain lions per year, those that prey on livestock or are deemed a threat to people. Mountain lions have been killed in California all along, just not for sport, and the cats targeted were those that were causing trouble, a more effective strategy than the random efforts of hunters. The pro-hunt crowd had no business flying the public safety flag; when they did, they only looked self-serving.

Could a scientifically sound management program that includes sport hunting be adopted in California without jeopardizing the state's cougar population? Maybe, yet I'm mighty skeptical that any proposed hunting plan would stand up to scrutiny. With only a rough idea of the state's cougar population, formulating an annual quota that is not too high might prove problematic. Besides taking into account the number of cougars killed annually through depredation permits, the quota must also consider the excess mortality resulting from the killing of females. Since kittens stay with their mothers for at least eighteen months, the true impact of killing a female is often underestimated, for the chance of kittens surviving on their own is slim. In addition, kittens may be killed by hounds in the course of trailing their mother.

Given the conflict that exists between predators and ungulates, state wildlife management agencies have time and time again aimed to maximize populations of deer and elk, sometimes above the carrying capacity of the land. Predators, however, are shown no such largesse. On the contrary, they have routinely been suppressed below minimum viable population. For example, Oklahoma has announced plans to institute a hunting season on cougars, despite the fact that they have only recently been documented in the state, no-one knows how many are present, or if a breeding population even exists. State wildlife agencies constantly bow to pressure and establish high quotas on lions to keep the population down and boost the numbers of deer and elk, routinely ignoring scientific data that show the quotas are too high. I'm not confident that California would act differently.

Mountain lions and other large carnivores naturally occur in low numbers and tend to regulate their own populations. Because they exist in low numbers, they are all the more prone to extirpation in a given area. They play a disproportionately larger role in ecosystems than other species and deserve to exist in numbers greater than the minimum viable population levels so often espoused by state wildlife agencies.

How many mountain lions are needed to ensure long-term survival in a given area? In an isolated area such as the Everglades or a small mountain range, it's been estimated that anywhere from fifty to five hundred are necessary to maintain genetic diversity. I'm a little leery of the lower figure—fifty seems like an awfully small number. That's about the number left in Florida, and those cats, like the old crowned heads of Europe, have exhibited telltale signs of inbreeding: kinked tails, low sperm count, and testicles that fail to descend.

If the number for population stability is closer to five hundred, then isolated cougar populations could be in big trouble regardless of legal protection. Given the low population density and substantial home range sizes of cougars, it takes a lot of land to support an assemblage of mountain lions five hundred strong. How much land? Several million acres, perhaps.

Despite the protections, several mountain ranges in Southern California have lost their cougar populations, as development fragmented the landscape and isolated them. The Diablo Range is larger, but even with ideal habitat and a strong prey base, it is unlikely that, with an area of about five thousand square miles, it provides a home for five hundred cougars. Perhaps it has half that. If so, the long-term future of the cougar in the range may depend upon the gene flow provided by lions entering from other regions. That may be cause for concern. A formidable geographic barrier, the San Francisco Bay, prevents lions from the North Coast Ranges from entering the Diablo Range. Likewise, cougars from the Sierra Nevada, fifty miles east, stand little chance of crossing the broad, domesticated San Joaquin Valley and reaching the area. To the west, development in the Santa Clara and Salinas Valleys has made it increasingly difficult for cougars to move between the coastal mountains and the Diablo Range. There appear to be several spots where lions can still move between those ranges, but most involve crossing Highway 101, one of the busiest routes in the state. That leaves the southern section as the best bet for habitat connectivity, but that region, though little developed, is sparsely vegetated and may not possess the larger prey base found to the north. If Diablo Range lions have to depend on recruits from outside areas, the future suddenly looks a lot less rosy, and I'd think three times before approving any hunting plan.

I worry about large carnivores. Spread thin across the land, they are particularly prone to extirpation. The jaguar, grizzly bear, and gray wolf in California have all been relegated to the forlorn annals of history. With apologies to the black bear, that leaves the mountain lion as the last large carnivore left. Perhaps we should continue to exercise care in how we manage cougars, letting the land tell us how many it can support. In California, the mountain lion has had a dramatic history. It's been portrayed as a rare, secretive, benign beast, as well as an abundant, aggressive, bloodthirsty killer. Its status has been equally complicated, for over the years it has been managed as an unwelcome predator with a bounty on its head, unprotected vermin, big game mammal, and finally, Specially Protected Mammal. It's had multiple status changes and multiple reputations. But what it may need most in the future is multiple lives.

October 2007

The Harder They Fall

The Beleaguered Plight of the California Condor

OCTOBER, 1985. IT'S 4:45 p.m. on a Sunday afternoon. I've been parked here since nine in the morning, in a dirt pullout at the edge of the Los Padres National Forest. I know this not because of the presence of any actual trees nearby—I'm standing along a ridge of dried grasses and scattered shrubs—but because a nondescript forest service sign says so. To a dedicated group of biologists and condor devotees, that sign holds significance far greater than its humble appearance would suggest. Since the 1960s, it has been the most reliable observation post for viewing the rarest and most spectacular bird in North America, the California condor.

The pullout is located along a lightly traveled road straddling a forlorn ridge overlooking the southern end of the San Joaquin Valley. The location is, if not quite in the middle of nowhere, miles from the amenities of civilization. The nearest community is Maricopa, a ramshackle town whose best days are behind it. The nearest city is Taft, twenty-five miles north. An oil town, Taft is larger than Maricopa and has fared better over the years, yet its main claim to fame is as the setting for *The Best of Times*, a Robin Williams film.

From this vantage point, a wide panorama extends in every direction. To the south lies the Sespe Wilderness, one of the last strongholds of the condor. To the west stand the San Rafael and Sierra Madre Mountains, also among the condor's final retreats. Looking north one can see the treeless, bone-dry Temblor Range, scarred by the San Andreas Fault. Beyond the Temblors, one hundred miles distant and out of view, the Diablo Range humbly rises. When staring east, the San Joaquin Valley lies below, while the Tehachapi Range provides a link between the coast ranges and the southern Sierra Nevada. This bowl-shaped area has, since time immemorial, served as a flyway for the California condor. The all-encompassing view from this spot has made it a beacon for wildlife biologists and condor watchers, particularly in fall, calving season on the ranches nearby. Condors forage here annually like clockwork, hoping to gorge on the remains of stillborn calves. The previous fall I had come for the first time with an Audubon group gathered to glimpse one of the fifteen free-flying condors left on earth. Scanning the skies with binoculars and spotting scopes, we viewed condors soaring along on thermals at distances of three miles, where they appeared as dark specks floating across the sky.

Something compelled me to return a year later. When I arrived in the morning, the pullout was conspicuously empty and remained so throughout the day. This was a far cry from the hub of activity here just a year ago, yet much had changed since then. During the previous winter, six of the fifteen condors had perished, a staggering 40 percent of the wild population. Worse, all were breeding adults. In addition, three other condors had been brought into captivity. As a result, where there had been five breeding pairs in 1984, there was just one in 1985, and a mere six condors left in the wild.

Several times during the day, I observed large birds soaring in the distance, but I couldn't tell if they were condors or golden eagles. As the afternoon wore on, I was contemplating the long drive home. I planned to leave at five o'clock.

4:50 p.m. For no particular reason, I aimed my binoculars toward the grassy hilltop one hundred yards to the northeast. Suddenly the lenses were overwhelmed by a huge, dark shape materializing out of the ether. For a magical moment, that bird and I shared a hillside, as I watched one of the last six free-flying condors glide low over the ridge and continue south toward the Sespe Wilderness, never once flapping its immense wings. Though I should have been ecstatic, I could not muster much enthusiasm. The California condor had been dwindling for over a century, this in spite of the fact that private conservation organizations, the state of California, and the federal government had expended years of effort and a small fortune to resuscitate it. All of those efforts were failing, and the California condor was on the threshold of becoming the most high-profile extinction in history. As electrifying as that sighting was, it was tempered with the realization that this magnificent creature was not long for this world. I had returned to get one good look at the California condor before it flew no more.

My introduction to the condor came in childhood, from a book, *Album of North American Birds*. Paintings and drawings of several dozen prominent species, along with a few paragraphs of text, adorned its pages. The painting depicting the condor was alluring: a bird perched stoically on the limbs of a dead tree, with others soaring in the background. Meanwhile, the drawing featured a condor peering out over the ledge of a cave along a massive cliff face, a gothic lord of a remote wilderness. The text fortified that image, portraying condors as Ice Age survivors that had retreated to an inaccessible wilderness, intolerant of humanity, a diminishing race whose numbers had shrunk to a mere seventy individuals.

California condors once flew throughout the Pacific Coast from Vancouver to Baja California. Lewis and Clark encountered them along the Columbia River; inland, they were known from the Grand Canyon, as well as the Snake River, possibly as far east as the Rockies. As the nineteenth century progressed, their range and numbers declined, so much so that by 1900, the bird had literally become the California condor, when the last sightings from Oregon ceased.

The decline did not go unnoticed; since the late 1800s, conservationists were championing its preservation. The first measure of protection came in 1905, when the California Legislature forbade the killing or capturing of condors, as well as the taking of eggs. (Condor eggs, due to a combination of size and rarity, had become valuable commodities, often fetching over one hundred dollars apiece, a heady sum in that era. Though the practice of egg collecting has since diminished, a century ago there was a vibrant market for the eggs of rare birds.) This law was enacted because in the previous thirty years, at least 111 condors had been taken from the wild and added to museums and private collections. That practice was especially reprehensible, for the institutions that could have worked to save condors were instead hastening their extinction by acting out of self-interest. At the same time, in the Southeast, ivory-billed woodpeckers were being collected in similar fashion, for obtaining museum specimens shamefully took precedence over saving the bird. Unfortunately, at that time a bird in the hand was worth more than two in the bush, and that attitude contributed to the decline of the condor.

The first study of the California condor was undertaken in 1906 by William Finley, who observed a breeding pair in Eaton Canyon in the San Gabriel Mountains north of Pasadena. Before Finley, information on condors came from anecdotal observations by naturalists and outdoorsmen, and while some may have been accurate, others were sheer fallacy. For example, there was a persistent belief that condors were predators rather than exclusive scavengers and thus posed a threat to livestock. Finley provided valuable insight into condor behavior, particularly in understanding the breeding cycle. He was the first to document the low reproductive rate of the species and make the connection between mortality rates and birth rates. Although he believed that shooting and collecting were the main causes of the condor's decline, Finley also speculated that predator control campaigns, particularly those employing strychnine, had taken a toll as well. Unless such threats could be curtailed, Finley foresaw a bleak future for the species.

The 1905 statute was effective in curbing the taking of condors and their eggs from the wild. However, additional conservation measures did not soon materialize. In the 1930s, the first population survey was conducted throughout the Los Padres National Forest. The survey revealed the importance of the Sisquoc River watershed, and in 1937, the Sisquoc Condor Sanctuary was established when a tract of national forest land was set aside in the San Rafael Mountains. The construction of a fire road, which would have greatly facilitated public access, threatened the area. Ten years later, the Sespe Condor Sanctuary was created in Ventura County. This area incorporated a number of active nest sites, and its establishment was primarily due to the efforts of one man.

In 1939, Carl Koford, a graduate student at UC Berkeley, began what would become an intense four-year study devoted to the California condor. Koford's work formed the basis for much of what we know about the species. He spent long hours in the field, taking copious notes, observing breeding pairs, and locating nests. Given the limited tools he had to work with, his study was nothing short of remarkable. The condor of my youth was that described by Koford: a rare, fragile creature, intolerant of humans and sensitive to the slightest of perturbations, threatened primarily by shooting and harassment. The salvation of the condor, according to Koford, required habitat protection and keeping the birds as free as possible from human intrusion. Though Koford was never affiliated with official recovery efforts, his body of work demanded attention, and even with his passing in 1979, his influence remained.

As the decades progressed, the role of the federal government grew increasingly larger. The California condor was among the first species protected under the Endangered Species Act. Initially, federal policy was congruent with the hands-off recommendations of Carl Koford and like-minded conservation organizations. Throughout the 1970s, additional habitat was protected, public awareness and support for condor preservation increased, yet the bird continued to decline.

The Condor Recovery Team, established in the 1970s as an advisory body to the United States Fish and Wildlife Service, correctly concluded that the laissez-faire policy was not working and began advocating for proactive management measures. This hands-on approach included the formation of a captive flock and breeding program (as both an insurance policy against the extinction of the wild population and a means to maximize the remaining genetic diversity of the species) as well as using radio telemetry to better understand daily and seasonal activity patterns. Those proposals sounded reasonable but were met with vociferous opposition from a coalition of individuals and organizations adhering to the recommendations of Carl Koford. That alliance argued against attempts to breed condors in captivity, an idea that first surfaced in the 1940s. The primary reason for their objection was the concern that emphasis on a captive flock would shift priorities and funding away from the wild population, especially regarding habitat protection. This fear was not without merit; it was hard enough to stave off threats such as oil and gas exploration, road building, and dam construction in areas utilized by an extant condor population. If condors existed only in captivity, the task of preserving habitat for future generations of condors could become even more difficult.

Another point of contention was the belief that condors were too sensitive to disturbance to breed successfully in captivity, and because of this, the idea of a captive breeding program was treated as folly, like NASA sending astronauts to the sun. Radio telemetry was opposed because that would involve capturing and handling condors, and many felt that this placed an unnecessary stress on a species they believed had a low tolerance for human intervention. They were convinced that the information obtained would not be worth the risk. The stage was set for a bitter, protracted battle. Conflict in itself was hardly new; every effort to preserve species or habitats has been met with rancorous opposition from people on the other side of the aisle. In the case of the condor, this was a civil war, pitting two groups dedicated to condors squarely against each other, each with a vastly divergent vision on how to save the species. Lawsuits were filed; insults and accusations were exchanged during heated meetings. The Condor Recovery Team eventually secured permission to initiate a radio telemetry program, monitor chicks, and capture a female condor to serve as a mate for Topatopa, the sole condor in captivity.

The era of hands-on management had scarcely gotten off the ground before a colossal mishap occurred. During a nest entry, a chick died from the stress of being handled, and this blunder nearly doomed the recovery team. The subsequent outcry was deafening, and the team's privileges were revoked. It appeared as if the recovery team had squandered its hard-won opportunity, and this might have been the demise of such recovery strategies, and even the condor itself, were it not for one timely observation.

In February 1982, researchers who had been observing a pair of nesting condors looked on in alarm as the egg (condors lay but one) tumbled off its rocky perch and splattered like Humpty Dumpty on the ground. In the aftermath, the pair began another courtship ritual and another egg was laid. Someone had finally documented that which had long been suspected by some (particularly the old egg collectors), never mentioned by Koford, and dismissed outright by others: California condors are capable of double-clutching; they can lay a replacement egg if the original fails. The ramifications of this could hardly be overstated. A captive flock could now be established without removing birds from the wild.

In light of that finding, the recovery team was given a second chance, an opportunity to take eggs from nests, incubate them, and raise chicks in captivity to establish a captive breeding program. Granted this reprieve, the subsequent achievements of the recovery team were stellar, for condors bred very well in captivity, something Carl Koford and many others doubted was possible.

Evidence of double-clutching arrived in the nick of time. Emerging in 1982, when there were still five breeding pairs left in the wild, it enabled the recovery team to collect over a dozen eggs. Had that information never surfaced or if permission to remove eggs from the wild had been denied, it is possible that the condor would by now be functionally extinct, given the disastrous die-off that hit the wild population in 1984–5 that left but one breeding pair intact. Yet as 1985 drew to a close, an acrimonious debate over how best to save the condor was still raging. The recovery team, which had been permitted to take into captivity three condors earlier in the year, pleaded to bring in the remaining six as well, arguing that all wild birds were in imminent danger. In addition, the captive flock was predominantly female, while five of the six wild birds happened to be males. It doesn't take a geneticist to see what's wrong with that picture.

Opponents of captive management feared that habitat protection would suffer if there were no birds left in the wild. Incredulously, they urged that birds from the captive flock be released to augment the wild population, despite the fact that free-flying condors were dropping like flies. It took another tragedy, the poisoning death of the last free-flying female, to tip the scales toward the side of the recovery team. The last wild condor was captured on Easter Sunday, 1987, and the irony of that transpiring on a day of resurrection was heavy, for it seemed as if the revival of the California condor was anything but assured.

I followed all this with frustration. At first my opinion rested in the Koford camp. As events unfolded, however, I adopted the viewpoint of the recovery team. My initial opposition to captive breeding was based on the dogma that condors wouldn't breed in captivity. Once this was disproved, my confidence in the recommendations of the recovery team rose.

Among the hands-off crowd, there was a strong resistance against handling condors for philosophical reasons. The idea of adhering transmitters to the wings of condors was an affront to many. While I understood those sentiments,

I had no issue with biologists making use of modern technology if valuable information could be obtained in the process. By then the condor had become something larger, a symbol, a mythic being instead of a flesh and blood species. Certainly, the condor lends itself well to imagery and symbolism. But at some point, you have to tease out the symbol from the living bird, and for some people the condor, despite (or perhaps because of) its impressive size, could not be viewed beyond the filter of its own image. The most telling example of this occurred during the 1985 debate over whether or not to bring the wild population into captivity following a winter that had seen six birds perish. There was a faction so opposed to the hands-on strategy that they preferred to relegate the condor to extinction rather than subject them to captive management. Their slogan was "death with dignity," and for the life of me, I could not fathom it. Yes, it's a sad day when an awe-inspiring bird that should be soaring freely must be taken into captivity for its own safety. Perhaps a condor endowed with a wing tag, whose every flight can be tracked, seems less wild than its predecessors. Maybe such practices smack of indignity. But extinction? Where is the dignity in that, especially in one that might be prevented? The condor was not passing away in an act of altruistic self-sacrifice or perishing on principle. It wasn't dying with dignity; it was just dying. Using technology to help preserve species seems worth the risks. The worst outcome would be for the condor to go extinct, yet that was the endgame for the "death with dignity" contingent. Dignity is arbitrary and subjective; extinction is unequivocal and final. What kind of people were these who would pull the plug on the condor because they had a philosophical conflict with the recovery strategy?

Some interesting revelations have emerged since the advent of hands-on management. As it turns out, condors are not the ultrasensitive creatures Koford portrayed them as being, and their ability to breed in captivity contradicted a falsehood that had persisted for decades. In other behaviors, condors are far from instinct-driven automatons. They are bright, inquisitive, and social, and juveniles benefit greatly from the presence of adults. In fact, the absence of adult birds hampered early reintroduction efforts. Juveniles raised in captivity began behaving in ways that were highly unnatural once released: roosting on the ground, perching on utility poles, gathering on the decks of mountain cabins. Although biologists had gone to great lengths to prevent them from imprinting on humans, it was obvious that those young birds needed to absorb the wisdom that only adult condors could provide. Lacking that influence, the curiosity of young condors could be their undoing. Early observers hardly referenced this intelligent, curious, and social side of their nature.

For as long as people have been studying the California condor, it was obvious that the bird was in serious trouble. Condor numbers were shrinking with each passing decade, as evidenced by range contraction—the disappearance of birds from Oregon, Northern California, and Baja California—and smaller flock sizes observed at foraging sites. Although it was obvious that the population was declining, it was unknown whether the cause was one of excessive mortality—too many birds dying—or reproductive failure. As time passed it became clear that reproduction was not a concern, for condors continued to fledge young into the 1980s. Some speculated that food shortages hindered reproduction, but there was never any evidence of that. Meanwhile, studies examining the role of DDT failed to show much of a link between it and nest failure in condors. It had long been suspected that mortality was more of an issue for condors, and as time passed, ample evidence supported this.

Early researchers contended that shooting was the major threat to the condor. Besides the unconscionable practices undertaken by private collectors and museums, condors were shot by misguided ranchers who viewed them as a threat to livestock, as well as a contingency of dunces whose idea of thrill-seeking consisted of blasting large birds out of the sky.

A potentially significant mortality source was the poisons used to rid the state of predators. Strychnine-saturated carcasses were scattered like Easter eggs, and they worked all too well, killing not only their intended targets but anything unfortunate enough to feed on them. This must have taken a toll, but we'll never know the extent to which poisoned baits affected condors, for the practice declined after the extirpation of wolves and grizzlies in the 1920s. The use of other toxins continued, targeting ground squirrels and coyotes, and though there is evidence that condors occasionally succumbed to their ill effects, in all likelihood the threat to condors was lower than in the era of strychnine. Condors also perished in collisions with power lines, as well as natural causes. None of these appeared to occur with great frequency, however, and it was not until the 1980s that the most serious threat of all was discovered, thanks to radio telemetry.

Before the advent of GPS technology, radio telemetry provided a cutting-edge look into condor habits in ways unimaginable to early researchers, whose most sophisticated equipment was a pair of binoculars. By affixing transmitters to condors, researchers were able to track the movement of birds on a daily basis. Telemetry soon illuminated how far they travel, when they are most active, where they roost, where they forage, where they nest, and other mysteries. Telemetry has been very useful in helping us understand how condors live. Yet its greatest asset has been in providing insight into how condors die.

Condors were first fitted with transmitters in 1982, rather late considering the technology had been available years before. The constituency opposing hands-on management was successful in delaying a radio telemetry program until it was nearly too late. Besides their earlier arguments, they claimed that all the necessary information could be acquired through less intrusive methods. On that they were never more wrong.

In March 1984, a condor was found dead at the base of a pine tree in the Sierra Nevada foothills. Its radio signal indicated that the bird had been motionless for a number of hours, a sure sign that something was amiss. Because it was fitted with a transmitter, the bird was located. Without that, the likelihood of happening upon a dead condor in a time frame that would allow the cause of death to be determined would be beyond minute, like locating a contact lens on a beach. The body was retrieved and necropsied, and the results revealed that it had perished due to lead poisoning. In addition to its having high levels of lead in its blood, X-rays revealed bullet fragments in its digestive tract. This was the first time that lead had been implicated as a cause of death among California condors. It would not be the last.

Unfortunately, only about half of the remaining wild condors had been fitted with transmitters following approval of the telemetry program in 1982 and the time the last condor was taken into captivity in 1987. During the disastrous winter of 1984–5, which saw six of the remaining fifteen birds perish, only one of the eight birds fitted with transmitters succumbed, while five of the seven unadorned birds died. For those birds, the cause of death will always remain a mystery, vanishing into the air like the great soaring birds themselves.

By 1986, lead poisoning had been confirmed as the cause of two more condor deaths. Given they would have over a centuries' worth of exposure to lead-contaminated carcasses, it's likely that lead has been killing condors steadily and stealthily since the arrival of firearms on the West Coast. Fortunately, the lead threat was identified not a moment too soon, and subsequently almost every aspect of condor management revolved around the omnipresent threat posed by lead. The first such management decision was to capture the entire wild flock and take them into captivity, for the powers that be realized they were dealing with a threat that would not be easily or quickly remedied.

California condors are more susceptible to lead poisoning than perhaps any other species. Being scavengers, condors rely exclusively on carrion. Moreover, that carrion is composed almost entirely of mammal carcasses, some of which are shot with lead ammunition. Lead bullets fragment into numerous tiny particles upon penetrating flesh, and even small fragments can poison a condor. To make matters worse, one tainted carcass can poison several birds because condors frequently feed in groups. This occurred recently in Arizona, where condors were reintroduced in 1996 north of the Grand Canyon. Several perished shortly after feeding on a coyote that had been shot. It's not hard to imagine similar scenarios occurring over and over. Ultimately, lead poisoning devastates condors so because they are among the slowest-breeding birds in the world, each pair producing at most one chick every two years. Being long lived (potentially, that is, as it is doubtful that any wild condor since the Gold Rush has experienced old age) condors do not even begin breeding until the age of six. If a pair of condors can defy the odds and successfully fledge two chicks, then they will have replaced themselves in terms of population numbers. During modern times, the odds of that happening grew ever slimmer.

Biologists are acutely aware of the devastating threat represented by lead in the food supply of the condor. Even before all wild birds were taken into captivity, they began placing clean carcasses in foraging locations in the hope that condors would feast on safe fare. Twenty years later, with release programs in place at five locations, biologists routinely set out uncontaminated carcasses to avoid the ever-present threat of lead poisoning. Additional precautions include fitting all released birds with transmitters, undertaken in large part to alert researchers to the presence of birds that may be ill or dead. If discovered in time, sick birds are doctored through chelation. So great is the lead threat that free-flying condors are periodically recaptured to test for lead levels in their blood. At some point, you come to the realization that all the time, money, and effort spent on reducing the lead threat is the price that must be paid if we're going to release birds into an environment where lead is present. After an ominous start, the Condor Recovery Team has achieved spectacular results, yet the overwhelming specter of lead casts a shadow over the entire recovery effort.

To address this issue, an outreach and education program was put in place, urging hunters to either bury the gut piles of their quarry or switch to nontoxic ammunition. Yet even if every hunter conscientiously buried every gut pile, there are bound to be animals that are wounded and succumb later, to be fed upon by scavengers. Besides, many people simply won't comply. The department of fish and game contends that about half of the deer shot annually in California are poached; it's hard to believe that anyone who refuses to comply with basic game laws would lift a finger on behalf of the condor. Besides game hunters, there are varmint hunters, who as a group may be even less likely to dispose of the carcasses of the coyotes and ground squirrels they shoot. In terms of switching to nontoxic ammunition, many remain reluctant to change, while others balk at the higher cost of nonlead bullets.

In 2003, the California Fish and Game Commission appeared to confront the issue by summoning Dr. Michael Fry, a toxicologist from UC Davis, to study the effects of lead on condors and other raptors. The commission is the five-member body entrusted to formulate rules and regulations governing California's game animals, as well as its nongame species.

Fry submitted an eighty-three-page report that showed well beyond a reasonable doubt that lead bullet fragments constitute a serious threat to the California condor. In January 2005, the commission met to review the study and vote on whether or not to ban lead, if not throughout the entire state, then at least throughout condor range. By a 3–2 vote, the commission declined. This was not surprising; with the commission composed of political appointees, anything was possible. Rather, what made me livid were the comments uttered by the head of the commission explaining the vote against the recommendations of an expert whose counsel they had sought. Rather than admit the truth—that the commission was unwilling to enact legislation that would be unpopular with a good portion of the hunting community—the spokesman instead attacked the validity of the report, claiming the science was insufficient. How this particular commissioner was able to differentiate good science from poor science escapes me; as he lacked a scientific background, I doubt he could tell a hypothesis from a hypotenuse triangle. Having a nonscientist refute a scientific paper is like honoring the opinions of a deaf music critic. The commissioner exposed his ignorance like a keynote speaker with his fly unzipped when he went on record as wondering why condors were sensitive to lead poisoning when red-tailed hawks were not. (The Fry Report analyzed the prevalence of lead poisoning in several other raptors.) Call me an idealist, but is it too much to ask that someone occupying a prominent position in the state wildlife management hierarchy possess at least a modicum of knowledge regarding the species he or she is entrusted to oversee? I'm not insisting upon a panel of PhDs, nor do I expect commissioners to be experts on condor biology, but the least they can do is put forth an effort to learn a little something about a species prior to convening to consider actions involving the fate of that species. By dismissing the Fry Report on scientific grounds, the commission turned its back on twenty years of steadily mounting evidence incriminating lead. At the very least, the commission should have acknowledged the report by accepting its findings. They didn't have to ban lead immediately; they could have allowed for a gradual phase-out in order to address concerns such as the cost and availability of nonlead ammunition. Instead, they took the easy way out. To give the appearance that they were addressing the issue, they requested a scientific study, which they, a panel of nonscientists, then dismissed as insufficient science. In the end, the commission merely covered its ass, pretending to confront an issue it wished would just go away. This entity, which during the 1980s may have been more protective of the California condor than any other governing body, had by 2005 become a milquetoast laughingstock whose credibility was at an all-time low.

Of course, the issue did not go away. More scientific studies ensued, and by the end of 2006, five more surfaced, each concluding that lead bullets represent an overwhelming obstacle to the restoration of the California condor. The culmination of this was a signed statement of scientific agreement by over three dozen biologists. In 2007 the state legislature passed, and Governor Schwarzenegger signed the Ridley-Tree Condor Preservation Act, which required the use of non-lead ammunition for big game and coyotes within the range of the California condor. It took over twenty years, but at last something had been done to counter the threat of lead poisoning.

At the same time, I think it would be prudent to make this legislation as palatable to hunters as possible by easing the transition to nonlead ammunition. Consider defraying the cost differential of nonlead bullets so that hunters don't feel as if they're paying extra for condor conservation. If some of the funding earmarked for condor recovery goes instead toward subsidizing ammunition, perhaps, as strange as that may sound, that's in the best interests of the condor. Passing laws isn't enough. Doing so runs the risk of alienating people and creating a backlash against condors. Of course there are always dyed-in-the-wool zealots who can never be pacified, who see subterfuge behind efforts to ban lead bullets, claiming it's a ploy concocted by the antigun lobby to infringe upon their Second Amendment rights. Never mind that the lead ban was proposed and endorsed by biologists, not gun-control advocates. Disregard the fact that some of these same biologists are not only gun owners but hunters as well. Suspend the notion that a lead ammunition ban does not in any way deny a person from hunting or otherwise using a firearm. Some of these people claim that the evidence linking lead to condor mortality is weak on two fronts, the first being a small number of condor deaths attributed to lead poisoning and the second a lack of lead fatalities in other species. To respond to the latter, the reason lead poisoning has not been implicated as a cause of death for other species is because there has been little effort to study the phenomenon. I wouldn't be surprised if subsequent research documented lead poisoning across a wide spectrum of predatory and scavenging species. That none of those creatures is plummeting toward extinction may be due to the fact that higher reproductive rates offset the loss of individuals succumbing to lead poisoning. With the lowest reproductive rate of any North American bird, a diet composed entirely of carrion, and a habit of feeding in groups, the California condor is by far the species most vulnerable to lead poisoning.

As to the small sample size, the fact that "only" a dozen condors (as of 2005) were found to have perished due to lead poisoning says a lot more about the scarcity of condors than the ambiguity of the lead threat. It's possible that this number would be significantly higher were it not for the chelation treatments administered to birds showing high lead levels. A generation ago, poisoned condors would simply have vanished into the black hole that condors have been falling into since the days of Lewis and Clark.

Viewed in flight, there is no bird like the California condor. Turkey vultures have a teetering lilt to their flight far removed from the steady flight of condors. Golden eagles are perhaps closest to soaring condors, as they spiral steadily and attain great heights. But for all their prowess, golden eagles don't give the lasting impression that condors do. For the condor, neither the fleetest nor the most agile denizen of the skies, is the most majestic. Their stability in flight has led some to mistake them for small aircraft. Condors float regally in the air. To see one suddenly appear in the midst of other soaring birds—ravens, hawks, vultures, even eagles—gives a lasting impression of their enormous size. From a distance, a condor is memorable. From close up, it's reverential.

January 17, 2004. I've spent the last three weekends trying to observe condors at Pinnacles National Monument. A half-dozen birds were released here in December, the first in a series of releases with the goal of restoring the great bird to a range it hasn't occupied for the better part of a century. So far I haven't seen one closer than a mile away. Today I've decided to try something different. Rather than set my spotting scope up in the High Peaks, I'm headed for a lower vantage point above Chalone Creek, about four hundred feet up the slopes of Mount Defiance. No hiking trails adorn this mountain; the only pathways up the steep slope are those fashioned by deer as they traverse this area of chaparral and patchy grass. Coming upon a level spot, I set up the scope and settle in for a day of condor watching.

Condors are not early risers, often remaining at roosts until midmorning. Today, a fog bank from Monterey Bay drifted inland, and as the overcast lifted, I notice two condors perched on a dead gray pine two miles east across Chalone Creek. Soon they are airborne. Though the birds are juveniles, a year and a half old, they have already attained adult size but lack the striking orange head of adults. Throughout the day, they disappear and reemerge behind a ridge. At one point, I count four aloft at once, almost the entire flock, though never do any approach within a mile.

3:15 p.m. There is perhaps one and a half hours of sunlight left, and soon the birds will be looking to roost for the evening. I'm just about ready to pack it in myself, but before dismantling the scope, I notice a large bird perched atop a power pole south of Drywall Slide, just outside the monument. Even at two miles, I see that this bird is either a golden eagle or a condor—nothing smaller. If it's a condor, it's displaying a disastrous preference for perches, astride a pole where electrocution is a possibility. Someone involved with the release program should be notified if that bird is a condor. Cranking up the scope to full power, I strain mightily to identify this bird. Unfortunately, when I reach sixty power, the bird's image wavers like a mirage on a desert highway. After five minutes, I back away. While relaxing my eyes, my vision drifts to the north. Suddenly I spy a large black shape flying low over Chalone Creek, a quarter mile distant, heading my way. There's no doubt about this bird: one of the young condors has decided to head west before settling down for the night. I fumble with the spotting scope, but as valuable as it is when viewing perched birds, it is unwieldy when trying to pick up a bird in flight. The condor is soon two hundred yards away when I remember that I have two shots left on the roll of film in my camera. As the condor approaches, it changes course fifty yards in front of me, veering off over a tight, steep ravine. As it does, I snap the final two shots. They reveal the condor below me, the afternoon sun illuminating the number sixty-six on the bird's wing tags. After I take the final picture, the condor changes course and heads back toward me. Not thirty feet off the ground, the great bird wheels in the air right in front of me, looks toward me, and with an incredibly loud flap of its wings, resumes course back up the canyon, seconds later completely out of sight.

It was a transcendent moment, and if I live to be one hundred, I will never forget the rich memory of the day the largest bird on the continent flew within a stone's throw of me. That this bird was conceived, hatched, and raised in captivity didn't matter. That it was monitored by biologists didn't bother me. That the bird was adorned with transmitting paraphernalia didn't lessen the experience. Standing alone on that slope, I experienced a condor much as people did a thousand years ago, when the world was big and wonderfully wild. It's easier now to understand why condors figured prominently in the religion of Native Americans. My wish is that everyone who admires condors be rewarded with such an experience. I have the same hope for those who see nothing special about condors, who view attempts to restore them as a waste of time and money. Such people should experience a close encounter of the condor kind before dismissing them so blithely. Anyone who could walk away from that and not feel something special has something other than blood coursing through his veins.

Nearly everything you've read or will ever read about the California condor references its historic past, usually by proclaiming the species an Ice Age remnant or Pleistocene relic. While this is technically true, it's misleading, for in evolutionary terms, the Pleistocene was just moments ago. So, yes, the condor is an Ice Age holdover, but so are crows, raccoons, and every other wild creature you can think of, as are humans. Opponents of condor restoration use the Ice Age relic argument to legitimize its extinction, claiming that the species is old, outdated, and naturally convalescing. That's bullshit. It isn't old age that hobbles the condor. It's large size.

The bigger they are, the harder they fall. While size has benefits, it brings with it burdens that make large animals particularly prone to extinction. Large creatures exist in smaller numbers, require larger tracts of habitat, are more likely to conflict with human activities, and have lower reproductive rates than smaller animals. Ten thousand years ago, our planet harbored a vast assemblage of immense and wondrous beasts, and North America boasted the most amazing collection of all: mammoths and mastodons, giant ground sloths, giant short-faced bears, lions, saber-toothed cats, dire wolves, horses, and camels. In the skies, the

California condor was a lightweight, upstaged by *Teratornis merriami*, a vulture with a twelve-foot wingspan, and dwarfed by *Teratornis incredibilis*, a bird twice the size of a condor, with a belief-defying eighteen-foot wingspan. Today, only the California condor remains, hanging on by a thread. The rest are gone, regrettably and irretrievably lost, leaving behind tantalizing remains in the pack ice of the arctic or the sticky goo of the La Brea tar pits.

Some complain that a handful of large, charismatic animals receive the lion's share of conservation funding while a menagerie of smaller animals and plants receive a pittance. Why should big animals receive a disproportionate slice of the pie? How come the California condor gets dollars while the Valley elderberry long-horned beetle gets pennies? Those are fair questions. I'm one of the last to trivialize the plight of smaller animal and plant species. They absolutely deserve more attention and funding. Yet I find no problem at all with a bias favoring megafauna.

Large animals often serve as either umbrella species or keystone species in their respective ecosystems. Some are both. An umbrella species is one whose protection covers the needs of a multitude of other species that share its habitat. When we protect such species, many others benefit. A keystone species is one with an unusually large role within an ecosystem, a species whose presence has a profoundly positive effect on the biodiversity and functioning of that ecosystem. Large animals, especially carnivores, often serve as keystone species. That being said, I cannot in good conscience label the California condor as either an umbrella species or a keystone species. Unlike most large creatures, habitat, while important, is less of an issue for the condor, so it is not a prime example of an umbrella species. Neither does it assume a major role in the ecosystem, for there are other avian scavengers, turkey vultures chief among them, to act in that capacity. It's quite possible that in the course of saving the condor, we won't be protecting a host of other imperiled species, if any. If that's the case, does condor preservation still deserve such a high priority, and if so, why? My reply is an emphatic yes, and my justification is simple: because they're large.

Large creatures may claim the bulk of species conservation efforts, but they have also suffered a disproportionate share of extinctions. The wild world is shrinking with each passing year, fragmented by agricultural, residential, and industrial development. With their considerable spatial requirements, large animals increasingly conflict with human activities, and this is particularly true for carnivores. Most of the world's big cats have experienced drastic declines in recent decades, while only two of the world's eight bear species appear to have a secure future. Large herbivores have fared only marginally better. While there have been some success stories, they are the exception rather than the rule and consist primarily of game species. We are hurtling toward a dismal, lonely future where large wild animals no longer exist, where the only sizable beasts remaining will be domesticated.

Can you imagine a world without elephants? Whales? Tigers? Polar bears? It would be as unacceptable as California without condors. If the condor is neither keystone species nor umbrella species, if its ecological role has been usurped by turkey vultures, so what? I chided the "death with dignity" contingent for loading too much symbolism on the wings of the condor, but perhaps they have a point. Condors have become something more than a species, more than a component of an ecological community, and to casually dismiss their symbolic value would be a mistake. Condors and other large animals are worth the effort to preserve not merely for whatever ecological niches they may fill but for the enormous roles they have played, and continue to play, in human culture. Religions, myths, and tales involving large beasts have been part of human societies since prehistoric times. One might argue that we've come a long way from the animistic religions of earlier civilizations, that today's technological world has little use for such remnants of bygone days, but that simply isn't so. Now more than ever, the magnetic pull exerted by formidable beasts such as grizzly bears, wolves, and condors tugs on our psyche as surely as the moon affects the tides. Televised nature programs are widely popular, and they are almost exclusively the realm of large animals: sharks, crocodiles, bears, and lions. We are spellbound by large beasts because their size kindles the imagination in ways smaller animals can't. They make the world seem bigger, wilder, and more mysterious. As they become rare, we value them more. You might even say we miss them, for a world full of people, pets, and domesticated animals can't make up for their absence. Evidence of this lies off the beaten scientific path, in the red-light district of cryptozoology, which concentrates on creatures that are rumored to exist. A cursory glance at the cryptozoological lineup reveals a pantheon of fantastic beasts, nearly all large: the Loch Ness monster, mokele mbembe, the dinosaur of the Congo, black panthers roaming the English countryside, the yeti, sasquatch, and a host of similar ape-men from around the globe.

Me, I don't believe any of those crypto-creatures exists. I think they're manifestations of what we've lost, a way of replacing a part of our world that has been tragically diminished, a world of mystery, a world of wildness, a world of large, wondrous beasts. Conventional wisdom admonishes us that we couldn't possibly live with them, but we're not doing very well without them. As those glorious large animals pass from the Earth, something deep in our soul dies with them. The bigger they are, the harder they fall. And the harder they fall, the further we fall.

The Last of the Mojave

Remnants from a Desert Past

THE MOJAVE. IT may be the most famous desert in the world, having served as a background for dozens of forgettable movies, long ago replacing the Sonoran as the Official Desert of Hollywood. The Mojave also houses military bases and bombing ranges. What red-blooded American desert doesn't? As the Saguaro cactus is in the Sonoran Desert, the Joshua tree is the symbol of the Mojave. It was in the Mojave that the earthly remains of musician Gram Parsons were pilfered and ignited in a funeral pyre and where Charles Manson and his devotees sequestered themselves while scheming to ignite a race war. The Mojave encompasses Death Valley, the hottest spot in the Western Hemisphere, if not the world. Beyond California, it makes its way east into Arizona and southern Nevada, surrounding Las Vegas and reaching southwestern Utah. In California its influence extends northwest beyond its geographic boundary, spreading north along the west side of the San Joaquin Valley on the lee side of the Diablo Range. It is an austere region, a sere no-man's land spliced by Highway 5. Rainfall averages less than ten inches a year here, and the natural landscape, what's left of it, is treeless, its grasses drying in March. Where the natural community persists, the vegetation is a mixture of desert scrub and shortgrass prairie. Such areas are few and far between, swept away by oil and gas development and agriculture. Petroleum deposits were discovered here over a century ago, while large-scale agriculture has been more recent. The desert that once carpeted the valley floor has retreated to the foothills to the west. These barren, destitute hills appear forlorn and lifeless. They broil under a merciless summer sun, with triple-digit temperatures day after day. Much of the landscape has been grazed, if not overgrazed, for generations. The few watercourses dribbling down out of the mountains are more often than not parched by the onset of summer, and many are infested with tamarisk, the tree that sucked the West dry. This land is a far cry from the inviting oak savanna on the west side of the range. But looks can be deceiving, for this region provides a home for a collection of imperiled species. And what a fascinating cast of characters they are: a squirrel that thrives in hundred-degree heat, the world's largest kangaroo rat, a mouse that acts like a wolf, a desert-dwelling lizard that is active for just several months a year, and a fox that doesn't need to drink.

The San Joaquin antelope squirrel (*Ammospermophilus nelsoni*) is one of four species of antelope squirrels, diurnal burrowing rodents occupying the arid regions of western North America. Antelope squirrels are supremely adapted to the hot, dry lands they occupy. With higher body temperatures, antelope squirrels are able not only to tolerate heat but remain active in temperatures that would wither other animals. They arch their tails, the underside of which is white, over their back to reflect the sun. When all else fails, they retreat to their burrows. Lastly, they obtain all the water they need from food. San Joaquin antelope squirrels need never drink, and though they are not unique in that, the fact that they are active during the heat of the day makes it all the more impressive. Their diet contains an interesting seasonal twist: in winter and spring, squirrels rely on green vegetation, high in water. In summer and fall they consume insects, better sources of moisture than dried grasses.

With their small size and white striping, San Joaquin antelope squirrels could be mistaken for chipmunks. They differ markedly from California ground squirrels (*Spermophilus beecheyi*), the familiar ground squirrel inhabiting much of the state. California ground squirrels are massive in comparison, carrying three to six times more weight, and have bushy tails, in contrast to the short, slender tails of antelope squirrels. Although there is some range overlap, the ecological relationship between the two species is unclear. It's been speculated that California ground squirrels may limit the range of antelope squirrels. Whether or not this is true is questionable; what's clear is that there are several factors, both natural and human influenced, combining to restrict the range and reduce the numbers of the San Joaquin antelope squirrel.

Historically, the range of the squirrel covered 3.5 million acres. Today, less than 700,000 remain intact, and while that number may seem large, it is misleading, for antelope squirrels have a spotty distribution and are not present throughout that acreage. Why squirrels are absent from otherwise suitable habitat is a mystery; perhaps large-scale rodent extermination campaigns are to blame. From the 1960s to the 1980s, planes dropped rodenticides over much of the region. Insecticides may have also played a role in the squirrel's decline by poisoning a significant food source. Today, the Panoche natural area on the eastern fringe of the Diablo Range supports what remains of the squirrel's northernmost population. Much of it is in public ownership as BLM land, thus there is a mandate to manage the land for the benefit of at-risk species such as the San Joaquin antelope squirrel. Only time will tell if it will do so successfully.

Kangaroo rats are indigenous to western North America, and while several species have adapted to the moister, cooler regions along the coast, the majority inhabit the drier interior. California happens to be ground zero for kangaroo rat diversity, for fourteen of the seventeen species of kangaroo rat are found here. Six are endemic, while two others barely extend their ranges beyond the state's boundaries. Many endemics have a highly restricted geographical distribution, which makes them prone to rarity. It is no surprise that as a group, kangaroo rats are well represented on the list of endangered species. This has not been lost on opponents of the Endangered Species Act, who wring their hands over efforts to preserve creatures they portray as disease-carrying vermin. In this case, the term kangaroo rat is not only an inaccurate misnomer but a public-relations disaster. Kangaroo rats are not rats at all, more closely related to ground squirrels, yet even if they were renamed kangaroo squirrels, I suspect their protection would still be met with derision. And that's a shame, because kangaroo rats are fascinating.

Within the Diablo Range, there are five different species of kangaroo rat. The one we're concerned with here is *Dipodomys ingens*, the largest and rarest, the giant kangaroo rat. Being referred to as the largest kangaroo rat might be akin to being labeled the world's tallest pygmy, for kangaroo rats are slight creatures, the largest weighing less than half a pound. Like the San Joaquin antelope squirrel, the giant kangaroo rat is supremely adapted to life in a harsh, dry world. It, too, never needs to drink, fulfilling its needs through a combination of diet and a handful of physiological and behavioral traits. Primarily seed eaters, giant kangaroo rats harvest seeds, cramming sizable quantities into their cheek pouches before returning to cure them outside their burrow. Once dried, they store them underground for future use. While kangaroo rats will avail themselves to green vegetation, they are capable of conjuring water from a dry seed diet. Kangaroo rat kidneys are highly efficient, four times more than those of humans. Their urine is highly concentrated, and their minute droppings nearly dry. Giant kangaroo rats also conserve moisture by remaining in their burrows during the day and emerging at night when the evaporation rate has lessened and airborne moisture, such as it may be, is at its peak. Interestingly, Heermann's kangaroo rats (*Dipodomys heermanni*) the most common and widespread kangaroo rat in the Diablo Range, do not possess such adaptations. Dwelling where moisture is more plentiful, they must drink to survive.

Given their nocturnal proclivities, kangaroo rats are not as readily observed as antelope squirrels. Not only are they nocturnal, they are far from active all night long, being out and about for short durations. On moonlit nights, they may wait until after the moon has set. I've seen kangaroo rat tracks on a handful of occasions, the most rewarding being a procession of prints left on the ground just outside my front door. It was only recently that I saw the real incarnation, as a group of biologists and I drove out of the Cantua Creek area in western Fresno County one evening. There, along a dirt road in the hills, several kangaroo rats hopped haphazardly out of our way, illuminated in the headlights. I couldn't tell if they were giant kangaroo rats or the smaller San Joaquin kangaroo rats (*Dipodomys nitraoides*). If they were indeed giants, I was not taken by their size.

If not impressive in stature, giant kangaroo rats may provide ecological benefits of far greater value than their diminutive proportions suggest, for they are considered a keystone species in the arid scrub and grassland communities they inhabit. An eight-year study demonstrated that plant productivity was anywhere from two to five times greater in kangaroo rat precincts than in areas where they were absent. They also serve as food for many birds, mammals, and reptiles, including the endangered San Joaquin kit fox, and their burrows provide refuges for species including the blunt-nosed leopard lizard and the San Joaquin antelope squirrel. The antelope squirrel, in particular, shares a great deal with the giant kangaroo rat beyond burrow use. So similar are their stories that their fates seem intertwined.

The historic distribution of the giant kangaroo rat mirrors that of the San Joaquin antelope squirrel, a territory that extended from the base of the Tehachapis north along the west side of the San Joaquin valley to an area south of Los Banos. Their preferred habitat of flat scrub/grassland and sandy, friable soils was well represented on the floor of the San Joaquin Valley, though seasonal flooding precluded them from ranging east the valley. Such inundation was not a problem along the west side or in the Panoche region, their last stronghold in the north.

Before 1950 there still existed over a million acres of giant kangaroo rat habitat. However, that dwindled after water projects opened up the west side of the valley to irrigation, for, like the San Joaquin antelope squirrel, the giant kangaroo rat is incompatible with irrigated areas or plowed fields. Other dreary causes of decline include petroleum development and the massive rodent control campaign cited earlier. As with the antelope squirrel, there are areas of quality habitat from which they are absent, and that absence may be the result of earlier extermination efforts. Currently, giant kangaroo rats persist on twenty-seven thousand acres spread out over six widely separated areas, and to make matters worse, those six areas are further split into smaller fragmented populations. The population surviving in the Panoche region is all that remains of a vast colony that once extended miles to the north and east, where suitable habitat no longer exists. Like many rodent species, giant kangaroo rat populations are prone to boom and bust cycles influenced by rainfall. As a result, the giant kangaroo rat, despite its scattered populations, is threatened not by inbreeding or low reproductive rates but rather by catastrophes such as prolonged drought and further loss of habitat. If enough habitat can be protected and restored, the giant kangaroo rat may long continue its role as a keystone species in the arid lands of central California.

Truth, so the saying goes, is stranger than fiction. As proof, I give you the Tulare grasshopper mouse.

The Tulare grasshopper mouse (*Onychomys torridus tularensis*) is a subspecies of the southern grasshopper mouse, one of three species of grasshopper mice inhabiting the West's drier regions. Pocket mice, harvest mice, and deer mice all bear a resemblance to grasshopper mice, and in the unlikely event that I would happen across one, I couldn't identify it without a field guide. However, it is not their physical appearance that sets grasshopper mice apart; it's their behavior, which strays beyond peculiar into fascinating. They may look like mice, but they act like wolves.

Their name might lead you to think they possess extraordinary jumping ability, but that's not the case. Also known as scorpion mice, they're named for their diet. While it is not uncommon for rodents to include insects in their diet, grasshopper mice go a step further, making them the bulk of their diet. The teeth of grasshopper mice differ from those of other mice by being sharper, for shearing, while their jaw muscles are enlarged, traits common to carnivores. Grasshopper mice secure their namesake prey by nibbling off the hind legs; they disarm scorpions by grasping the tail and biting off the stinger. Along with invertebrates, grasshopper mice have been known to subdue larger prey such as lizards, frogs, small birds, and rodents up to three times heavier than they. Yet this predatory nature also has a paternal side, for males help raise the young. Most charmingly, grasshopper mice vocalize, standing on their hind legs, snout pointed skyward. The high-pitched sound is audible to human ears, and those who have heard it liken it to a howl.

Unfortunately, grasshopper mice share other traits that are less advantageous with larger carnivores. Not only do they possess large home ranges—a male's may cover seven acres—they also persist at lower densities. As a result, grasshopper mice are not nearly so plentiful. The Tulare grasshopper mouse originally ranged from the southern end of the San Joaquin Valley north to Merced County but is known from few locales. The Panoche region is one of those. As of now, the Tulare grasshopper mouse has no legal protection, and it is hoped that efforts to protect species such as the giant kangaroo rat and the San Joaquin kit fox will benefit this intriguing little beast as well.

The blunt-nosed leopard lizard (*Gambelia sila*) haunts me. Over the course of the past dozen years, the creature has migrated from the fringe of my consciousness perilously close to the forefront. And it all started so innocuously.

In August 1995, my father and I drove to a ranch he was leasing in the foothills north of Coalinga. I had never set foot on the place before, and as soon as we arrived, I could see to my disappointment that it was a far cry from the property he leased in the northwest portion of the range. This ranch consisted of several thousand acres of rolling hills and gullies, its short grasses parched under a withering summer sun. The property ran parallel to Highway 5, that ceaseless hub of activity linking Northern and Southern California. Overhead, massive transmission towers loomed. A vast field planted in cotton marked the boundary of the property. There was not a tree on the entire ranch, and it was dry. I imagine hell would seem moist in comparison and perhaps even cooler.

We came to set out salt blocks, which we hauled in the back of a pickup. Dirt roads laced the ranch, and as the truck lurched along, I sat on the passenger side, window down to combat the heat. Beneath a transmission tower, we discovered the carcass of a golden eagle, looking as if it had been freeze-dried. Later we saw a squirrel burrow, while in front of it sat a large lizard the likes of which I had never seen before. As we approached, the lizard scurried into that subterranean retreat, and while I did not get a long look, I saw enough to determine that this lizard was too large to have been a skink, fence lizard, or side-blotched lizard, too hefty for a whiptail, and definitely not an alligator lizard. When I got home, I took out a field guide and recognized it as a blunt-nosed leopard lizard.

Originally, blunt-nosed leopard lizards occupied the same arid scrub and grassland as the three aforementioned species. The lizard probably had a larger distribution, being known from farther north in Merced County, and it may even have ranged as far as Corral Hollow in San Joaquin County. Many of the factors that brought about the demise of the three mammal species mentioned earlier also impacted the leopard lizard. Agricultural conversion took a heavy toll, for it cannot survive in cultivated areas, nor can it tolerate habitats with dense vegetation, natural or otherwise. Indirectly, rodent control efforts probably hurt the lizard by removing the source of the burrows it depends on for shelter. The loss of habitat has been a long and ongoing process in the story of the blunt-nosed leopard lizard, despite the fact that it was among the first species protected under the Endangered Species Act.

Initially, the blunt-nosed leopard lizard was considered a subspecies of the long-nosed leopard lizard (*Gambelia wislizenii*), a large lizard widely spread across the deserts of North America, from Texas to California, from Mexico to southern Idaho. In the San Joaquin Valley, there arose a unique form with an abbreviated snout. Today, the Tehachapi Mountains form a geographic barrier between the two species.

Blunt-nosed leopard lizards rely on rodent burrows as a refuge from a variety of predators as well as a permanent abode for the surprisingly long portion of the year when they are inactive. Adult lizards are active from spring to early summer, during which time they feed, court, and breed, with females laying one, and occasionally two, clutches of eggs. By midsummer, most adults have retreated underground, and even though weather conditions may be optimal for activity, they generally remain inactive after breeding. It is not clear why adult lizards retreat so early in the year. Perhaps, after gaining enough weight and breeding, the risks of remaining aboveground and vulnerable to predators outweigh the benefits. For the hatchlings, adult inactivity is most welcome, for leopard lizards eat smaller lizards, including their own kind. Hatching in July and August, young leopard lizards remain aboveground until cooler weather arrives in fall, growing rapidly, safe from the threat posed by adults if they were on the scene.

Besides rodent burrows, leopard lizards require open ground, for they fare poorly in areas of thick vegetation. It may be that such plants hinder their ability to detect prey, move quickly, or spot predators. They prefer gentle terrain where they can take advantage of their speed. In foothills they are absent from slopes exceeding thirty degrees, preferring washes and plateaus. Areas prone to flooding are avoided, for dormant lizards would drown there. Tilled soil is thoroughly inhospitable, although lizards have been known to recolonize fallow fields adjacent to occupied habitat.

My fascination with the species involves several factors. One is the improbability that such a desert lizard persists in central California. It's not the only one, though, for yellow-backed spiny lizards (*Sceloporus uniformis*) and desert night lizards (*Xantusia vigilis*) are also found in the southern Diablo Range. Its rarity, of course, is another, drawn as I am to a whole host of critters on the impoverished side of the tracks. The blunt-nosed leopard lizard shares something in common with species many times its size in that even where it is found, it is not common, and nowhere is it abundant. An acre of prime habitat may harbor a single lizard. That low threshold renders the lizard prone to extirpation in a given area. But there is something else about the lizard that draws me, an aura of mystery. The range of the species, particularly in the north, is little known. Is it possible that there are remnant populations yet to be discovered along the eastern flank of the Diablo Range? You would think not, for the desert influence recedes imperceptibly with each northward mile, subtly changing from scrub and short grass to taller, thicker grasses such as wild oats, the type of vegetation incompatible with leopard lizards. On the other hand, how many surveys for the species have been conducted in the region? Not many, I'll bet.

I pored over the handful of records for blunt-nosed leopard lizards in Merced County, the northernmost area where they have been documented. Several were particularly tantalizing: a 1970s sighting from Jasper Sears Road, west of Highway 33, and one from the 1930s, east of San Luis Reservoir (which had yet to be constructed), not ten miles from my home. In 2005, I made several fruitless attempts to find the species in the Lower Cottonwood Creek wildlife area and in the vicinity of Los Banos Creek Reservoir. With those failed efforts behind me, I sought them out where they were more likely to be found.

Thirty miles southwest of Los Banos, the Panoche Hills rise, a series of dry, weathered slopes and gullies, a landscape where trees are as sparse as people. Here, the eastern edge of the Diablo Range meets the floor of the San Joaquin Valley in a merging of two distinct bioregions. In and of themselves, the hills are unimpressive, for they appear no different than any of the other windswept foothills along the 150-mile eastern front of the range. Yet they differ significantly on at least two counts: they constitute a sizable tract of public land in a mountain range dominated by private ranches, and their unassuming contours still harbor the blunt-nosed leopard lizard.

Several large tracts of BLM land carpet the region, and on this day, I descend Jackass Pass, a washboard-bottomed dirt road linking the Panoche Valley to Highway 5. I park at a pullout and climb out of the car on this, the first day of June. It is a sunny morning, mild but by no stretch of the imagination cool. At nine thirty, it is seventy-five degrees, the minimum temperature at which leopard lizards become active. It will take temperatures above one hundred to force them back into their burrows, but this day will barely exceed ninety degrees, perfect for leopard lizards, if not for me. The temperature is ideal, the time of year is right, and I am in what looks like ideal leopard lizard habitat—dry, flat land with scattered vegetation. I am parked near the confluence of Panoche Creek and Silver Creek, though this late in the season, neither is running. Unfortunately, the creek channels are lined with tamarisk, a thorough infestation that may explain the utter lack of water in the streambed. I'm focusing on rodent burrows, specifically the entrances, where leopard lizards often bask. Yet while there is no shortage of burrows, I see no lizards. For the next several hours, I continue searching, wandering several miles. Occasionally, I spy a lizard as it scurries to the safety of a nearby shrub, but those invariably turn out to be side-blotched lizards (*Uta stansburiana*), a common species. I notice a miniature skull atop a patch of withered grass—that of a kangaroo rat, I assume. At a rare pool of standing water, I inadvertently scare the hell out of a coyote pausing for a drink.

The afternoon wears on. If there are leopard lizards here, I'm not seeing them. That's certainly possible, for not only are they scattered sparsely across the terrain, they blend in well with their surroundings, and those that run are fleet and quick to vanish underground. Still, I have to admit to a certain amount of dejection. As I walk back, my mind wanders toward the prospect of quenching my thirst with an overpriced Sobe Green Tea at one of several gas stations clustered around the I-5 interchange four miles west. I'm within a hundred yards of the car when I belatedly notice a lizard scramble into a burrow not ten feet away. I curse myself for letting my guard down, for had I paid attention, I would surely have gotten a good look. It's one of life's ironies that the harder you search, the less you see, while the object of your attention reveals itself once you stop looking. Philosophers say more or less the same thing when contemplating the meaning of life, while self-help gurus advise likewise in the quest for love. Me? I'm just trying to find blunt-nosed leopard lizards.

If I have been haunted by the blunt-nosed leopard lizard, I have been teased by the San Joaquin kit fox (*Vulpes macrotis mutica*). Kit foxes are among the smallest members of the dog family, tipping the scales at a mere five pounds. They are creatures of dry, open country, ranging from West Texas north to Idaho's Snake River plain, and west to the Mojave Desert. California once harbored two endemic subspecies of kit fox. The long-eared kit fox (*Vulpes macrotis macrotis*) inhabited Southern California but was driven to extinction over a century ago, disappearing even before the grizzly and the wolf. A hundred years on, it has been all but forgotten.

The San Joaquin kit fox has fared only marginally better, holding on in the San Joaquin Valley as one of the state's most prominent endangered species. Despite this status, the kit fox has a greater geographic distribution than any of the other four species covered earlier. Not only is the fox found farther north, into Contra Costa County, it is found farther west in the Salinas Valley and has even been documented in the Santa Clara Valley near Hollister. It is the only one of the five species mentioned here with even a remote possibility of being discovered on my property, and in fact one was reported just a mile south on Whisky Flat in 1979. How often itinerant kit foxes wander through the oak savanna of the flat is unknown, but their presence nearby on the edge of the San Joaquin Valley is indisputable. Numerous sightings have been tallied along Jasper Sears Road, as well as in the Los Banos Valley to the south. Although agricultural conversion has usurped much of its habitat, the fox is not entirely incompatible with human activity. In its stronghold in the southern end of the valley, it frequents the suburbs of Bakersfield, existing well within the city limits, and has been known to den in culverts and other man-made structures.

The sandy, friable soils of the valley floor suit it well, for kit foxes reside in underground dens. The heavier clay soils found at higher elevations are less conducive to digging. Likewise, the wide-open spaces and low-rolling hills are more to their liking than the steep-sloped chaparral and oak woodlands common in much of the range. Primarily nocturnal, the kit fox subsists on a diet of rodents, lizards, and insects.

Although the fox enjoys a rather large geographic distribution, it has declined, and while habitat loss was a factor, it was not the only one. Predator control efforts aimed at coyotes may have hit kit foxes harder than their intended target. Large-scale rodent eradication campaigns diminished the food supply and killed foxes outright when foxes preyed on poisoned rodents. Kit fox numbers are also stifled by the presence of two of their larger relatives, one native and the other exotic. Coyotes kill kit foxes, not as prey but as competition for food. This trait is common among canines; where wolves are present, they limit coyote populations with an effectiveness the USDA can only achieve in dreams. Coyotes may aid kit foxes, however, by targeting red foxes. These nonnative interlopers are larger than kit foxes, more adaptable, and capable of out-competing them for food. Following a wide tradition of canine intolerance, they may kill kit foxes as well. Being the runt of the litter, the kit fox gets it from all sides.

Besides the ability to persist in the face of at least some habitat alteration, kit foxes display a tendency toward habituation, particularly in the suburbs of Bakersfield. They also have a reputation for being bold; a friend related that as he camped one evening in the Griswold Hills, one approached the campfire. My only good look at a kit fox occurred one afternoon as I drove down Highway 33 on my way to the Carrizo Plain. As I approached the town of Taft, something crossed the road and entered a vacant lot behind a Kentucky Fried Chicken on the edge of town. Pulling over to the side of the road, I whistled to get the creature's attention, and as it turned toward me, I saw a clear view of a kit fox.

That happenstance sighting behind a fast food restaurant set my mind wandering off on a peculiar tangent. Why do so many fast food outfits feel compelled to have a mascot? I can forgive KFC and Wendy's, for at least their totems were real human beings with a connection to their respective franchises. But Jack in the Box? In his current incarnation as a smug, smarmy, hipper-than-thou CEO, Jack's character has even less appeal than the restaurant's food, which is no mean feat. Yet Burger King managed to upstage Jack by concocting perhaps the creepiest character ever to appear in an ad campaign. Their depiction of a king—silent, mouth agape in what my mother would call a shit-eating grin—is so disturbing that their commercials ought to have a PG-17 rating. I blame the entire sordid phenomenon on McDonald's. What better way to market mediocre food to kids than by luring them in with a clown possessed with a simple, singsong rhyming name? I read recently that Ronald McDonald was more recognizable to children than practically everyone this side of their own parents and was giving Santa Claus a run for his money. The ad executives who conjured up Ronald McDonald ought to have chains ten times as long as Jacob Marley's by now. Not content with one icon, McDonald's spawned an entire troop of fast-food peddling mascots. There was the Hamburglar, a bumbling, inept little fellow with the supremely annoying habit of mumbling unintelligibly. As he is dressed curiously in both prison garb and bandit mask, we're led to believe that his incarceration stems from an uncontrollable fondness for McDonald's hamburgers. What a ridiculous item to risk doing hard time for. Then there was the Grimace, an amorphous purple blob with an asinine look on its face, an amoeba come to life. Blessedly mute, this lower life form evidently possessed a complicated digestive tract, for it seemed to subsist solely on milk shakes. But why the name Grimace? I can only hope that some conspiratorial ad-person with both a conscience and a wicked sense of humor named the character for the queasy feeling that comes from dining regularly at the Golden Arches. And don't even get me started on Mayor McCheese. It's a long drive from Pacheco Pass to the Carrizo Plain; on this day, maybe a bit too long.

I don't particularly enjoy driving, but I have to admit that cruising the two-mile stretch of road from my house to the highway is something I never tire of, especially at night, for there is always the possibility of seeing something memorable. A badger, ringtail, or spotted skunk would be a pleasant surprise; a mountain lion would be something special, but the finest sighting of all would be a San Joaquin kit fox.

Within a span of a couple of months in 2005, I twice had tantalizing encounters with creatures that may have been kit foxes, and the circumstances surrounding each were nearly identical. On both occasions I was returning home around midnight, pulling off the main highway, and driving down the access road. Before I reached the gate, a small canine darted out and trotted in front of the car. Although it was fox-size, it was no gray fox. Gray foxes have a spine of black fur down the middle of their tails; this one didn't. Only the tip was black, as if dipped in ink, and I got a good look on both occasions. Hoping to capture its attention, I tried to mimic the sounds of a rabbit, hoping the fox would stop, turn around, and afford me a better view. Unfortunately, this ploy failed both times, for the critter skittered beneath the gate and wandered off into the veil of night.

Fox-size, large ears, black-tipped tail—it had to be a kit fox, right? Well, no, not necessarily. While the animal in question was definitely not a gray fox, that doesn't mean it was a kit fox. In fact, it may not have been a fox at all. Born in spring, young coyotes attain fox size by late summer. One of those encounters took place in August, the other in October. Young coyotes bear a striking resemblance to kit foxes, down to the black-tipped tail. Though kit fox ears are comparatively larger, the ears of coyotes are pretty conspicuous, too. Had those sightings occurred in winter or spring, I would be confident calling them kit foxes, for by that time yearling coyotes are noticeably larger than foxes.

There are common threads weaving through the stories of these five species that go beyond adaptations for living in a dry environment. All are California endemics. In fact, the original distributions of all are remarkably similar; you could assign one range map to the first four species, for only the kit fox shows much deviation. All were more at home on the floor of the San Joaquin Valley than in the foothills to the west, which may provide only marginal habitat. But the most troubling commonality is that all five are seriously at risk.

The causes of decline for each are depressingly similar. Large-scale rodent control programs and insecticide applications have had devastating effects, in ways both direct and indirect. Although grazing may be benign, or in some cases even beneficial, to the ongoing survival of these creatures, overgrazing is not, and much of the land has long been overstocked. Habitat loss, not surprisingly, has been the overriding factor, and it has reared its ugly head through numerous guises. Urban expansion is one, as communities became towns, towns became cities, and cities expanded out into the open spaces that were long the realm of the animals. Yet urban expansion has not accounted for most of the habitat loss. And though petroleum extraction has tarnished a large chunk of habitat, it was not the primary culprit, either. No, the overwhelming agent for habitat destruction can be summed up in a single word: water.

Clear-cutting a forest, polluting a coastline, or draining wetlands all meet with a considerable amount of public ire, as they should. But watering a dry landscape? No one, it seems, is outraged by such a prospect, despite the fact that the consequences of watering arid lands leads as surely to their diminishment as the chainsaw does to a forest. Face it, does anyone bemoan the loss of a desert? The construction of the California Aqueduct, a four-hundred-mile canal transporting water from Northern California to Southern California, had just such an effect on the west side of the San Joaquin Valley. Suddenly, a windfall of cheap water was available, and land that was once practically worthless was brought into agricultural production on a vast scale. Melons, pistachios, almonds, alfalfa, cotton, and other crops sprouted where before only meager grasses and hardy shrubs grew. Was this not progress, and how could it possibly be a bad thing?

Progress, like beauty, is in the eye of the beholder. The beneficiaries of that water received some very favorable terms on the amount of money they pay for irrigation water. Perhaps this would seem reasonable if the lessees were small family farms. However, the reality is that corporations such as Chevron, Tenneco, and Southern Pacific Railroad own much of this land. If your idea of progress is the spread of giant agribusiness, then this is it in spades: large tracts of land planted in monocultures, irrigated with subsidized water, owned by absentee landlords, some of whose fortunes are so vast that they farm only as a tax write-off. So it is that a substantial government subsidy has landed in the laps of people among the least in need of government assistance, who as a group are staunch opponents of government spending. This didn't dissuade them from lustily supporting the heavy expenditures put forth by both the state and federal government to turn their parched real estate into something considerably more lucrative. So much for standing on principle. Granted an influx of cheap water, a bevy of crops was produced on lands far too marginal to otherwise support them. Cotton, for example, expanded in acreage in the desert on the west side of the San Joaquin Valley. Irrigating cotton in California seems a bit perplexing when cotton can be raised on rainfall alone in the South; it seems ass-backward when Southern farmers are paid *not* to plant their fields due to a glutted market exacerbated by California production.

Yet beyond habitat alteration and government subsidization, the most damning argument against irrigating the west side of the San Joaquin Valley is that it's ill-suited for irrigation. Underlying the western floor of the valley is an impermeable layer of clay soil. As irrigation water sinks below the surface, it stops when it reaches the clay and has nowhere to go but back up. Unfortunately, it returns with accumulated salts and minerals, which become concentrated through the process of irrigation. Without a vast and expensive drainage system to carry away that water, laden with excessive salt, minerals such as selenium, and pesticide residue, such lands become bleached, salt-encrusted wastelands, incapable of supporting anything, even the hardy desert plants that grew there before. Far from being progress, this is a sorry state of affairs where short-term thinking and avarice prevailed, aided and abetted by money, politics, and power. Someday, I hope wiser decisions will be made and incentives created for retiring lands that should never have been brought into production in the first place. Perhaps some of that desert landscape can be restored, and maybe these unique and fascinating creatures will return to stand on solid ground.

There are deserts that beckon to people due to their austere beauty. Photographers flock to Monument Valley in Arizona, Death Valley, and Utah's slick-rock canyons. Movie producers film against a backdrop of Saguaro cactus or Joshua trees. The Panoche natural area, however, is no such place. I admit the area doesn't lend itself to a splashy first impression. If desert beauty is sublime, that of Panoche is sub-sublime. Forlorn, bleak, destitute, it looks impoverished, even for a desert, the kind of site counties value as a landfill, or the state would covet as a prison location. Passersby probably regard it as a godforsaken no-man's land. I've wandered the area some, and it's definitely an acquired taste. You could spend days walking across gulches, dry washes, and ridges, and see hardly any wildlife. But looks can be deceiving. For all its lifeless appearance, the Panoche natural area might be the most ecologically important area in the entire Diablo Range. This is especially true for endangered species. Of the five imperiled species mentioned here, only the San Joaquin kit fox is known to exist farther north. For the other four, the Panoche region represents the northernmost outpost of a range that once ran unbroken from Merced County to the Tehachapi Mountains almost two hundred miles south. If these creatures are to recover, especially in their northern haunts, this area is absolutely essential. Before I became aware of this, I saw nothing special about the Panoche area. Now, I view it differently, through a newfound light of respect, for it is in fact a repository, an unassuming haven for the last of the Mojave.

On the Road, Again

Pondering the Effects of Highways and Byways on Wildlife

I'VE DONE IT. You've done it. We've all done it. Not indulging in some guilty pleasure but running over an animal. It may have been a portly 'possum, a low-flying bird, or in the spirit of Loudon Wainwright III, a simple skunk that was hurtled into oblivion. Me, I've slowed down for deer, braked for snakes, even swerved for tarantulas against my arachnophobic impulses. My track record is very good but not unblemished. Just recently a ground squirrel inexplicably decided to cross the pavement at the approach of my car. Halfway across, it had a fateful change of heart, and its time on this globe came to an abrupt end courtesy of my left front tire. Of course, I blamed the squirrel. The indecisive little bastard should've stayed on the side of the road. The whole unpleasant experience got me thinking about roads, wildlife, and the consequences of mobility.

The open road. Is there anything more American than a vast ribbon of highway? What better symbolizes freedom than getting into your vehicle and driving anywhere you choose? Half a century ago, the development of the interstate highway system helped foster such attitudes. That was the era of the Sunday drive and cheap gas. Cars became extensions of the personality of their owners, straddling the divide between machine and status symbol. Speed was seductive, and this led to tragic consequences. Until the death of Princess Diana, perhaps the most infamous car crash was the one that claimed the life of James Dean on a lonely stretch of Highway 46 near Cholame, just south of the Diablo Range. The days of the open road faded fast as a swelling population led to traffic jams. Two-lane highways quickly fell into obsolescence, and even newly constructed ones required expansion to handle the oncoming torrent of vehicles. Commuting became a lifestyle, as people increasingly worked outside the communities in which they lived, traveling hellish distances between home and job daily.

Perhaps that's why Californians are such rude and impatient drivers. Outside their cars, Californians are fine. Friendly? That might be a reach, but at least civil. That civility wears off behind the wheel, and I often wonder if overcrowding and the harried lifestyle of commuting are to blame.

I drive at or just above the speed limit and avoid the fast lane. Nevertheless, even in the slow lane, I've been subjected to tailgating and flashing headlights. As I putter along at sixty-five or seventy, I'm surrounded by motorists whizzing by at eighty, driving way too close for comfort, and using turn signals about as often as they do snow chains. Is it the rat race that gives these people their Jeckyll-and-drive personalities? I find it incredulous that, as prices soar toward $4.50 a gallon, people continue driving as if gasoline grows on trees. In the 1970s, the federal government instituted a speed limit of fifty-five MPH to encourage conservation. I can't imagine such a scenario today, even if gas soared to ten dollars per gallon. We'll see businesses close on the Sabbath and the return of Prohibition before that. Such a mandate might provoke California into secession, for as God is my witness, we Californians love to drive fast. The effect on wildlife is devastating, and this is evident along Pacheco Pass.

Highway 152 runs from the Central Valley to the coast on its journey from Highway 99 to Highway 1. Pacheco Pass Highway is the stretch bridging the gap between Highway 5 and Highway 101, the busiest north/south routes in California. Traffic along the pass consists mostly of vehicles driving between those two highways. Unfortunately, those motorists tend to take their Highway 5 mentality with them, careening along. Nightfall does not deter people from barreling along at warp speed, but this is no urban roadway. There are no lights strung along the length of the pass, and the area, though not wilderness, is lightly developed and a natural landscape. Drivers career through the pass as if the prospect of a deer crossing the road is the furthest thing from their minds. As a result, it has become a mecca for roadkill. Skunks, raccoons, coyotes, ground squirrels, and deer are the primary victims, but barn owls, bobcats, gray foxes, and badgers all pay a price, too. When we think about roadkill, we picture mammals squirrel-size and larger. But vehicles take a heavy toll on a number of critters too small to notice as they expire beneath the weight of our tires.

It was late February, and a storm was brewing. A friend from Bitterwater was planning on driving a lightly traveled stretch of road during the deluge. As to what could possibly coax anybody out on such a night, I offer these two words: spadefoot toads.

Spadefoot toads are superbly adapted to life in a dry region. Much of the year is spent underground, either in the burrows of other animals or those they dig themselves, courtesy of a hard, black protuberance, or "spade," on their hind feet. Rains herald a breeding frenzy, and eggs are subsequently laid in vernal pools, slow-flowing streams, and stock ponds. Tadpoles develop rapidly in order to transform before their watery home evaporates. Of the five species in North America, only one, the Western spadefoot toad (*Spea hammondii*), is found west of the Great Basin. Primarily an occupant of low-lying valleys, the toad has lost much of its habitat to land conversion and is becoming increasingly scarce. I had hoped to find it in either Henry W. Coe State Park or Pacheco State Park during my surveys, for the species had never been recorded in either, but I didn't. In fact, I had never seen one before.

There were four of us addled enough to search for spadefoots on this rainy night, and we met at the east entrance to Pinnacles National Monument. We gathered in a single vehicle and slowly headed south on Highway 25 through a driving rain. Slowly would be an understatement, for I doubt we exceeded ten miles per hour as we drove directly down the middle of the road, trying to illuminate the entire roadway with our headlights. After a short while, we stopped. Something resembling an acorn appeared in the glow of the headlights. It was a spadefoot toad. It was small, smaller than the Western toads I'm familiar with, and its vertical, catlike pupils bespoke of its nocturnal nature. The tiny black "spades," tough as toenails, looked as if they had been implanted. As we resumed driving, we spotted amphibians with increasing regularity. There were ensatinas, slender salamanders, and California tiger salamanders, but the most numerous were spadefoot toads, of which we counted seventy-five. One productive stretch of road contained over two dozen. They sat there, still as stone, in the middle of the pavement. When I moved one to the side of the road, it promptly returned to the asphalt. One of us spotted the headlights of an oncoming car in the distance, and the scramble was on—we each retrieved as many toads as we could and placed them out of harm's way. In the two hours we were out, we encountered all of three vehicles. Had this road been busier, I can only imagine the carnage that would have ensued among the toads, which seemed hell-bent on remaining on the pavement. If this is typical behavior, it's no wonder spadefoot toads are rarely seen anymore near Hollister. Highway carnage has been the number one mortality source for at least two rare animals in the United States—the Florida panther and the ocelot. It can also devastate regional populations of amphibians, some of which migrate en masse during wet weather. As I drove home that evening, I was never more attentive.

The impact of roads on wildlife extends beyond collisions. Studies have shown that some species avoid roads. Grizzly bears and wolverines are two such animals. Many forest-dwelling creatures are similarly leery. Roads may also serve to artificially delineate home-range boundaries for species such as mountain lions. Similarly, roads often disrupt wildlife corridors, separating populations and leaving them subject to extirpation, one area at a time. I don't know when tule elk were reintroduced to the area surrounding San Luis Reservoir south of Highway 152. Yet as long as they've been there, I have yet to see them north of the highway. I can only surmise that the four-lane highway and its attendant traffic serve as imposing obstacles, perhaps too daunting to risk crossing. If that's true, the highway serves as a barrier to elk reestablishing populations to the north. The ability of roads to fragment habitat for creatures large and small is a phenomenon that has only recently received much notice, but it may be a larger problem than we suspect.

While it's easy to imagine the disruption caused by a bustling four-lane highway, it's harder to envision problems presented by lightly traveled two-lane roads and dirt roads. Such routes often possess a charm and bucolic atmosphere the larger highways lack. However, the off-the-beaten-path charisma of these roads less traveled often attracts a less than honorable contingent who would otherwise have less access to natural landscapes. The cast of characters includes poachers, collectors, marijuana farmers, and my pet peeve, litterbugs. The activities of poachers and illegal wildlife collectors are self-evident, their transgressions varying in intensity. Pot farmers are castigated here mainly on the basis of their environmentally destructive growing practices. In the Diablo Range, many plantings are large and require copious amounts of water. This often means diverting water directly from streams, and in a dry climate, that can have a profoundly negative effect on a multitude of critters, from fish and frogs to invertebrates. In addition, the application of pesticides and herbicides serves to further foul the landscape, not to mention the debris and garbage left behind by those who tend the gardens.

Unfortunately, debris and detritus follow roads as surely as Monday follows the weekend. It's bad enough that rural roadsides are disgraced with fast-food wrappers, beer cans, and plastic bags by those too lazy to deposit them in a trash receptacle or recycling bin. What's worse is the use of rural roads as dumping grounds. Twice in the past year, abandoned vehicles have graced the entrance to the access road off Highway 152. Along Mount Hamilton Road, soiled sofas, broken appliances, and enough junk to make Fred Sanford blush is routinely deposited along the pullouts. This refuse is often toppled over the edges of ravines, making the extraction of those items more costly and difficult. Too lazy to hold a garage sale, too cheap to dispose of things responsibly at the county dump. Is there a punishment too severe for those who litter so egregiously? I say throw the book at 'em.

The effects of litter on wildlife are bad enough, yet roads also attract a more innocuous type of trash: biopollution. The disturbed soil along the edges of roads provides a toehold for a number of aggressive, nonnative plants, and while some never extend beyond the vicinity of the roadway, those that do can have disastrous effects. Yellow star thistle (*Centauria solstitialis*) is one of the worst such weeds, blanketing extensive areas of open country, choking out native plants. Unlike some of the nonnative grasses, which can at least be utilized by some native species, star thistle is useless, and livestock spurn it also, making it a foe of ranchers as well. The proliferation of roads, even rarely used dirt roads, allows this pesky plant to colonize new territory, and once established, it has proven tough to eradicate.

If you build it, they will come. I'm not talking about a baseball field. I'm describing the relationship between road construction and the people that inevitably follow. Roads make human residency possible, and that occupancy puts a strain on natural areas. The people that choose to dwell in rural areas are as diverse as their surroundings, and in some cases, it's clear that they were not drawn to the country by any love of nature. Some may be misanthropes, others may be stuck due to circumstances, and then there are those who come to conduct dubious activities undetected. From all of the above, there is little thought or concern regarding the effects of their residency on the land.

Of course, many people are drawn to the country out of love for the land, yet even with such admirable values, things can get complicated. Maybe a mountain lion kills a pony. Perhaps a coyote nabs a cat or a fight breaks out between a dog and a badger. Dogs may keep all sorts of animals from their territory, while free-roaming cats prey on a wide array of animals. Purposefully or not, people often end up feeding wildlife, leading to habituation, which is never in the best interests of a wild animal. It's not a good situation for people, either, for habituated animals can become nuisances and sometimes dangerous.

Even people with the best of intentions alter habitat, and sensitive creatures may unceremoniously vanish as a result. I've wrestled with the issue of responsible land ownership on my property for years. Because the land was in a natural state when I acquired it, I can't tell myself that the land is better off now that I'm around. I've tried to improve upon it by removing nonnative plants, all the while aware that the road to my home aided their dispersal. As a symbolic gesture, I've allowed a spur of dirt road to revert to nature, perhaps an act of atonement. There are many other like-minded property owners who act as land stewards, but in most cases, the land ethic begins and ends with each individual property owner. It's challenging to protect land beyond the immediate future, for each parcel is subject to the whims of the current occupant. Each time land is split, this dilemma appears, and roads allow all of this to transpire.

If I were to walk out my front door and head south, I would cover thirty miles before my shoes touched pavement on Panoche Road. If I continued, I would travel almost forty miles before reaching another, Highway 198. Heading north is a different matter entirely, for less than a mile distant lies Highway 152, Pacheco Pass Highway. Crossing this stretch of road would be no mean feat. Not only does this four-lane highway represent a formidable distance to cross, in the center stands a rigid concrete barrier running for four miles from the bottom of the grade at the Pacheco Creek Bridge to a point near the top of the pass. A similar section is also found to the west. Such barriers were erected to prevent the horrendous head-on collisions that used to plague the pass, and without a doubt that structure has saved lives.

Yet there is also something bothersome about that concrete wall. Straddling the center of the highway, I am only slightly exaggerating when I claim that a driver can touch it as he or she drives by, for there is no shoulder or median there. Any animal crossing the highway must be able to leap over that wall, while the momentum would land it squarely in the path of oncoming traffic. Only a handful of animals are capable of clearing that concrete wall. The rest must scamper back if they are going to live to see another day. Although carcasses are strewn liberally throughout the length of Pacheco Pass, I wonder if there are more in the area of the concrete divider.

That barrier was the product of an era when wildlife concerns were not even remotely considered when planning or augmenting roadways. Only in the past decade have such issues surfaced, and there is much to learn. Which species are most vulnerable to traffic? Which abandon areas around roads? To what extent do roads fragment habitat? Hopefully, future road construction will be undertaken with the effects on wildlife in mind. In the meantime some interesting solutions have emerged. Tunnels and overpasses designed for wildlife have been constructed in a handful of locations. Properly designing and situating such features will require further research. Nothing in the world of construction comes cheap, and it would be a waste if ill-designed projects were installed or worthy ones situated in areas of little benefit. I suppose anything would be an improvement over the current situation, because highways through wildlife habitats typically provide nothing. Along the entire length of Pacheco Pass, there are but three locations where animals can travel safely between lands north of the highway and south, and all are beneath the bridges of creek crossings. Hopefully that situation will improve. If we as a species are determined to leave a large footprint on the landscape, the least we can do is watch our step along the way.

August 2007

Water, Water, Everywhere

Low Tide at San Luis Reservoir

THERE IT SITS, gleaming in the sun, a vast, shimmering body of water, nine miles long, five miles wide. Hills surround it on three sides; those to the west are generously suffused with blue oaks, while those to the north and south are barren, covered with annual grasses. From the vantage point of a passing automobile, the scene seems as natural as the waves lapping the beaches on Monterey Bay, yet it is all a grand illusion. That twelve-thousand-acre body of water is a fraud. The sordid truth is: San Luis Reservoir is a fake lake. And not just any fake lake—San Luis Reservoir is the most improbable body of water in the country.

What about Lake Mead or Lake Powell? Those enormous reservoirs, though unnatural, were formed by damming a natural feature, the Colorado River. Even the woebegone Salton Sea, anomaly that it is, owes its existence to periodic over-flows of that same river. San Luis Reservoir, on the other hand, is far more con-trived, a testimony to artificiality. The imposing dam, three hundred feet high, is absurdly overqualified to hold back the flow of the meager creeks that trickle into its basin, for Cottonwood Creek and San Luis Creek are seasonal streams, too ephemeral to even support a fish population. It would take forever for those streams to fill the massive reservoir. No, the water in San Luis originates from the Feather and Sacramento Rivers. Therein lies San Luis Reservoir's other dirty little secret: she's not a true blonde. All that water glistening in the afternoon sunlight was taken from the delta, arriving via the California Aqueduct and the Delta Mendota Canal, stored at the O'Neill Forebay and lifted by pump turbines into San Luis Reservoir.

The roots of San Luis Reservoir go back to the State Water Project, the ambitious water development plan hatched during the 1950s. Over the next several decades, California was replumbed, and water was diverted, transferred, and allocated from one end of the state to the other through a series of canals, aqueducts, pumps, and reservoirs. Work began on San Luis in 1960; it was completed in 1967 and filled in May, 1969. Thus it was that San Luis Reservoir became the largest off-stream reservoir in the United States, the country's largest holding pond.

Today, motorists careening past the reservoir are inured to its presence, its having been part of the scenery for forty years. If they even give it a second thought, perhaps some know it's not a true lake like Mono Lake or Lake Tahoe. Most, however, probably assume it's a natural feature, a massive lake miraculously welling up in a sun-drenched land averaging ten inches of rain per year. There is a great disconnect among Californians in distinguishing the real from the illusory as they contemplate the countryside. When the subject is San Luis Reservoir, no one felt the repercussions more keenly than Paula Fatjo, in whose life the artificial became all too real.

Although Paula was a Californian by birth, her roots permeated deeper in California history than most. Her great-great grandfather was Francisco Pacheco, who in 1833 acquired the Rancho Ausaymas Y San Felipe and later Rancho San Luis Gonzaga as land grants from the Mexican government. Born in 1920, Paula left California as a young woman, spending time in New York City as a debutante. She was not long anonymous, drawing the attention of media mogul Walter Winchell, who stopped sharpening his claws long enough to praise her beauty. She returned to California in 1948, settling down in the venerable adobe ranch house on family property along the eastern front of the Diablo Range. Her tranquil life was disrupted, however, when plans for San Luis Reservoir were drawn up, for her historic home stood in the middle of what was envisioned as a grand reservoir and pillar of progress. That property was sacrificed for said progress when the state condemned a hefty chunk of her land under eminent domain. Paula attempted to have the adobe home moved uphill to the top of Pacheco Pass, but the structure did not survive the trip. Paula had another modest home built in its stead and lived the rest of her life there. She was an accomplished equestrienne, though as time went on, she was less able to ride. By the time I acquired my property, Paula was just past seventy years old but ailing. An acquaintance knew her; he tried to arrange a meeting between the two of us, but Paula passed away in December, 1992.

Ironically, Paula bequeathed her ranch to the very state that condemned her property. It was testimony to her character that she willed her land to the state of California, to be protected in perpetuity as a park. Whatever ill will she may have harbored, and she certainly had ample justification for a heady dose of resentment, none was evident in her final wishes. I'd like to think she got a point across, though, by stipulating that her land be preserved and protected. I think about Paula's ordeal when property rights advocates whine over the Endangered Species Act. Never in the history of the act has any property been condemned and usurped—literally taken away—as it was in the case of Paula Fatjo when the powers that be felt her land would be better served as a vast storage tank. I have never heard the name Paula Fatjo invoked during any property rights dialogue, and I doubt I ever will, since the movement seems more concerned with regulatory restrictions than with actual examples of land seizure.

To my regret, I never met Paula Fatjo, but thanks to her largesse, I have come to know her land well, for Pacheco State Park opened in 1995 and is a short walk from my home. Climbing the ridge to the east, on land passed on by Paula, I can see the placid waters of San Luis Reservoir several miles to the east. Its size is impressive; its volume in stark contrast to conditions throughout the rest of the range, where water—especially underground water—is a precious and mysterious commodity.

If you were to count the residents in the Diablo Range, I doubt you'd find more than a couple of thousand people. I'm not including those living in the foothills lining the valley floors; I'm speaking of those in the interior of the range, whose water comes from wells. There are reasons that population is so meager, a major one being lack of water. Over the years, development proposals have come and gone, but mostly gone. The Diablo Range gives up her groundwater as reluctantly as a family secret. No one believed that water could be so elusive, yet well after well was drilled, and most were as dry as beef jerky. Faced with that harsh reality, ambitious developers found their plans dangling in the dry breeze.

When I purchased my property, the seller had to provide a well productive enough to meet county requirements. This he did, and in 1992 I took title to fifty-five acres. When it came time to build, things went smoothly until we got to the well. The well had been drilled, tested, and inspected but not developed. Transporting water from that well to the home site a thousand feet away would require pipes, pumps, and holding tanks, all of which cost money. I called a local drilling company for an estimate. When the figure came back, I was stunned to see it sit at almost $70,000. But there was more: besides the hefty price tag, the well itself was, in the eyes of the expert, a poor one, literally a ne'er-do-well. When it had been tested ten years previously, it had pumped water at the rate of 2.51 gallons per minute; the minimum requirement was 2.5, so it passed with all the luster of a D-minus student. Furthermore, there was no guarantee the well would churn out even that paltry amount when tested again prior to occupancy. It was his opinion that I would be pissing away seventy grand on a bum steer, a hydrological Edsel, a well that could fail a subsequent inspection and dry on a regular basis. He strongly suggested I dig another well. I strongly wanted a second opinion. I called another company, another expert came out, and he too advised that another well be drilled.

There are many services in life that are guaranteed, in which payment is contingent upon results satisfactory to the customer. Well drilling is not one of them. Drillers are paid to dig, and they charge by the foot. If they drill four hundred feet and charge fifty dollars per foot, you will be billed twenty thousand dollars whether they strike water, oil, or sandstone. As a result, selecting a drilling site becomes tremendously important. I finally asked the consultant the question that had been plaguing me all afternoon.

"How do you guys decide where to drill?" I envisioned some technician equipped with some state-of-the-art device similar to a Geiger counter poking around my property.

"We don't. We drill where you tell us to."

"Where *I* tell you to? How am I supposed to select a well site?"

"Hire a dowser."

"You mean a water witch?"

I vaguely remembered hearing stories of old-timers armed with nothing more than a willow branch. Farmers seeking water for their hillside apricot orchards greatly coveted their talents, and their ability to find water was legendary. For me, it seemed a little too legendary, a rural myth.

"Yes. I know a guy down in Salinas. I'll give you his number."

"Is he a good witch or a bad witch?" I asked in a tone of voice significantly lower than that of Glinda in *The Wizard of Oz*.

"He's good, real good. The best I know. Nobody's perfect, though."

That last statement rang in my ears like a church bell as I took down the number and prepared to summon a witch.

Following a phone conversation involving terms and payment options, the witch and I agreed to meet outside the coffee shop at the Casa de Fruta along Pacheco Pass Highway. I had never hired a witch before; if nothing else, the affair promised to be interesting. He arrived right on time, in a big boat of a car. As I approached the vehicle, I was puzzled, for there were three people inside. Behind the wheel was a man of about sixty; on the passenger side was a woman of perhaps fifty. Alone in the back was a heavy-set man who appeared to be in his sixties. He was ashen, peaked, and his breathing was labored. My grandfather had passed away at the age of ninety-one several months before, and on the last day of his life, he looked better than this poor guy, who of course was the witch. After saying hello, I sidled up to the driver and inquired about the health of the dowser. I was told that, while yes, he was ailing, it would not deter him from the task at hand. I reminded him that my property was a long way from a hospital and my rusty CPR skills had never been put to the test. I admired his dedication, but still felt uncomfortable about dragging him out on a ninety-degree day, for he was in no condition to move about.

As it turned out, he performed his duties without ever leaving the backseat. This he did with the aid of a large black, rubber-coated divining rod. I had never seen one before—if you had told me the object in question was some kind of pleasure enhancer, a Mr. Spanky Valentine's Day special, I would have believed it.

Our first stop was the well that I had been advised to abandon. He took a reading there, and he, too, proclaimed it to be too poor to depend on. From there, we set off to find another potential drilling site. He took readings near the proposed building site but got nothing. As we drove downhill, he suddenly got a strong reaction from the divining rod and told the driver to stop.

"There's water down there, lots," he said excitedly. "You tap into that, you'll be able to plant a vineyard!"

In truth, I had no plans to plant anything, least of all a vineyard. I just wanted to take a shower every now and then and enjoy the simple luxury of indoor plumbing.

"How do you know how much is down there?" I asked.

"Experience. You do this long enough, you know not just how much water's there but also how far down it is."

"How far down is it?" I asked.

"About three hundred feet." That wasn't bad, considering the hilly topography.

"Here," he continued. "You give it a try. See if you have the Gift. Only about one in ten people do, you know."

He handed me a smaller plastic divining rod. Judging by the looks of it, he got the Pamela Anderson model—the old pro—while I got the Paris Hilton version, which consisted of two thin, flexible shafts emanating from a cylindrical base.

"Grab one in each hand, hold them apart at chest level, and keep the base facing forward. Start walking toward that tree. If you've got the Gift, that base will be pulled down any second now."

I did my best to curb my considerable skepticism and went through the motions, not for a minute believing anything out of the ordinary would occur. Yet at that very instant, I felt the divining rod surge down like a magnet reacting to steel. Ever the cynic, I wondered if perhaps the old dowser had some remote control device to manipulate it. But why would he? After all, he was going to get paid the same whether he found water or not—hell, I paid him up front. Of course, he could have been pulling my leg, but I achieved the same results later after he left.

I marked the spot with a surveyor's stake, and a week later the drilling company arrived and dug a $13,000 hole. The witch said we'd have to dig three hundred feet to find water; the driller hit it at three twenty five; the witch claimed the well would produce seven gallons per minute; it produced five. So, he was a bit optimistic. But the important thing was that there was water after all, and if it wasn't quite as much as he predicted and was a bit deeper, who cares? The well passed with flying colors. Had he not found water, I shudder to consider the predicament I would have been in.

He let me keep the divining rod. I took it out several times on my parent's property. In my hands, it produced consistent results; however, when others tried it, nothing happened. I was accused of trickery, but I had nothing up my sleeve. It's reassuring to know that if I ever lose my day job, I can always hire myself out as a water witch.

I rarely support altering natural landscapes. However, I'm conflicted when it comes to stock ponds in the Diablo Range. Natural ponds, lakes, and wetlands are extremely rare in the Diablo Range. There are, however, thousands of man-made stock ponds. Many serve as important habitat for native species, which have lost considerable habitat to development. The property south of mine is an example. There, a pond an acre in size sits in an open basin surrounded by grassy rises and scattered oaks. On a spring afternoon, it is a thing of beauty, set amid wildflower fields and valley oaks. Swallows, phoebes, bluebirds, and kingbirds snatch insects above the water's surface; orioles and red-winged blackbirds cackle from the branches of the oaks. Red-legged frogs—I've counted as many as a hundred at a time here—peer back at me with suspicion as they rest on the surface of the water, while Western pond turtles bask on a log. In winter, migrating waterfowl flock to the pond, and you never know what the sky will bring—I've seen greater white-fronted geese, Eurasian wigeons, and hooded mergansers there. None of those species would remain without that pond.

Of course, not all ponds are beneficial. Many are poorly situated or ill-constructed. Some are home to bullfrogs, which pose a threat to native amphibians. Many have been stocked with fish and, as such, become useless to amphibians, which tend to disappear where fish are introduced. Yet there are scores of ponds with none of those negatives that provide tangible benefits for native species. In fact, both California red-legged frogs and California tiger salamanders owe their continued existence in the range in large part to the breeding habitat provided by stock ponds. As much as I'd like to see landscapes returned to their original state, it's hard for me to champion pond purging on any level higher than a case-by-case basis.

However, in the case of something as egregious as San Luis Reservoir, I just can't muster much enthusiasm. Where others see an inland sea beckoning under a sunny sky, I see a quirk, something hopelessly out of step with its surroundings, like a head full of jet-black hair on an octogenarian. California's hydrology has been nipped, tucked, and face-lifted beyond recognition; at least one dam impedes the flow of nearly every major river; canals and aqueducts charmlessly transport water from one end of the state to the other, while the extensive marshes and wetlands that were once prominent are but shadows of their former selves, as are the riparian forests that once lined the unbridled rivers. Tulare Lake is not even that; in terms of sheer surface area, what was once the largest body of fresh water west of the Great Lakes is today nothing more than a pitiful, pesticide-laden sump, an inland sea so dead that even its outline no longer appears on contemporary maps. We have taken water from where it was and placed it where it was convenient for us, and we have done so without a trace of humility. If anything, we've glorified such intrusive meddling. At San Luis Reservoir, the dam and pumping plant are both named after someone, while the state has declared the stretch of Pacheco Pass Highway along the reservoir—and only that portion—a scenic route. Apparently the canyons, mountains, and alluvial plain of Pacheco Creek beyond lack the luster of a phony lake.

This celebration of man's domination over nature evidently appeals to many but not to me, for I see it as a sacrifice, not a triumph. There's a couplet from the song "The Night They Drove Old Dixie Down": "Just take what you need and leave the rest/but they should never have taken the very best." That summarizes how we Californians have treated our land in our insatiable thirst for water. It's not that we proceeded with water development; it's that we did so with a gusto and zealousness that exceeded our needs. Instead of realizing what was patently obvious even a century and a half ago—that California is a dry land that cannot support a forever burgeoning population—we pushed the envelope. We wanted water, water, everywhere, and by hook or crook, we were going to get it. Nearly a century ago, Hetch Hetchy Valley was dammed—inside Yosemite National Park, for God's sake—because San Francisco "needed" the water. At the same time, the Owens River was hijacked and diverted four hundred miles south to Los Angeles because it, too, "needed" the water. The massive state and federal water projects of the 1950s and 1960s, which brought us the California Aqueduct and San Luis Reservoir, were foisted upon us because California "needed" the water. And just when you thought one humongous holding tank would suffice, in less than the span of a single generation, plans were drawn up for yet another gigantic off-stream storage facility, Los Banos Grande Reservoir. That was proposed in the 1980s and was to inundate the Los Banos Valley, just south of the present San Luis Reservoir, with another rivaling San Luis in size. Although that monstrosity was never realized, there's no such thing as a dead water project, and I have little doubt that several consecutive dry years will resurrect it, once again on the grounds that we "need" more water.

Evidently, we Californians are a needy bunch. But it's hard to take such claims seriously when conservation has been such a small part of the equation. We live in a world of excess, where conservation is, if not a four-letter word, then an afterthought, whether the resource in question is energy or water. Proponents of water development argue that it's a waste to allow a river to flow untapped to the sea, but one could just as easily argue that water diverted is equally wasted. Witness the profusion of water-hogging lawns and lush landscaping, practices such as watering during the heat of day, and automatic sprinkler systems that blast away even during rainstorms. It's not hard to find water being wasted; try locating a river that hasn't been tapped. For so long, we have paid so little for water that we have taken it for granted and, in the process, confused what we want with what we need. All those easy come, easy go water projects have made us profligate, and the cost of that excess has been borne by the fresh water ecosystems of the state, which are a tattered remnant of what they once were. We always "need" more water yet are loath to use the resource more efficiently, preaching the gospel of conservation only during drought. All those dams, canals, aqueducts, and reservoirs, all those billions of dollars of state and federal money, and what do you know…we still need more water. And we always will because the clamor for more water has always been about accommodating more people into the state. Long ago we hitched our star to the siren song of population growth, and no political figure on either side of the aisle wants to touch that issue with a ten-foot dowsing rod. We have chosen to cram as many people as we can into a dry, drought-susceptible land, rather than exercise restraint. To continue that into the future would be a dicey proposition, for the quick fixes have all been taken. You can look at our water system as an example of ingenuity and innovation, if you choose, but it's hard for me to look beyond the irresponsibility, unsustainability, and hubris behind it. That's what I see when I gaze upon the blue surreal waters of San Luis Reservoir.

Perhaps that's a lot of animosity to foist on the shoulders of one body of water, even one as large as San Luis Reservoir. Maybe the time has arrived for me to come to terms with the reservoir, since it's not going to disappear anytime soon. So recently I've tried to view the reservoir in the best light I can dredge up. Here goes:

Its expansive waters attract an abundance of waterfowl that would otherwise be absent. Likewise, wintering bald eagles owe their appearance to this large body of water. I can at least be grateful that the area surrounding the reservoir is public land; if it wasn't, the hillsides flanking it might be carved into home sites and the obligatory golf course. As recreation areas go, it is not overly developed, and that's good. The reservoir may even be responsible for the return of tule elk to the area, since much of the surrounding land is publicly owned and large enough to support a herd. And because San Luis is an off-stream reservoir, you could argue that it's less destructive than dams along rivers, which completely alter the hydrology and the fresh-water ecosystems that were present.

Work on San Luis began before I was born, so I have no memory of what the area looked like prior to its incarnation as a massive storage tank. Had I been born a generation earlier, I would have opposed its construction; instead, I was hell-bent on cracking the Santa Claus mystery at the time the reservoir was completed. So, I must rely on imagination to envision the area as it once was. If I go back to the days of the old ranchos, I see a plain at the base of the hills, where herds of pronghorn and elk graze. If I head forward to the 1950s, the elk and pronghorn are gone, but the plain is still there, and the area is in a mostly natural state.

This leads to a hypothetical question: What if San Luis Reservoir had never been built? I'd like to think that Paula Fatjo would have left her lands to the public regardless. Given her mandate for preservation, I can see that land managed as a natural area, but who knows? Maybe the experience of having her land taken away motivated her to protect her remaining holdings. Had the reservoir never materialized, maybe she would have sold the ranch piecemeal. I can see an alternate fate for that land: all that property, adjacent to a four-lane highway linking the Central Valley to the Bay Area and Silicon Valley jobs. If not for the inland sea that is San Luis Reservoir, there might be instead an ocean of stucco houses, each and every one mind-numbingly similar, surrounded by shopping centers, car dealerships, and fast-food franchises. A whole new city, west of Los Banos, yet another bedroom community in a region chock-full of bland nowheres. Given that potential outcome, the reservoir doesn't seem quite so bad after all. There are worse fates than inundation, and one is never too old to learn the backstroke.

December 2007

It's a Small World

Why the California Tiger Salamander Is So Important

It was a mild February morning, and I decided to go for a hike. The year was 1986, and I had recently purchased my first camera. I was eager to put it to use, and that morning was as good a time as any. A recent storm had just passed, and early wildflowers were coloring the slopes.

My destination was Joseph D. Grant County Park, a gem of a property below Mount Hamilton. I began on the floor of Hall's Valley and headed south on the Hotel Trail. The trail follows the eastern edge of the valley floor before climbing a gentle ridge of grassland and oaks. Toward the top, a stock pond that had been all but dry the previous autumn was full, its margins skirting the trail. As I walked past, I glanced into the shallows to see something breach the surface. I assumed it was a newt, for California newts are plentiful in the Diablo Range. But this was no newt. It was larger, not brown like a newt but black, with cream-colored spots. Though I had never seen one before, I could tell at once that this was a tiger salamander. I waded into the water and grabbed it, observing the comically small, beady eyes before placing it ashore. I took a couple of pictures, returned it to the water, and continued hiking. I had no idea how exceptional that sighting was.

My next such encounter took place a year and a half later, under bizarre circumstances. That August afternoon, I was mowing the lawn of the house I was living in on the west side of Morgan Hill. It was a one-acre property in an area where the suburban and the rural come together. Wildlife was common there—deer, raccoons, and coyotes were seen frequently, and occasionally mountain lions were reported. If I had to live in a land of stop signs, garden gnomes, and streetlights, that was as good a place as any. The downside was that there was a lawn to mow, and as I did so that day, I noticed something moving in front of the mower. Turning off the engine, I was surprised to see a tiger salamander making its way through what it must have seen as foreign terrain, a land awash in manicured (more or less) lawns, asphalt, and automobiles. I took the salamander inside and placed it, for the moment, in an empty apple box. I delved into the garage and retrieved a terrarium that had been out of use for several years. I then collected a layer of sand from the backyard sandbox, followed by some soil. A pie tin that would never be returned to Marie Callender's was appropriated and filled with water in preparation for the terrarium's newest tenant.

Shortly after being placed in new surroundings, the salamander acclimated by disappearing. Just hours into residency, I checked in on my new charge, only to find an empty terrarium. It couldn't have escaped. I lifted the pie tin, expecting to see the salamander huddled beneath it, but saw nothing other than a hole that had been dug below the sides of the tin. In that hole rested the salamander. Thus I had learned the first of several lessons about tiger salamanders. From books I learned that they belong to the genus *Ambystoma*, or mole salamanders, named for their preference for spending time underground. From experience I learned they are highly nocturnal, for it was rare to see the salamander during the day or even at night if lights were on. In the wee hours, I would get up for work, and more often than not, the salamander would be active. At first I fed it pillbugs, but I later replaced those with mealworms. One morning I tried something different. I was wondering if it would eat out of my hand. I doubted it would, figuring it would be cautious in my presence, and if it did, I thought it would munch slowly and deliberately, like a horse chewing a carrot. I picked out a mealworm and dangled it in front of the salamander's snout. To my surprise, the salamander snatched it in a burst of speed that would have done the swiftest lizard proud. For seven years, that salamander resided in my terrarium, until one day it surfaced no more. Its final lesson to me was one of longevity, for the salamander was probably ten years old or more when it died, a long life span for something so small.

Though I did not realize it then, those salamanders I stumbled across were not ordinary tiger salamanders. One of the most common and widespread salamander species in North America, tiger salamanders of one subspecies or other are found throughout the country. Beyond the border, they exist from Calgary down into Mexico. Those inhabiting central California are different, however, isolated geographically by four hundred miles and separated physically by five million years. Different enough, genetically and behaviorally, to be classified as a separate species, the California tiger salamander.

That five-million-year separation resulted in a species uniquely adapted to California. For example, breeding takes place as ponds fill in winter. In other regions, tiger salamanders breed in spring and summer. Given the long dry season, California tiger salamander larvae transform quickly, in two and a half to four months, while those in wetter areas may take over a year. Permanent water is scarce; vernal pools and sag ponds fill with rainfall and dry long before the end of summer, and any larval amphibian that is going to be successful must be able to grow quickly. Consequently, California tiger salamanders often transform before July, some as early as May. They can also accelerate their development as ponds start to evaporate. While this is a very useful adaptation, it is not foolproof, for there are limits to how quickly larvae can grow. Sometimes ponds dry early, and they perish. The capricious nature of water in California probably explains why neoteny—the tendency to persist in larval form as a breeding adult—has never been observed in California tiger salamanders but is well documented in tiger salamanders from other areas.

California tiger salamanders belong to the genus *Ambystoma*, mole salamanders, so named for their habit of spending much of their time below ground. The burrows of ground squirrels are their preferred neighborhoods, but they also use those of gophers and kangaroo rats. And while they can use cracks in the soil or dig their own retreats if soil conditions are right, areas that lack burrowing rodents are unlikely to contain California tiger salamanders.

There is a misconception that, because California tiger salamanders breed, hatch, and spend the larval stage of life in water, they are primarily aquatic. Yet while breeding ponds are absolutely essential, adults come to water only briefly to breed in the aftermath of winter rains. The vast majority of their lives are spent on land, underground. In fact, during drought years, female salamanders may forego the pilgrimage to breeding sites. (Males show up regardless. Boys will be boys.) Moreover, not all waters are useful to the California tiger salamander. Rivers and streams, even the most placid, slow-flowing creeks, are never used. Only the truly still waters of ponds will do.

In 2001 I began a survey of ponds in Henry W. Coe State Park to determine the presence of breeding amphibians. A park-wide search for the California red-legged frog was the catalyst for this, but two years into the study, I found myself distracted. I had covered over half of the ponds in the park, and while I found red-legged frogs in a number of them, the California tiger salamander was noticeably absent as 2003, the third year of the survey, approached. It was during that winter that I became obsessed with California tiger salamanders in a way that few people, I imagine, have ever been.

Why, I wondered, had I not come up with a single tiger salamander during two survey seasons in Coe Park? Were the little devils more wary and elusive than tadpoles, able to avoid the net? Were they hanging out in deeper water out of reach? Or were they truly absent? I pondered such questions during the course of the winter.

On a cold, overcast day, I returned to Grant Park and the pond where I had first seen a California tiger salamander seventeen years before. I took a seat at the water's edge, looked out over the pond, and waited. I kept my eyes on the surface, hoping for a salamander to rise. I waited and waited but saw nothing. I returned the next week and the week after, only to receive the same disappointing results. I felt like an investigator at Loch Ness, scanning the water fruitlessly for hours on end. I realized the only way I could quench my curiosity would be to conduct a salamander survey at Grant Park. Thus, in the spring of 2003, I surveyed Grant Park.

During two survey seasons at Coe, many things had turned up in my net, but only one, the larvae of California newts, could possibly be mistaken for a California tiger salamander. Fortunately, I was, by that time, well acquainted with larval newts, which possess a tried and true diagnostic feature—a pair of dark lines running down each side of the back. However, I didn't know exactly what a larval California tiger salamander looked like—field guides place heavier emphasis on identifying adults. My method of identification involved the process of elimination: if it wasn't a newt, it had to be a California tiger salamander, for those are the only possibilities in the Diablo Range. At the second pond in Grant Park, I struck gold when I brought up in the net a feathery-gilled larval salamander with tiny, beady eyes and not a trace of striping on its back—a California tiger salamander.

Over the next several months the field experience paid off, and my knowledge of the species grew. A pattern emerged. I rarely found salamanders in large ponds surrounded by cattails or filled with clear water. Ideal as such ponds may have been for red-legged frogs and turtles, they were less inviting to California tiger salamanders. Rather, salamanders turned up in the most modest ponds, those with the color of coffee doused with cream, often with barren shorelines. I entered one such pond at the end of March. Small, devoid of vegetation, and thoroughly turbid, it was as unappealing as you could imagine. No sane person would even think of drinking from it, nor would it cross the mind of even the boldest bather to dip their skinny in. No self-respecting red-legged frog would dream of inhabiting such a forlorn body of water. As I entered the water, a cow pie floated past. Yet this tiny pond was a prolific tiger salamander pond. More often than not, the best salamander ponds were shallow, murky, and lacking vegetation, very different from those preferred by red-legged frogs.

The ability to use such stock ponds turned out to be a boon for the species, for the vernal pools and seasonal wetlands that the salamander used for breeding for eons vanished rapidly. The California tiger salamander evolved in the fertile valleys and rolling hills of central California—in fact, it occurred nowhere else. Unfortunately, this was to become some of the most highly coveted land in the country, not only for agriculture but for urban and suburban expansion. Virtually every prominent city between Santa Barbara and Sacramento is built upon land that at one time was prime salamander habitat. The Salinas Valley, the Bay Area, Wine Country, and the Central Valley were all at one time strongholds for the species, but those landscapes have been irrevocably altered. What habitat remains has become fragmented and vulnerable, and these days the salamander relies heavily, and in some places exclusively, upon ponds constructed for livestock.

While habitat destruction deserves the brunt of the blame for the decline of the California tiger salamander, there were other factors at work. Nonnative predators have certainly played a role, especially fish. When introduced to ponds where salamanders breed, fish devour larval salamanders with impunity, leaving none to transform to adulthood. Even tiny mosquitofish (*Gambusia* spp.) can devastate a breeding pond by feeding on the eggs.

But the most unorthodox threat to the California tiger salamander is posed by nonnative tiger salamanders. Tiger salamander larvae from other parts of the country were widely used as live bait throughout California. Some that didn't meet their fate on the end of a hook were released; at least one enterprising individual freed them in hopes of establishing a self-perpetuating colony that could be gathered and sold for profit. Unfortunately, those salamanders not only survived but interbred with their California cousins, muddying the gene pool. As a result, hybrid salamanders are now known from several locations, the most glaring example occurring in eastern Monterey and western San Benito Counties, where the California tiger salamander has been nearly hybridized out of existence. It is no longer legal to sell tiger salamander larvae as bait precisely because of such genetic contamination, but to a large extent, the damage has already been done.

I netted California tiger salamanders throughout Grant Park, and I soon found them at Coe Park, although in smaller numbers and in one area only. As the survey progressed, I became increasingly interested in the species, for I had come upon a creature every bit as rare as, and even more cryptic than, the California red-legged frog. While following a creek or scanning a pond, I often saw red-legged frogs as they basked along the shore or stared at me from the safety of a floating mat of algae. With tiger salamanders, I had no such luck coming across adults. By the time the survey was completed, I had entered ponds hundreds of times and spent hours in the water, but I never again had an experience like I did on that February day in 1986 when I saw an adult surface in a pond. Given their largely underground existence and nocturnal nature, their presence might go undetected were it not for the brief period of their life cycle when they exist as larvae, confined to ponds.

For so inconspicuous a creature, the California tiger salamander was thrust into the national spotlight halfway through the survey. In 2004, the US Fish and

Wildlife Service announced its intention to list the salamander as a Threatened Species under the Endangered Species Act. This was no sudden occurrence; herpetologists first petitioned for its protection in 1994. The official response to that petition was that listing the salamander at that time was "warranted but precluded," which meant that the service agreed that the species needed protection, but due to a backlog of cases involving other species and a lack of funding, the species would not be listed then. Like a restaurant patron without a reservation, the salamander would have to wait its turn. Ten years later, when it finally had its day in the sun, it did so amid controversy. Lawyers representing opponents of the listing tried to sprinkle doubt over the testimony of biologists. They pressed them for figures when asking how much of the species' historical range had been lost or how many California tiger salamanders remained, questions that were impossible to answer precisely. When biologists admitted as much, their opinions were criticized as flawed science. Yet even if one of them had been able to pluck a number out of thin air, who would have been able to interpret what that number meant relative to the degree of vulnerability faced by the California tiger salamander? Suppose a biologist claimed there were ten thousand California tiger salamanders left. That sounds like a lot, but we're used to population figures from larger animals. Ten thousand grizzlies in the continental United States would be a robust population; ten thousand California condors might be more than have ever existed at any one time. But ten thousand salamanders over a twenty-five-thousand-square-mile area is a small number. Besides, there's more than numbers involved in assessing the risk of extinction. There are other variables at play, among them habitat destruction, and a species with rigid habitat needs may be in deep trouble regardless of the size of its population if that habitat is lost at an accelerating pace. A large population can be very vulnerable if it is disconnected and fragmented into a number of small, isolated groups that may be at risk.

Besides legal objections, a wave of derisive media articles from across the country lambasted the decision to protect the salamander. The California tiger salamander became the latest poster child for opponents of the Endangered Species Act, the kind of critter they love to hate: small, innocuous, of no economic benefit, and virtually unknown to the world outside field guides. No less a presence than the *Wall Street Journal* piled on, dispatching a reporter to cover the effects of the listing on vintners. I'd never read anything in the journal before; it always seemed to be a stodgy publication read solemnly by middle-aged men whose worldly concerns never ventured beyond their investment portfolios. Plus, it didn't have a sports page. After reading that particular article, however, my perception changed. I had assumed the journal espoused high journalistic standards, yet the article I read was a hatchet job in which the reporter emphasized the inconvenience the listing posed to wine growers but made no attempt to present another side to the story. In a telling display of biological cluelessness and editorial oversight, the reporter actually referred to the salamander as a reptile, a blunder many fifth graders wouldn't commit. If the journal vets its investment advice with the same degree of precision, I think I'll keep my savings in coffee cans beneath the porch.

That article was just a taste of the scorn those who oppose the Endangered Species Act hurled toward the salamander. The strongest and most visionary of our nation's environmental laws, the act has long been under fire from those who would profit from its rescission. Many attempts to castrate it have been undertaken over the years, and its opponents are quick to discredit the act, claiming it to be ineffective and plagued by flawed science. Here, I want to refute them and specify exactly why the California tiger salamander, and a flotilla of equally anonymous species, should be protected and preserved.

When the Endangered Species Act was signed into law by President Nixon in 1973, the list of taxa thus protected—the charter members—consisted of less than one hundred species. It contained plenty of large, charismatic creatures: bald eagles, alligators, wolves, grizzlies, and condors. It was rather thin on reptiles and amphibians, with just a couple of each represented, while invertebrates and plants were absent. Despite the inclusion of roughly two dozen fish species, you'd be correct if you detected a bias toward birds and mammals. Hard as it may be to believe today, the act enjoyed bipartisan support and was met with scant opposition. Indeed, several politicians who had voted in favor of the act's passage backtracked later, claiming they thought the act only applied to prominent species. It did not, however, and as time passed, the safety net of the act came to cover a growing number of species that many people had never heard of. The backlash against regulations protecting such species grew louder, and by 2004 the California tiger salamander was the latest in the list of those unheralded species that had many questioning why their protection was so important. Why, indeed, save the California tiger salamander?

The tried and true response to this line of questioning has always been the utilitarian argument: you never know which species may someday prove useful, so to stand by idly while a species vanishes could be a rash, foolhardy course of inaction. Many of our most effective medicines are derived from wild animals and plants, and undoubtedly more medical breakthroughs await discovery. As species disappear, they take with them potential curative properties.

Likewise, since we don't fully understand the complexities of ecological relationships, we can't always predict the effects the loss of one species can have on the rest of an ecological community. Perhaps the loss of one species or another might be negligible, but there are cases in which the disappearance of a species has a disastrous effect on the overall health of the ecosystem. If you believe such pivotal roles belong solely to large animals, consider the role bees and other insects play in pollination.

The conservation community has long touted such practical arguments for species preservation, but there is a risk involved in adopting such a stance. It implies that the rationale for preservation lies in each species' usefulness to humanity. It would be hard for me to convince skeptics that the California tiger salamander should be protected on utilitarian grounds. Perhaps there's some aspect of California tiger salamander physiology that will someday help remedy some human malady. I'm just not anxious to put my eggs in that basket. I believe in halting extinctions on different grounds. Some would call it a moral imperative, and although that sounds a bit heavy, the shoe otherwise fits. I've always wondered why religious groups, especially those grounded in the Old Testament, have been indifferent to and occasionally hostile toward species preservation. Some believe fervently in Creation, yet stand idly by as Creation is disassembled, piece by piece, one species at a time. The story of Noah's Ark is among the most familiar of all biblical passages, and while I'm no Old Testament scholar, it's safe to say that Noah was given a mandate to preserve and protect all species, large and small, useful or not, including the problematic and dangerous. Call it, if you will, the original endangered species act.

Think of a piece of music. Though some sound similar, each is in some way unique. Now imagine that recordings could vanish. The discs and tapes would disintegrate, the music never heard again. If such a catastrophe was possible, you would probably go to great lengths to prevent that, even if it entailed some sacrifice. You would do so not because music stimulates the economy or confers medicinal benefits. No, you would preserve it because music enriches your life in a profound way, and without it your world would be diminished.

Each species is like a melody. Each is unique, and though some resemble others, each is an entity unto itself, with a story all its own. When a species vanishes, that story is lost forever, and every time that happens, the world becomes a little more impoverished and shrinks. It's a small world, and it's getting smaller with each extinction. The day may come when the only wild things left will be the adaptable species that prosper in our presence—coyotes, striped skunks, and crows, along with a depressing litany of nonnative species. Some argue this is how it should be, a perverted application of survival of the fittest. I couldn't disagree more. *The Wall Street Journal* looks at the California tiger salamander and sees a ludicrously protected, insignificant creature that's become a ward of the government and an impediment to individual rights and economic progress. I look at the same creature and see an animal with an incredible story to tell to those who are willing to listen. Five million years of separation have given us a salamander unlike any other, a creature ideally suited to central California: a salamander that breeds in the dead of winter, emerging during the harshest of storms. A salamander that spends most of its life in burrows dug by mammals; a salamander that, despite its need for moisture, shuns the lush coastal forests in favor of the dry interior; a salamander that, upon departing from its natal pond, may move a mile or more into upland habitat; a salamander that may forego breeding during drought and that can, if all goes well, outlive the vastly larger creatures with which it shares the landscape. This is not about saving the lives of individual animals nor is it about animal rights; it concerns the future of an entire race, one five million years in the making. To consign it to premature extinction is unacceptable, even if the California tiger salamander delivers no direct benefits to mankind. In all likelihood it will never help cure the common cold, much less Alzheimer's disease or cancer. But then, neither did Bach, Bing Crosby, or the Beatles.

A Tale of Two Creeks

Streams as Portals to Discovery

ONE OF THE drawbacks to living in the Diablo Range is a lack of flowing water. I love the grassy slopes and oak savannahs, but I long for rivers and streams. There are numerous creeks, but most dry well before summer's end. Rivers are even harder to come by—there exists but one, the San Benito River, flowing through the entire range, but dubbing the San Benito a river is a bit of a stretch, for it is to rivers as Pluto is to planets.

Along the boundary of my property runs a seasonal stream, fed by winter rains and habitat for Western pond turtles and California red-legged frogs. It ceases flowing in May and dries completely by July, save for a handful of tiny, shaded pools. Though it flows for over four miles, it has no name. The Diablo Range is riddled with such nondescript watercourses as well as more substantial ones. This is the story of two prominent creeks, and though they share similar origins, the differences between the two are at once stark and disturbing.

Coyote Creek begins its journey to the southern arm of San Francisco Bay as a two-pronged entity. The east fork meanders down from chaparral-covered hillsides south of Isabel Valley, while the middle fork originates below Castle Ridge, contorting itself vigorously before joining the east fork. The blending of their waters forms Coyote Creek, one of the most important watersheds in Santa Clara County. It is dammed twice before its waters reach the floor of the Santa Clara Valley, at Coyote Reservoir and Anderson Reservoir. Below Anderson Dam, the creek continues through Coyote Valley and past downtown San Jose before emptying into the bay. Throughout its flatland course, stately cottonwoods shade its banks, remnants of a riparian forest that add a tinge of authenticity to a region that has been thoroughly transformed. Recently, efforts to rehabilitate the creek near its urban setting have borne fruit. Extensive streamside habitat has been preserved as a county park, and cleanup efforts have resulted in a healthier creek than that which ran through a generation ago. That's encouraging, but I am little acquainted with the lower stretches of Coyote Creek. Above the reservoirs, however, I have known it since childhood, when my grandparents took me there for picnics.

The Coyote Creek of my youth was a fortuitous revelation. The clear, gurgling waters teemed with life: frogs sunbathing on gravel shores, turtles basking on boulders, garter snakes slithering into the current. Tadpoles were everywhere, seeking refuge under algae, leaf litter, and stones; minnows darted back and forth in the shallows, and trout swam in the deeper pools.

Because of such outings, Coyote Creek became a special place, a land of discovery. It was a door to a different world, a land of limitless possibility, where anything could be found around the next bend. As does so much in life, those carefree days of picnics and creek exploration ended not with a bang but with a whimper. I don't know when our last outing occurred, nor do I know why they ceased. All I know is that they did, and it would be over thirty years before I returned. By then, my grandparents were gone, and I ventured to the creek alone to survey amphibians.

I drove slowly up Roop Road as it followed the path of Coyote Creek. I was pleasantly surprised at how little things had changed over the years. Here and there, a home had been built, and a barbed wire fence now stood between the creek and the road. Several pullouts evoked a strong sense of familiarity, and I felt certain those were the very spots we parked at years ago. I continued upstream and parked near the old bridge.

I planned to walk from the confluence of the east and middle forks back to the bridge, a distance of six miles. I started on higher ground, hiking up Mahoney Ridge before dropping into the confluence. There, whatever meager traces of human activity remained had vanished. Miles downstream, the creek had been dammed twice, and Lord knows what might have been discarded into its waters as it approached San Jose. This upstream section, however, had never known such insults. Logging or mining had never damaged it, and although the surrounding hillsides had formerly been grazed, there appeared to be no residual damage done. I was glad to see that the Coyote Creek of my youth remained intact—natural, unsullied, and very much alive.

I alternated between walking along the bank and wading. The creek contained ample water but was barely flowing, and its waters were clear as glass. That clarity allowed me to identify tadpoles, as well as anything else residing in the stream. There were fish: schools of California roach, native minnows that were everywhere. In deep pools were Sacramento suckers, bottom-dwelling fish approaching a foot and a half in length. More impressive were Sacramento pikeminnows, sleek, fleet, and at two feet long, the largest fish in the watershed. They are frequently mistaken for rainbow trout, which are more common upstream along the middle fork.

Besides fish, a variety of birds called the streamside habitat home. Common mergansers, mallards, and wood ducks floated past in the serene waters. The melodies of dozens of different songbirds echoed through a riparian forest of willow, sycamore, and alder. Beneath the water's surface, the black shells of California floater, a native mussel, were a common sight. Western pond turtles were still common here, despite their disappearance from a number of compromised watersheds throughout the Pacific Coast. Garter snakes were frequently seen, while fence lizards and whiptails scurried across boulders and dry washes on higher ground.

But it was the amphibians that drew my attention. Chorus frog tadpoles were everywhere, while the tiny black tadpoles of Western toads massed in schools in shallow water. Larval California newts were seen here and there, while yellow-legged frog tadpoles were possibly the most abundant amphibians present. That was good news, for the foothill yellow-legged frog, despite its lack of federal protection, may be more at risk than its celebrated relative, the California red-legged frog. The frog is still found in the foothills and mountains of California and southwestern Oregon but is gone from much of its historical range; the Southern California population may be extirpated. Like many at-risk species, the frog is restricted in its habitat requirements, found exclusively in creeks and streams. Unlike red-legged frogs, it neither breeds in nor inhabits ponds, lakes, marshes, or wetlands. Its granulated skin is almost toad-like; its unexceptional size and muted color don't tend to leave a vivid impression. In Coe Park, the frog is found in only two watersheds: the Orestimba Creek drainage and Coyote Creek. A recent statewide survey for the species revealed that there may be as few as thirty streams left with as many as twenty adult frogs. Coyote Creek must be one of them; it's certainly one of the strongholds for the species in the Diablo Range. As much as anything, their ample presence confirms the health of the creek.

San Carlos Creek tumbles off the slopes of San Benito Mountain, the highest peak in the Diablo Range at almost a mile above sea level. Flowing northeast, it wends its way down through brush-covered mountains and onto the austere foothills below, a ribbon of water in a parched landscape less populated today than it was a century ago. Near the head of Vallecitos Canyon, the creek changes identity, becoming Silver Creek, emptying into Panoche Creek downstream. Panoche Creek continues into the San Joaquin Valley until it reaches the Mendota Pool, where Fresno Slough and the San Joaquin River meet. The San Joaquin flows north, taking its water and sediments to San Francisco Bay. There are dozens of creeks trickling down off the eastern flank of the Diablo Range—Garzas Creek, Salado Creek, Orestimba Creek, and Cantua Creek, to name a few. They are all meager, flowing most heavily following winter rains and tapering to a trickle by summer. San Carlos Creek would hardly merit a footnote in a discussion of even these paltry streams were it not for its particular curse. For although San Carlos Creek courses down through some of the most remote terrain in central California, it has the dubious distinction of running through the abandoned New Idria quicksilver mines. And even though the mines are no longer active, and the people all but gone, the toxic legacy lingers, flowing down through its tormented waters.

In 1853, ambitious prospectors hoping to find gold or silver in the southern Diablo Range instead discovered cinnabar, from which they could obtain mercury. Though not what they were looking for, it nevertheless represented a considerable financial opportunity, for mercury was highly valued as a means of extracting gold. Within a year, mercury mines were up and running at New Idria, in time to cash in on the gold rush occurring nearby in the Mother Lode.

Eight years later, William H. Brewer visited the New Idria mines as part of the United States Geological Survey team appointed to map and document resources in the recently admitted state. He devoted an entire chapter in his journal to the team's foray to New Idria, where they found a bustling community living in isolation several day's ride from the nearest neighboring outpost. They spent several days touring the mines, and Brewer took side trips up to nearby summits. What Brewer recollected most, apart from the oppressive heat (they visited the mines in July), were the extensive workings of the mines and the boom or bust nature of mineral extraction. He felt the most hazardous jobs were not those of the miners but of the men cleaning the chambers adjacent to where the cinnabar ore was heated and processed. The vapors of sulfur and mercury made for a horrific atmosphere; one's health could be ruined in the course of a week. Yet the wages were so high—twenty dollars a day, perhaps ten times as much as those of a miner—that there was never a shortage of laborers. This was perhaps the first mention of the detrimental effects of mercury mining in New Idria.

Besides its value in gold extraction, mercury would later be used for a variety of industrial purposes, in fungicides, and in explosives, particularly during World War I and World War II, when the United States military was the primary customer. The New Idria mine was the second largest source of mercury in the United States, surpassed only by the New Almaden mine south of San Jose. The New Idria mine remained active until 1972, when demand for mercury waned. By the time the last flask of mercury had been hauled out, it marked the end of a 118-year run. What remained were residences, outbuildings, storage sheds, and miles of tunnels and shafts. Unfortunately, those downtrodden structures were not all that was left behind.

In order to obtain mercury in liquid form, it was necessary to roast cinnabar ore in furnaces at an ungodly temperature approaching six hundred degrees Celsius. This heated ore was processed in condensers where liquefied mercury could be harnessed. After processing, the ore was discarded nearby in an ever-growing tailings pile. Over one hundred years of mercury mining produced one hell of a slag heap—over a half-million cubic yards' worth. But it's much worse than an eyesore. Unfortunately, mercury extraction was never a precise discipline, and the discarded ore, jumbled together in a mountainous pile, still contains mercury and a host of other toxic chemicals. But instead of being bound in strata of rock, they lie exposed on the surface, where they leach into the soil and downhill into San Carlos Creek.

As if the massive tailings weren't enough, thousands of feet of tunnels and mine shafts have become a conduit through which groundwater seeps. As it courses through those neglected tunnels, that water accumulates a veritable witch's brew of heavy metals, including aluminum, arsenic, iron, magnesium, manganese, and nickel. This toxic torrent spews out of portal 10 before emptying into San Carlos Creek a hundred yards downhill. Between this groundwater effluent and the tailings pile runoff, San Carlos Creek had hit the toxic daily double.

The keen eye of William H. Brewer took no notice of San Carlos Creek, at least nothing he recorded in his journals. Its deteriorating condition must have been obvious to the miners over the years, yet no record of that exists. Given the dangerous working conditions, the laborers probably viewed the tainted creek as the least of their worries. Their drinking water came from the pure waters upstream of the mines, where a portion of the creek was dammed.

The first hint that something was amiss in San Carlos Creek didn't surface until the 1950s, when an employee of the United States Geological Survey examined a stretch of creek downstream from the mines and found it not just fish-free but entirely lifeless. In 1975, a rancher whose cattle grazed downstream became concerned that the odd-colored waters might be detrimental to his herd. He contacted the California Regional Water Quality Control Board and registered a complaint. Thus innocently began the tragicomedy of errors and apathy that has swirled around efforts to purge the acid mine drainage oozing into San Carlos Creek.

The board responded to the complaint by dispatching several employees to inspect the area. They took samples from six sites along the creek, including the clean waters above the mine, at portal #10 (the point of discharge), and several miles downstream. They found that while the upstream section was suitable for livestock use, water in the mines and downstream was not. Domestic use was out of the question. It found the owners of the mine, the New Idria Mining and Chemical Company, in violation of State Resolution 70–205, which states that water discharge shall not cause a pollution of ground or surface waters. They recommended that the company should try to contain the runoff. But with toothless words like "recommend" and fuzzy terms such as "should try to," it's hardly surprising that the company ignored the notice. This could hardly have placated the rancher who worried about the creek—after all, chemical analysis confirmed his suspicion that the water wasn't fit for even cattle to drink. Yet he didn't press the issue, and the pollution of San Carlos Creek would have gone completely unaddressed were it not for the determined efforts of the Woods family.

In 1981, back when the terms "cheap land" and "California" could still be uttered in the same sentence, the Woods family, tired of renting and disillusioned with their crowded existence in San Jose, decided to leave the city and make a go of it in the country. For the price of a luxury sedan, they purchased two hundred and forty acres downstream from the mine. The property consists of a canyon with surrounding hillsides draped in scrub oak, manzanita, and gray pine. Through the bottom of the canyon, flanked by cottonwoods, flow the defiled waters of San Carlos Creek.

They planned to build a pair of modest residences. Power would not be an issue, for utility poles had been erected decades before along New Idria Road to service the mines. Water, on the other hand, was a different story. They assumed they could tap into the creek, but a subsequent visit to the stream revealed an unexpected surprise. Its waters ran orange, and it doesn't take an advanced degree in chemistry to conclude that such water is wholly unfit for household use. Drilling a well was out of the question, for the ground below the property contains a thick layer of bedrock that is not easily penetrated. In order to obtain water, they would need to improvise. Water for drinking and cooking came from a cistern that collected rain during the winter. This was supplemented by water purchased in five-gallon bottles during summer and fall. For cleaning and bathing, creek water could be used, but only after first passing through a home-made filtration system that did an admirable job of removing most of the contaminants. Even so, that water is far from pure, and while it may suffice for toilets, there are legitimate long-term health concerns about using such water for other purposes. By the spring of 1988, Mrs. Woods, the family matriarch, had had enough. She embarked on what would become a lifelong odyssey to find an agency and a party responsible for cleaning the creek.

Like the rancher thirteen years earlier, Mrs. Woods began by writing a letter to the California Regional Water Quality Control Board. The board responded by sending a three-person team to the site. They took samples from eight locations, from just upstream of the mine to several miles below it. They tested for nine inorganic constituents, six of which (aluminum, arsenic, iron, magnesium, manganese, and nickel) were detected. Samples taken above the mine showed very little presence of those metals; those below the mines showed elevated levels, in some cases alarmingly so. They concluded that the mine discharge was a pollutant affecting the creek, one that was not regulated by a NPDES (National Pollution Discharge Elimination System) Permit, and the ongoing runoff was a violation of State Resolution 70-205. In July, the board sent the mine owners a copy of the inspection. The mine owners were "recommended" to submit a report with a work plan and time schedule for cleaning the creek, and a response was requested by the end of August.

Here, the story takes a similar turn to how the events unfolded in 1975, right down to the tepid recommendation issued to the mine owners from the board. Yet things had changed in thirteen years. The mine had changed hands. In 1986, a consortium of businessmen formed a partnership called New Idria Associates and purchased the 868-acre site for $400,000. Moreover, the issue had aroused the ire of Mrs. Woods, who would neither suffer fools nor be brushed off so easily.

By November the board had not heard back from New Idria Associates. They sent a second letter, and lo and behold, they finally got a response. But instead of a reply from New Idria Associates, the owners of the property, the board received a response from something called Futures Foundation.

The letterhead of Futures Foundation contains an interesting symbol on the bottom right-hand corner of the page. The image appears to be that of a mountain or, with a bit of imagination, a pair of weathered hands steeped together as if in prayer. At the apex of all this, the letter F appears twice, in capital form, interlocked in the mode of the yin-yang symbol. To achieve this effect, an upright F is connected to one that is not only upside down, but backward. And despite all the other imagery present, that upside down, backward F pretty much sums up the Futures Foundation.

The Futures Foundation was formed as a rehabilitation center for those jailed for drug offenses. However, they don't claim to rehabilitate people. Though they operate as a nonprofit organization, they are not licensed and receive no oversight. According to their founder, they are structured less like a business than like a family, which sounds harmless if you picture the Partridge Family and much more disturbing if you think of the Manson Family. The members, predominantly male, were housed at one of several rented dwellings in San Jose, in addition to the facilities at New Idria, which in 1986 they began leasing from New Idria Associates. In exchange for room and board, members were asked to pledge a two-year commitment to the family, during which time they were expected to work at the compound to keep the family financially solvent. Over the years, those duties came to include a smorgasbord of small business ventures, including electronics assembly, auto detailing, trash hauling, and a dog breeding business that specialized in rottweilers.

Despite the warm insinuations of a family atmosphere, there was certainly no hospitality extended toward the outside world. From the time they arrived in New Idria, they assumed a paranoid stance that worsened as time passed. I experienced this in November 1986 when I drove up New Idria Road to San Benito Mountain. As I was driving through the old mining town on a public road, one of the family members gave me the evil eye, glaring as if he had just caught me breeding his prize rottweiler personally. He stared at me until I was out of sight.

This, then, was the organization that finally responded to the letters issued by the California Regional Water Quality Control Board. Future's response emphasized that, while they too were concerned about the creek, it was a problem they had inherited rather than caused. Being a "struggling, nonprofit organization," they couldn't afford to clean up the creek or even hire an engineer to devise a plan to do so. They emphasized that they were not miners and thus exempt from resolution 70-205. They claimed they tried to devise solutions to improve the creek, such as diverting the tainted water pouring out of portal 10 but were concerned that doing so would cause hardship for downstream ranchers, since that would reduce the amount of water by half. Better, I guess, to have a lot of toxic water than a little pure water. If you're trying to find the logic in that line of thought, you're not alone.

The board ignored their response, since it came from a tenant rather than the owners of the property (and responsible party), New Idria Associates. In January 1989, with Mrs. Woods on their heels, the board informed New Idria Associates that they had two weeks to submit the overdue report or risk a fine of $1,000 per day. That got their attention. They promptly announced they had hired an engineering firm to devise a remediation plan and requested a thirty-day extension. Perhaps symbolically, the board agreed to an April 1 deadline.

On April 21 the engineering firm hired by New Idria Associates submitted the report and announced that they would soon provide a work plan to remedy the situation. However, they challenged resolution 70-205 by asserting that their clients were not involved in mining and were maintaining the property as an agricultural preserve. In truth, this steep land of rock and chaparral was god-awful grazing land; furthermore, the only crop that could be profitably grown there was cannabis, so taking New Idria seriously as an agricultural preserve is as believable as picturing Siegfried and Roy as Hell's Angels. Still, the ball was rolling, and after fourteen years, it appeared as if San Carlos Creek would finally get its due.

Then things unraveled. The remediation plan devised by the engineering firm was never implemented, possibly because in May, 1991, New Idria Associates sold their "agricultural preserve" to Futures Foundation Family, Inc. The struggling nonprofit was able to scrape together enough dog-eared bills to purchase the controversial property they had been leasing for five years. Apparently, things were going so well they added a third F to their title, and while this made for a crowded letterhead and cluttered up the yin-yang symbolism, at least they got that all-important word "family" into the title.

In the meantime, the only real family living in the watershed retested the water running through their property, and it continued to show high levels of contamination. The Woods family contacted Futures, their new neighbor, and offered free labor and equipment to divert the tainted water flowing from portal 10. Yet Futures declined this and every other overture from the Woods family in subsequent years. With a secure water source of their own—the small upstream reservoir constructed years ago to supply the miners—the welfare of those living downstream was of little concern to them. This is the same organization that, five years earlier, had argued against diverting sullied mine water because cattle might be deprived. This stance is especially reprehensible because there had been a verbal agreement between the Futures Foundation and the Woods family. The Foundation's plan to establish their thoroughly unconventional rehabilitation center in rural San Benito County was, to say the least, highly controversial and met with a great deal of opposition. The Woods family agreed to add a voice of support to the Foundation at a time when the county was leaning toward denying them permission to operate there. In return, the Foundation agreed to allow them access to clean water in the reservoir upstream from the mines. Once Futures became established in New Idria, however, they went back on their word. Ask any member of the Woods family what those three Fs stand for and the response will leave blisters on your ears.

Meanwhile, the board tried to contact the party that held the mineral rights to the property. Mining law is convoluted, and while Futures Family Foundation owned the land, the mineral rights belonged to someone else. The board spent several years tracking down the holders of those mineral rights, hoping to have them contribute to the cleanup. This chase led them to Wyoming and Ohio, yet no degree of culpability was ever established and no money was ever procured.

In 1996, Coastal Advocates, an environmental group based in Santa Cruz, took up the cause. They bypassed the state, petitioning the EPA to address the mine discharge. Coastal Advocates emphasized the dangers posed by mercury in all its various forms, from inhaled vapors to the extremely toxic methylmercury. Mercury is especially dangerous because it accumulates as it passes through the food chain. Small amounts of mercury multiply significantly with each link. By the time it gets to the fish people eat, the levels are high enough to pose a threat to human health.

In 1997, the EPA came to New Idria to investigate the creek, to a decidedly mixed reception. On the Woods property, they were treated to welcome signs, coffee, and pound cake. At Future's, the welcoming committee consisted of snarling rottweilers, a video surveillance system, and semiautomatic weapons. Somewhat unnerved, agency personnel took samples above the mine, in the mines, and at numerous spots downstream up to seventeen miles distant. Besides testing the waters, they also collected stream sediment samples and samples from the tailings pile. They found the water upstream from the mines to be healthy. However, at the mine and downstream, it was in woeful shape. Levels of mercury, zinc, iron, nickel, and sulfates exceeded federal water quality standards, in many cases drastically so. Predictably, the highest levels of contamination were found at the mine, yet alarming levels of mercury were found throughout the watershed, including the most distant sample site, seventeen miles beyond at the Panoche Creek confluence. As a result, the EPA declared the New Idria Mine a Superfund site in 1998.

While that represented a milestone and vindication, it's one thing for a location to be designated as a Superfund site and another to actually have it remedied. Lying in a remote, unpopulated area, New Idria went to the back of a depressingly long line of areas in need of rehabilitation. Meanwhile, researchers from UC Santa Cruz came to San Carlos Creek to study mercury in all its nefarious guises. Like the EPA study, that conducted by the UC Santa Cruz group found disturbingly high levels in the creek. However, they took the analysis further by identifying the various forms taken by mercury throughout the creek, something the EPA did not do. Methylmercury, the most toxic form, is produced through bacterial metabolism. It is a highly potent neurotoxin and truly frightening stuff. It is this that magnifies through the food chain as it passes from plankton to invertebrates to fish to people. Methylmercury was discovered in high concentrations not merely in the surface waters but also in stream sediments well downstream from the mine. The researchers concluded that the specter of methylmercury haunted the watershed far downstream, including the Mendota Wildlife Refuge, the San Joaquin River, and San Francisco Bay, San Carlos Creek's ultimate destination.

In 2002 hope surfaced again when the State Water Resources Control Board conducted hearings to determine which of the state's eight hundred sullied waterways should receive priority for federal cleanup. Despite considerable lobbying by the San Benito County Board of Supervisors, recommendations by the UC Santa Cruz team, and access to a file of evidence collected by the Woods family that approached biblical proportions, the state deemed San Carlos Creek a low priority, not under consideration until at least 2015. The county threatened to sue the state; that prompted the head of the board to visit New Idria. Supposedly, he was impressed, and he left promising action.

Unfortunately, he didn't say when, and the events of 2002, which seemed to hold such promise, turned out to be yet another case of *cleanus interruptus*, something the Woods family had experienced before. The most recent sliver of hope for creek cleanup took place in 2006, when an Ohio-based plastics manufacturer stepped forward as a partial responsible party after they became aware that San Benito County received a $200,000 grant to hire a legal firm to ferret out those responsible for the acid mine drainage. In fear of being outed, the corporation, which never operated the mine but rather purchased a company that did, came forward on its own. The company was also involved in the New Almaden Mine cleanup, yet that took fifteen years to resolve, and in this case, the company's liability may be limited, since it was only involved in New Idria for five years.

It is May 2008, and I have returned to New Idria to see firsthand what I've read about in documents and reports. The Futures Foundation is becoming a part of the past here, for although the foundation still owns the land, it is in arrears in property tax payments and no longer maintains a rehabilitation facility on the premises. As a result, there is no one left to give me the evil eye, much less the finger. The buildings, decrepit and vacant, have been vandalized, and the only hints of modernity are numerous yellow signs posted on buildings warning of hantavirus. But the buildings are none of my concern; my interest lies in the mining residue.

My tour guide on this occasion was Kate Woods, who is all too familiar with the history of New Idria, living in the ominous shadow of the mines. Our first stop was the tailings pile. In my mind's eye, I pictured an orderly set of pyramid-shaped piles of red rock standing drearily atop a plateau. My imagination proved accurate only with regard to the color of the stone.

"There's your tailings pile," Kate announced.

"Where?"

"That hillside," she replied.

Until then, I had had no idea how to visualize half a million cubic yards' worth of spent ore, and it was with dejected awe that I surveyed the scene before me: an entire hillside of mining detritus, sliding hopelessly down toward San Carlos Creek. I could see now that removing all this would be practically impossible; to somehow cover up and stanch the leaching would be more realistic, but even that would be a formidable task, much more daunting than addressing the effluent spewing from portal 10. Cleaning this Superfund site would certainly, to use an ever-popular political spin, create jobs.

On higher ground, I witnessed the infamous portal 10 exude its vile discharge, a toxic ribbon of orange liquid. It arrives at a woefully inadequate settling pond before spilling over en route to the mixing zone, where the acid mine runoff enters San Carlos Creek. There, pure and poisoned waters blend, and it is as stark as it is accessible, lying twenty feet from the road. Above, San Carlos Creek runs clear and clean, as a mountain stream should. Where its waters collide with those of the mine drainage, it becomes something entirely different, a turbid torrent of rust-colored liquid. If a mountain could bleed, this is what it would look like.

The next morning I followed the tainted creek through the Woods property. Kate had piqued my curiosity by mentioning that she had startled a frog as it rested along the banks of the creek last fall. It was the only frog she'd ever seen in the creek, and best of all, it had only one head, two eyes, and four limbs. I deluged her with questions: Did it have an eye stripe? Was its skin smooth or granular? Did it dive down into the water and seek cover beneath a stone, or float along the surface once it jumped away? I had a hunch she had seen a foothill yellow-legged frog. They inhabit several streams nearby, and I thought this frog may have dispersed from above the mixing zone, where San Carlos Creek is healthy. Finding a frog in the polluted stretch doesn't refute the fact that the stream is severely degraded. After all, tainted water won't immediately kill a frog, but it would keep them from reproducing, for neither tadpoles nor eggs could tolerate its toxins. The exciting prospect about finding that frog was the possibility that a viable population may still exist upstream and could once again thrive throughout the creek if it were ever cleaned.

Walking up New Idria Road, I was struck with the area's subtle beauty, so easily missed from inside a car. Here and there, eroded sandstone erupted from the steep hillsides, pocked with small grottoes. One was particularly spacious, precisely the sort of location a pair of condors might choose for a nest site. Though it was late May, a profusion of wildflowers decorated the roadside— larkspurs, Indian paintbrush, penstemon, and yarrow were all familiar friends that I see to the north. The lavender and yellow lilies that I saw, though, were different than those in my area. The same was true for a glorious native thistle that sent out a bubblegum-pink blossom that could stand toe to toe with that of the finest rose. Best of all, however, were the yuccas, Our Lord's Candle (*Yucca whipplei*), with towering stalks draped with dozens of fragrant white flowers.

Lining the creek was a riparian zone of cottonwoods, a streamside forest that pulsed with birdsong and the drillings of woodpeckers. But that's where the beauty ceased. At my feet, the creek ran a surreal orange. For a quarter mile I followed it, yet the only life I saw in its tormented waters was an occasional water strider darting along the surface. It was otherwise as lifeless as a current of Clorox. It reminded me of a public service television commercial that aired during the 1970s, in which an elderly Native American man grimly witnesses one polluted landscape after another, the last of which, I believe, is a river. In the final scene, a close-up of the old man's face, a tear runs down his wizened cheek. My guess is that, after witnessing the tailings pile, portal 10, and the mixing zone, he would have been wailing out loud long before he got this far downstream, for what should have been the most vibrant part of the mountain was lifeless. There should have been dragonflies hovering over the creek and a host of insects in its waters. I don't know if the creek ever supported fish—if it did, it was probably restricted to small species such as sculpins and California roach. Foothill yellow-legged frogs should be basking along its banks, and two-striped garter snakes (*Thamnophis hammondii*), a declining Southern California species not found north of here, should be slithering along the watercourse.

During its preliminary site assessment in 1997, the EPA analyzed sensitive environments downstream of the mine, concentrating on the potential effects of the creek on four species: the blunt-nosed leopard lizard, San Joaquin antelope squirrel, giant kangaroo rat, and the San Joaquin kit fox, all of which inhabit the watershed at lower elevations. However, all four desert-adapted species derive water from food sources and do not depend upon streams for drinking. As a result, the agency concluded that the beleaguered creek had little effect upon those creatures. However, no study has ever addressed the creek's effect on wildlife in general. What about the effects of the creek on aquatic organisms or terrestrial animals drinking its fouled waters? While the influence on aquatic organisms might be obvious—they are absent from the creek—the effects upon land animals might be more subtle. I sifted through several studies measuring pH levels and the presence of various heavy metals throughout San Carlos Creek, but all I really needed to do to gauge how damaged the creek was to walk the stream and observe its sterile waters.

Almost half a century has passed since someone first observed San Carlos Creek and beheld something fishy, or fishless, as the case may be. As I stand on the banks of the stream and peer into its murky, odd-colored waters, it dawns on me that, despite over thirty years of complaints, investigations, studies, and hearings, not one penny has been allocated to clean the creek, even though everyone agrees that the creek is polluted and that the cause of the pollution is discharge from the mine. This begs the question: Why has nothing been done to fix San Carlos Creek?

Maybe because there has never been a public outcry. San Carlos Creek flows through the spine of the Diablo Range, one of the least populated areas in California. Only one household uses its waters, and the Woods family, despite all their pluck and determination, will never be confused with the Hearsts or Chandlers. When the creek finally reaches civilization, it does so at Mendota, a small, dirt-poor ag town that most Californians have never heard of. By the time the creek's mercury-laden sentiments reach the San Francisco Bay, they mingle with those of other tainted watersheds, and the connection is blurred. But I have another theory as to why San Carlos Creek still languishes.

A room common to many will be swept by no one.

Although that proverb is centuries old, it is as pertinent now as ever, not only as a commentary on public restrooms but also on the fate of San Carlos

Creek. From the jurisdictional side of the equation, county, state, and federal government have all failed it. San Benito County has at times shown genuine interest in the welfare of the creek, but this concern runs hot and cold and is dependent upon the makeup of the board of supervisors. Most of the time, I get the feeling the county wishes the issue would just go away, that the creek be annexed into neighboring Fresno County, where it could be ignored by a larger entity. The state has been even more reluctant to take up the creek's cause. They have repeatedly requested rather than demanded action on the part of those holding title to the mine. When they did lay down the law, they did so meekly, with little follow-through and no enforcement. The same criticism could be applied to the federal government, for the EPA has all but admitted that the creek is a low priority.

The proprietary side of the ledger is even more farcical. Since the 1970s the property has been owned by the New Idria Mining and Chemical Company, the New Idria Land and Development Company, New Idria Associates, and (cue the circus music) Futures Foundation Family, Inc. As if that weren't enough, toss in several mineral rights holders as well. Every one of those has denied any responsibility and dragged their feet in complying with the law. Special mention must be given once again to Futures, the current owners, who could serve as poster children for poor land stewardship. One could sympathize with the plight of a nonprofit organization with no connection to mining having to pay for the sins of their predecessors. But the braintrust (such as it is) at Futures can hardly be cast as victims. They were well aware of the existing pollution and the legal imbroglio surrounding the creek when they were leasing the property, yet they decided to purchase it anyway. *Caveat emptor.* At this point, you can be forgiven if you come to the conclusion that the leadership of the foundation is a few French fries short of a Happy Meal. You may also wonder how a struggling nonprofit organization that can't even afford to hire an engineering firm to devise a remediation plan for the creek amassed the capital necessary to purchase the property. While the foundation dabbled in a number of money-making schemes, none was as egregious as their trash-hauling enterprise. They transported all sorts of detritus to New Idria to be recklessly and illegally dumped. Much of that refuse was toxic. When these shenanigans came to light in 2002, the state fined the foundation $150,000 to cover the cost of cleaning the pollution they had only themselves to blame for.

After that, the future for the foundation looked increasingly dicey. The "family members" dispersed, leaving New Idria once more abandoned. In 2006, the foundation put the 868-acre albatross up for sale, attempting to unload it for a cool $7 million. They may as well have asked for $7 billion. When asked about the toxic baggage that comes with the site, the real estate agent offering the property put on a spin that would do a dervish proud: if sixty-eight acres are contaminated, doesn't that mean that eight hundred acres are fine?

I could go to great lengths to explain the inaction plaguing San Carlos Creek and still fail to achieve the clarity of one profanely eloquent word: fuckery. That is how Kate Woods describes the cast of dubious characters and litany of events her family have witnessed over the last quarter century. If you're going to live in New Idria, you're going to need a strong sense of humor. Unfortunately, time has taken its toll. Mrs. Woods unfortunately passed away without seeing a single step taken to restore the creek. Her children have had their hopes raised and throttled too many times to honestly believe they will ever witness the watershed healed in their lifetime. My prediction? We'll see contestants named Red, Lefty, and Skeeter on the *Jeopardy!* Tournament of Champions before that creek gets cleaned.

As a child, I followed Coyote Creek and entered a world of wonder. As an adult, I followed San Carlos Creek and entered a world of negligence, dishonesty, and apathy. Creeks are truly places of discovery. Unfortunately, not all discoveries are pleasant.

February 2008

Fear and Loathing in Tres Pinos

San Benito County's War on the Coyote

IN NOVEMBER 2001, a weekly newspaper based in Hollister, the seat of San Benito County, ran a feature that brought to light something the board of supervisors and certain politically influential citizens wished had remained in the dark. The perpetually shallow-pocketed county had, since 1999, spent $50,000 annually contracting the USDA's Wildlife Services program to address an alleged coyote problem. "Wildlife Services" is one of those Orwellian euphemisms, like President Bush's Clear Skies Initiative, that tends to confuse people about its agenda. The name borrows heavily from that of the US Fish and Wildlife Service, the federal agency overseeing our national wildlife refuges and the Endangered Species Act. Yet protecting wildlife is about the last thing the USDA's Wildlife Services Program is designed to do. Its previous moniker, Animal Damage Control, provided a more accurate portrayal of its activities: to kill wildlife deemed a nuisance to agriculture or property. Whether or not the animal in question is a native species or an exotic invasive makes no difference—they're all treated like vermin. As a result, bobcats and gray foxes, California natives, are dispatched with the same impunity as nonnative, invasive starlings and feral hogs, both ecological black eyes. The list of species taken during a given year may exceed twenty in some counties. Raccoons, striped skunks, and opossums are heavily represented, but the most prominent species on the list, particularly in San Benito County, is the coyote. From July, 1999, until November, 2001, USDA trappers reported

197

killing 2,773 coyotes in the county, more than twice as many as in any other county in California. San Benito County: we're number one.

No mammal native to North America has adapted to the human conquest of the landscape as spectacularly as the coyote. Most carnivores have seen their numbers diminish and their ranges contract, yet coyotes are not only more abundant now than during the time of Columbus, they have expanded their range considerably. Originally an animal of the West, the coyote has managed to make its way to the farms of Ohio, the swamps of the Southeast, the forests of Maine, even into New York City. Not only has it managed to accomplish that without the aid of any government program or private conservation organization, it has done so in the face of widespread persecution. How did the coyote manage not merely to survive, but thrive under such conditions? Certainly, the wholesale clearing of forests in the East and Midwest provided open habitat more to the coyote's liking. But the main factor behind the coyote's rise was a government program of a different sort—the bounties enacted to rid the east of its top carnivores, mountain lions and gray wolves. By 1900, that had been accomplished, and it was not long before coyotes began showing up in places they had never been seen before.

Coyotes filled the void left at the apex of the food chain, and they proved to be nothing if not supreme opportunists. Eastern coyotes are larger than their Western counterparts, sometimes exceeding forty pounds. Some have suggested that larger size may be the result of crossbreeding with wolves in the waning days of their tenure in the East. If that's correct, the Eastern coyote may be a modern phenomenon that arose as a consequence of meddling with the top of the food chain.

Out West, where coyotes have been part of the fauna since time immemorial, the scenario was different. Although the war on predators got off to a later start on the western front, it was administered with more virulence. In addition to wolves and cougars, the West had grizzlies, not found back East. With far-flung settlements and plenty of wide-open space, eradicating predators in the West required something beyond the state and territorial bounties that proved sufficient in the East. Livestock associations instituted their own bounty systems, but these were not very effective. As their political clout grew, they began lobbying the federal government for assistance in taming the West. Soon after 1900, the United States Biological Survey was established under the Department of the Interior. This agency, the progenitor of today's Wildlife Services Program, employed a variety of tactics in its battle against animals deemed injurious to agriculture. Among the weapons in its arsenal were bounty hunters, traps, explosives, poisons, and later, aerial gunners. The gospel of predator control was preached with religious fervor, approaching a fever pitch in the 1920s, when even the National Park Service shamelessly hopped aboard, eliminating wolves in Yellowstone. By the time World War II ended, victory was in sight. Mountain lions had been diminished, jaguars were pushed back to Mexico, grizzlies were gone save for the few remaining in Yellowstone and Glacier National Parks, while wolves were not even afforded those sanctuaries. Like the armies of Germany and Japan, the formidable enemies had been vanquished. It was time to shift focus, and coyotes were about to command the bulk of the agency's attention. But while coyotes were small in stature, they proved to be more than a match for anything the USDA could throw at them. If wolves were like the German Army, coyotes were like the Viet Cong.

For over half a century the USDA has been killing coyotes in numbers approaching one hundred thousand annually, yet if there is so much as one county from which they've been expunged, I'm unaware of it. Besides colonizing the East, coyotes have continued to prosper in the West, flourishing in the absence wolves. They've been shot, poisoned, blown up, gassed, burned, clubbed, and strangled. Yet there are more coyotes than ever. What explains the coyote's resiliency in the face of such onslaught?

For starters, the modest size of the coyote works to its advantage. Coyote territories are vastly smaller than those of wolf packs, so a given area of land can support many more coyotes. Destroy a pack of wolves and you've rid the species from a sizable area; kill a similar number of coyotes and you haven't made a dent in the population. Although coyotes are social, they don't form packs as large as those of wolves. Wolf social structure leaves them vulnerable to mass poisonings and aerial gunning, whereas coyotes, with looser bonds, are harder to kill en masse.

Dietary differences also favor coyotes. Wolves are more carnivorous, favoring medium- to large-size prey. This leaves them highly vulnerable to poisoned carcasses, which could potentially wipe out an entire pack. But the coyote's habit of incorporating many items into its diet—smaller animals such as rodents, lizards, and insects, as well as some occasional vegetable matter—makes large-scale poisoning less effective.

Coyotes also utilize a variety of habitats—deserts, plains, mountains, and woodlands are all called home by the coyote. Nor do such haunts need to be far from human activity or in pristine condition, for coyotes take to farmlands as well as they do wilderness. In fact, some of the densest populations known have been in suburbs, where, subsisting on a diet of garbage, pet food, and occasionally pets, unnaturally large concentrations have built up.

Yet perhaps the main reason coyotes triumph in the face of persecution is that female coyotes often respond to increased mortality by producing larger litters. That's as good an explanation as any for the abject failure of an effort that has cost US taxpayers millions of dollars over the last half century. Those who staunchly defend the efficacy of coyote control remind me of parents who swear by hitting their kids. If it's really so effective, why do they have to keep doing it?

Native Americans often cast the coyote in the role of the Trickster, much as Aesop portrayed the fox. Today, the coyote is frequently viewed as an irrepressible force, as indestructible as the cockroach. I've had enough run-ins with coyotes to appreciate their intelligence and versatility. I've observed them in all hours of the day, usually alone, sometimes in pairs, and occasionally in groups of three. Whenever I see one, I try to remain still and silent and observe it as it goes about its business, whether that be following its nose in haphazard fashion, pouncing on voles in a field, or yapping for reasons known only to the coyote itself. Unfortunately, their keen senses are usually quick to detect me, and they typically trot off. But not always. On one occasion, a coyote bayed, yelped, and howled from a respectful distance until I left. While it was unquestionably reacting to me, what exactly it was intending to communicate, I'll never know. But my most fascinating encounter with a coyote played out in silence.

It was a mild November afternoon following the first season of the survey in Coe Park. Although the survey season had ended, I was curious to visit some of the ponds toward the end of the dry season to get a feel for seasonal changes.

One such pond was situated near the top of Grizzly Gulch, a two-hour hike from the parking area. On this day, however, I was in no hurry. I stopped by several other ponds before I arrived in midafternoon. My appearance surprised three coyotes in a field south of the pond. Two immediately departed, swiftly scaling the side of Wasno Ridge. The other, to my surprise, remained. After inspecting the pond, I looked out to see the coyote still present. As I unpacked my camera, I began slowly walking toward the coyote, about twenty-five yards away. Proceeding at a glacial pace, I approached within ten yards before it moved away. Yet even then it didn't move far, just several feet beyond. At that point, having taken enough photos, I sat down in the shade of an oak. To my surprise, the coyote reclined as well. We sat there, that coyote and I, forty feet apart, for an hour. I watched as it reacted first to the calls of a crow, then later to the intrusive buzz of a low-flying plane. This animal showed no signs of disease—in fact, it appeared to be the epitome of health. Although it behaved like a habituated animal, it was miles from the nearest campground or habitation.

Historically, the constituency lobbying hardest for coyote control has been sheep ranchers. Sheep have been grazing the West for over 150 years, and you couldn't release a more defenseless, predator-attracting animal onto the land unless you started herding hamsters. Small, weak, slow, and unintelligent, spread far and wide across the open range, sheep succumbed to a variety of predators, from bears to eagles to bobcats. Coyotes, however, posed the greatest problem, especially after wolves were eliminated. Yet the glory days of sheep ranching are behind us, and while the industry is still extant, it's not what it used to be. This rings particularly true in San Benito County, where you'd be hard pressed to find a sheep ranch anymore. No, the ranchers calling for the coyote's head there are, believe it or not, cattlemen.

I've often wondered what kind of reaction I'd get from ranchers operating in the Yellowstone region, where wolves are present, if I mentioned that California cattlemen were complaining about losing stock to coyotes. Unlike their counterparts in the East and the Rockies, the coyotes frequenting central California are among the smallest, tipping the scale at little over twenty pounds. While it's possible that coyotes occasionally take calves, it's pretty hard to believe that coyotes are doing damage enough to warrant a $50,000 per year control program. Even some fellow San Benito ranchers were skeptical, adding that they had never experienced problems with coyotes.

Neighboring Santa Clara County has no coyote control program, nor has there been much of a clamor for one. How is it that coyotes can so devastate San Benito County, yet leave Santa Clara County unscathed? For twenty-two years my father ran cattle in Grant County Park and, during all that time, could not recall a single incident of coyote depredation. It's certainly not for lack of coyotes, for they are as common there as anywhere. Moreover, the ten-thousand-acre park is a wildlife sanctuary, where hunting, even varmint shooting, is prohibited. If any area should serve as a powder keg for coyote/livestock conflict, it would be Grant Park, yet there has never been a problem.

Closer to San Benito County, my property is part of a greater cattle lease encompassing a thousand acres. I've been intimately familiar with the area for nearly two decades, and while I see coyotes frequently, I have never seen evidence of any problem with livestock. The same holds true for neighboring Pacheco State Park, which has had a grazing program since its inception in 1995. It begs the question, what's going on in San Benito County?

Peer a little longer into the looking glass and you may conclude that something besides livestock depredation may be feeding San Benito County's enthusiasm for coyote control. The county fish and game commission heartily supports the effort, ostensibly to boost deer numbers. Now, I might understand, if not condone, a county embracing a predator control program if hunting brought a significant amount of revenue to county coffers. Yet in San Benito County, deer hunting ranks somewhere between piano tuning and lemonade stands as an economic engine. In spite of this, the county chose to proceed directly into the business of altering its own ecosystem when it bought into the coyote control program. It did so without demanding any data or reasonable proof that there is, in fact, a dearth of deer in the county and that coyotes are a significant component of that decline.

While deer numbers in the county were higher in decades past, this doesn't mean that the current population is in jeopardy. Statewide, the deer population peaked around the middle of the twentieth century and has since tapered off.

Biologists attribute the midcentury spike to a scarcity of mountain lions, which bounty hunters targeted from 1907 until 1963. By the 1950s, the cougar population was nearing its ebb, and without the big cat, the deer population rose to unnaturally high levels. With the termination of the bounty in 1963 and subsequent statewide protection, cougars have increased, and the deer population is at a more sustainable level. The glory days of decades gone by were not a reflection of a healthy ecological community but rather of a dysfunctional one lacking its top predator. While I'm sure that some in San Benito County would love to return to the good old days, they know they can't supersede state law and begin killing mountain lions. So, they do the next best thing—go after the second tier on the food chain, coyotes.

Yet while deer comprise the bulk of the cougar diet, coyotes are far more general in their feeding habits, utilizing everything from fruit to carrion. Coyotes will prey on fawns, but nowhere have they been shown to deplete a population of deer. Numerous stomach content analyses reveal that deer make up only a fraction of the coyote diet, and some of those were likely scavenged as carrion rather than killed. In the Midwest and East, deer numbers have soared in the wake of the disappearance of cougars and wolves. There may now be more deer in those regions than at any time since settlement, and this unnatural population explosion has occurred in the midst of an expanding coyote population. If coyotes were truly a limiting factor—remember, Eastern coyotes are nearly twice the size of their California counterparts-—those deer populations would have been held in check.

In San Benito County, a much-ballyhooed incident occurred several years ago when a wildlife rehabilitation center released five fawns back into the wild. Allegedly, two were immediately taken by coyotes. This event has been used as evidence of the detrimental effect of coyotes upon the local deer population. However, the very scene itself was highly unnatural, for in the wild, fawns are accompanied by their mother. Anyone who believes a doe is incapable of protecting her offspring from coyotes is underestimating the power of maternal instinct. I have seen many coyotes flee from people, vehicles, dogs, and other coyotes, but I have never seen one run so fast as the one I witnessed being charged by a doe looking after her fawns.

Coyotes and deer have inhabited the Diablo Range for millennia in stable coexistence. If predators were threatening the deer population, an area such as Coe Park, a ninety-thousand-acre nature reserve where both species are fully protected, should serve as a litmus test. Yet in fifteen years of observations and discussions with park rangers, I have seen no evidence nor have I heard anyone associated with the park infer that the deer population is crashing.

In the aftermath of the newspaper revelations, tensions ran high in the community. Meetings that were supposed to be open to the public were scuttled or rescheduled. Some tried to frame the issue as city dwellers versus rural folks, long-time county residents versus newcomers and outsiders, ranchers versus environmentalists. The county agricultural commissioner weighed in, ridiculously invoking public safety as a justification for retaining the program. At the boiling point, some lunatic affixed an eyeball, presumably that of a coyote, to the antenna of the newspaper editor's car. Mamas, don't let your cowboys grow up to be babies.

In the wake of the bad publicity, the board of supervisors announced they would not renew the contract with the USDA once it expired. Several supervisors cited fiscal reasons as the overriding factor. Yet the problems with the program extended well beyond budgetary concerns.

The fundamental problem with the program is that it was hastily adopted, with scant evidence to support the claim that coyotes are either killing livestock or adversely affecting the deer population. A coyote feeding on a calf carcass may merely be scavenging but, in such instances, not receive the benefit of the doubt. Determining the cause of death is important, yet I doubt anyone investigated further once a coyote was sighted. Likewise, the presumption that coyotes negatively impact the deer population rested solely upon anecdotal evidence, supported by not so much as a shred of data. Given the amount of public money involved, is it asking too much that someone actually check those assumptions?

The amount of money spent on the program has rubbed a lot of people the wrong way. Some opposed the idea of a perpetually cash-challenged county earmarking funds for such a program while more pressing needs went unheeded. They felt that coyote killing aided only a handful of county residents, who as a group were among the least in need of public assistance. It's ironic that many of the program's supporters, judging by their letters to the editor on a variety of topics, wholeheartedly endorse limited government, a free enterprise system unfettered by regulations, and individual responsibility. Through such a viewpoint, attempting to solve problems through taxation and government programs is at best seen as frivolous and, at worst, viewed as an example of that horrible *S* word: socialism. Yet the USDA Wildlife Services Program is all that and more— a bureaucracy devoted to its own perpetuation, a government subsidy that is in essence a welfare program eagerly embraced by many who have the wherewithal to solve their own problems. Coyotes merit no special status, nor are they classified as game animals or furbearers, subject to seasons and bag limits. On the contrary, they are considered varmints and can be killed in any number at any time of the year. But why do it yourself when you can get the government to do it for you, for a song?

In an attempt to defuse the financial debate, one of the more zealous supporters of the program pointed out that the county would not bear the brunt of the costs but rather would receive reimbursements from a state gas tax. While this may have appeased some county residents, it did nothing to alter the fact that the program was still completely publicly funded—it just shifted the cost onto state taxpayers. By doing so, it further opened the debate to people outside the county, for all Californians were supporting the dubious policies of San Benito County.

Regardless of who picks up the tab, the economics of the coyote control program deserve to be called in to question. Larger and better-funded entities than San Benito County have tried to defeat the coyote, and all have failed. All the persecution and money spent have been no more effective than killing no coyotes at all, for the creature abounds in numbers greater than ever. Killing coyotes results in more coyotes. You'd have to go a long way to find a better example of pissing money away. In a desperate attempt to salvage the program, the agricultural commissioner unbelievably cited public safety as justification for its continuation. While it's true that coyote attacks are not unprecedented—a three-year-old was killed in Southern California in 1981—those few incidents of coyote aggression have occurred in areas where coyotes have become habituated, where they've been fed and associate people with food. The San Benito County program was initiated to eliminate coyotes from rural ranches far from town, yet the suburbs are where efforts should be focused if public safety is truly a concern. Of course, the public safety issue was a red herring, for coyotes pose far less of a threat to people than dogs, and a case could be made that a burgeoning deer population—the ancillary goal of some of the proponents of coyote control—represents a more serious risk to human life than coyotes ever could. Strike a coyote with your vehicle and all the damage is borne by the coyote. Hit a deer and things get more serious. Collisions with deer claim more lives annually than all predator attacks in the United States combined. Last week, chances are more people died hitting deer than have been killed by coyotes in the past two centuries. In addition to being a threat to public safety, deer aren't exactly free from agricultural conflict. San Benito County vintners complain of deer munching their vines, and depredation permits have been issued to cull excess deer from vineyards. Rural and suburban gardeners view deer as a much greater menace than coyotes for their raids on flower beds and vegetable gardens. I have nothing against deer—I'd like there to be as many as the land can support. I just can't condone manipulating ecosystems by removing predators, real or contrived, in a misguided attempt to maximize their numbers.

Many of the essays in this book are devoted to imperiled species. This is not one of them. Coyotes will persist, even flourish, whether San Benito County wants them to or not. Yet ironically, while an ongoing war on coyotes will have little effect on the coyote population, it may take its toll on a handful of other species caught in the crossfire.

USDA Wildlife Services employs many methods in its pogrom against coyotes. Unfortunately, not all are species-specific. While the act of denning—locating a den and killing the pups—may be inhumane and cruel, at least it kills only the target species. Poison baits and neck snares, the options of choice in San Benito County, kill indiscriminately and thus are more ecologically damaging. In addition to threatening bobcats and wandering dogs, the snares represent a hazard to two species uncommon enough in the region to merit special status: badgers and San Joaquin kit foxes. Snaring a kit fox in the hapless attempt to control coyotes is not just negligent and irresponsible; it's a violation of the Endangered Species Act. The USDA is not above the law, but who oversees the USDA? Its own trappers, apparently, perform this role of self-regulation, which both you and I know is as effective as a midday fireworks display. How plausible is it that trappers are going to admit to snaring badgers and kit foxes in violation of state and federal law? When questioned about the procedure for discovering other animals in snares set for coyotes, one trapper responded that such animals are released. But freedom is of little solace to an animal that's already dead, and as much as I'd like to put faith in his answer, I have a hard time believing it. Call me cynical, but I can't see a USDA employee going to all that trouble.

Unfortunately, San Benito County is hardly unique. When it comes to predator control, counties across the country flock like absentminded sheep to an ecologically backward, scientifically unsound method of wildlife management. It was predator control that created this abundance of coyotes by wiping out wolves. Wolves kill coyotes out of competition and do so with an efficiency that puts the USDA to shame. To this day, no strategy mankind has devised has put a check on coyote populations quite like the presence of wolves. One of the consequences of wolf reintroduction into Yellowstone was a 50 percent reduction in the coyote population shortly thereafter.

It was predator control as well that created the ecological imbalances in which rabbit and rodent populations surge, which in turn necessitates another offensive to control them, often through poisons and chemicals that rise through the food chain. Where does it all end? Such scorched-earth policies are bad for an ecosystem, and I find it difficult to believe they're even justifiable economically. Eradication campaigns and control programs appeal to people because of their aggressive, take-no-prisoners nature. They give the appearance of doing something when they are supremely ineffective, even counterproductive. There has to be a better way.

In San Benito County, that way should have included a thorough investigation into the problem. Perhaps some of the depredation incidents blamed on coyotes were instances where calves had died of other causes and coyotes were merely scavenging. If coyotes were killing calves, maybe the problem was confined to a handful of areas, and perhaps only such locations should receive specific attention.

Attention, of course, means money, and many contend that taxpayers shouldn't foot the bill for something that ranchers can take care of themselves. However, I'm not even going to espouse that argument. I don't mind having my tax dollars support the plight of ranchers as long as it's done in an ecologically responsible way. Thus, predator problems should be addressed as much as possible through nonlethal methods. I suggest putting money into such solutions before resorting to killing native animals. Lethal control has its place as a last resort, and then it must be administered specifically, killing the target species only. There is no place for poisons or snares. If a war is to be waged, let it be fought against an army of invasive, nonnative species.

As for the effect of coyotes upon the deer population, the county again should have requested proof before contracting with the USDA. If the county is going to take a more active role in game management, instead of goosing deer numbers by killing coyotes, perhaps they should look at the bigger picture and endorse the restoration of two native species, tule elk and pronghorn, to the county. Those seeking to increase deer numbers only are too modest in setting their sights; they need to think big and return those magnificent species that were driven out in the not too distant past.

The time is ripe to see ranchers in a new light, not merely as producers of stock, but as land stewards. It's not only what you farm; it's how. Rewarding those who adopt conservation measures on private land is something that is very much in the public interest. It is not realistic or fair to expect ranchers to bear the full cost of such actions, though some admirably do. Providing incentives such as tax breaks or direct financial assistance will give ranchers and landowners a real reason to support conservation efforts and promote biodiversity.

On a national level, the Farm Bill could do much more toward promoting land stewardship and ecological restoration. Nonprofit organizations such as Defenders of Wildlife have gone a long way toward promoting tolerance for predators by offering compensation for stock losses attributed to wolves and grizzlies. There are far more dubious provisions in the Farm Bill than a proposal to coexist with predators, and it may be cheaper in the long run than maintaining control programs. There are those who in principle oppose such an expanded role for the government. Their opposition rings hollow, however, if they on the other hand support government-funded predator control programs.

The more things change, the more they stay the same. The local newspaper that broke the coyote control fiasco changed hands in 2005. In a microcosm of what is happening to television and radio stations, as well as the print media nationwide, it was purchased by a company that already owned the local papers in nearby Morgan Hill, Gilroy, and the daily paper in Hollister, thereby cornering the market on local print news.

After the board of supervisors nixed the coyote control program in 2003, several ranchers retained the USDA's services, paying for them out of their own pockets. By 2006, they had grown weary of that and approached the board of supervisors with the intent of once again having the county absorb the cost of the program. This time, there was scant coverage of this about-face in the local paper. Evidently, new ownership didn't consider the item newsworthy. Maybe they didn't want to ruffle the feathers of any prominent supporters of the program. So, the USDA Wildlife Services program, bureaucratic, ineffective boondoggle that it is, was welcomed back with open arms by San Benito County. The only thing that changed was the price tag, which soared from $50,000 per year in 2001 to $70,000 in 2006. What was it that Santayana said about those who forget the past?

November 2013

How Green Is Thy Valley?

Color Blindness in the Battle to Keep Big Solar Out of Panoche Valley

HALFWAY BETWEEN MONTEREY and Fresno, on the lee side of the Diablo Range, lies Panoche Valley, a ten-thousand-acre plain bordered on the west by the crest of the Diablo Range and on the east by the parched Panoche Hills. That rain shadow location gives it a stark, austere appearance, for the oaks lining the mountains to the west recede well before the slopes reach the valley floor, yielding to a grassland that is treeless save for cloistered bands of cottonwoods lining the washes and shade trees buttressing the few and far between ranch houses. Though it lies close to the very center of the state, it seems out of context, a sliver of West Texas transplanted to California. It's a land of big skies, wide-open spaces, and lonely roads. Picture a landscape to *Wichita Lineman* and you've got Panoche Valley. Though less than twenty miles from Interstate 5, Panoche attracts few visitors. Isolated, sparsely populated, the valley looks much as it did a century ago. But all that is poised to change, and radically.

Despite it being tucked in a back pocket of California, it was inevitable that someday, someone with big plans would discover Panoche Valley. That day came several years ago when Michael Petersen fixed his gaze like the eye of Sauron on the sere valley and saw green. Petersen was the CEO of Solargen, a solar energy company seeking to construct a facility not in the sun-drenched deserts of southeastern California, Nevada, or Arizona, but in central California. After Petersen took a flight over Panoche Valley, he could hardly believe his good fortune in stumbling across a veritable Shangri-La for solar generation, a location blessed with not only abundant sunshine but transmission towers as well. In his exuberance, he blurted out that God must have created Panoche Valley to be a solar farm. Me, I'd like to think She had other plans.

Petersen envisioned blanketing the entire valley with solar arrays, but the valley is made up of multiple properties and not all owners were willing to sell. But he did find some takers, and although he had to scale back the original blueprint, the revised facility was still formidable: a 399-megawatt solar farm covering almost 5,000 acres on the north end of the valley.

Ten miles east of Panoche Valley lies the San Joaquin Valley, a region where the landscape today looks nothing at all like it once did. Its wetlands have been drained, its rivers dammed, tapped, and replaced by a series of canals and aqueducts to slake urban thirst and accommodate intensive agriculture. Its prairies and desert scrublands have been watered, plowed, disked, and furrowed, replaced by orchards, vineyards, and row crops. The southwestern portion has been riddled with oil wells for over a century. The amount of natural land remaining on the valley floor is abysmally small, perhaps as little as 1 percent. Worse, that paltry fraction exists in scattered fragments, many of which are too small to maintain populations of native species for any appreciable length of time. Of all the natural communities once present on the floor of the valley, wetlands are the most well-preserved, thanks largely to duck hunters. Yet even the remaining wetlands are but a shadow of what they once were, and as far as upland habitats go—the grassland and desert scrub communities essential to so many species—the situation is even worse. Today, in fact, the closest equivalent to the natural landscape of the San Joaquin Valley doesn't even lie on the valley floor, but on the Carrizo Plain. Although the Carrizo has a long history of grazing, it has never hosted irrigated agriculture, oil development, or urbanization. While the San Joaquin Valley was undergoing wholesale changes, the Carrizo Plain remained much as it was, and its previously unheralded landscape became something special, a relic for a host of plant and animal species once common but now disappearing from the San Joaquin Valley. Fortunately, the ecological importance of the Carrizo Plain was recognized decades ago, culminating in its designation as a national monument. Today the plain supports an impressive list of at-risk species, as well as reintroduced herds of tule elk and pronghorn, two iconic species that, due to their large spatial requirements, will never again roam free across the San Joaquin Valley. Some call the Carrizo Plain a national treasure, California's Serengeti, a place unlike any other. On the basis of sheer size, they're correct. But on a smaller scale, one hundred or so miles north lies a place very similar. That place is Panoche Valley.

The problem with Panoche Valley is that it doesn't *look* like vital wildlife habitat. There are no wetlands, streams, or forests. Hardly a tree in sight. What it does have are barbed wire fences, cattle, forlorn roads, the occasional ranch house, and massive transmission towers. Isolated, yes. Wilderness, no. Some drive through and see nothing so much as a godforsaken wasteland, a monotonous landscape where cows and road-killed ground squirrels are the only signs of life. Yet that is a misperception, for even in its less than pristine state, the Panoche Valley may be the most crucial area for wildlife conservation in the Diablo Range, not because of an abundance of wildlife but because so many of the species that persist there have vanished elsewhere. Go back several centuries and Panoche Valley was not at all unique. Millions of acres of similar habitat blanketed the San Joaquin Valley. But then came the wholesale transformation of the valley. By 1950 only half of the original habitat remained. By 1980 that number had dwindled to 7 percent. Today, it hovers near 1 percent. Generalist species that do well in varied habitats suffered little as the valley was altered. A few—crows, coyotes, raccoons, striped skunks—even benefitted when the land shifted from arid to cultivated. But for species with narrow habitat needs and little ability to adapt, those that evolved in the short grass prairie and desert scrub of the San Joaquin Valley, the loss of habitat was devastating. Like the Carrizo Plain, Panoche Valley became unique by staying the same while the world around it was turned upside down.

Solargen's proposal to blanket Panoche Valley with several million solar panels attracted attention in 2009, after the company applied for the necessary permits to operate in San Benito County. The county was thrilled with the idea, taken by the promise of jobs and revenue. Solargen aided mightily in feeding such notions, for although short on experience—this was the fledgling company's first foray into the solar power production field—they were well-versed in politicking.

They told the board of supervisors and local business leaders the project would be a boon to the local economy, providing scores of jobs and revenue to both county coffers and local businesses. The board of supervisors unanimously approved the project.

On the PR front, Solargen hoped to quell opposition to the project by insisting they would construct the plant in an environmentally sensitive manner. They brandished their good-guy image by pointing out that they fund efforts to preserve land for conservation. If they had painted themselves any greener, they'd have been a Saint Patrick's Day parade.

Not everyone bought that rosy picture. A group of local citizens arose to voice their concerns. How would the meager county roads handle the heavy equipment and extra traffic during construction? What about the effects of dust after thousands of acres were scraped bare prior to installation of the solar panels? How much water would be pumped, and how would this impact the aquifer they all relied on? How about the twenty-four-hour lighting schedule during construction, which would tarnish an area known for its brilliant night skies? Worse, consider the prospect of staring out your window and forever beholding over a million solar panels, as if Christo had gone insane.

Concerns about the project's impact on wildlife went beyond the local level and were expressed by several large environmental groups. While all supported solar power, they unanimously agreed that the location of this project was disastrous. The Audubon Society had years earlier designated Panoche Valley an important bird area, providing habitat for a number of declining species such as mountain plovers, horned larks, ferruginous hawks, and burrowing owls. Defenders of Wildlife and the Center for Biological Diversity contended that the site was out of the question due to its importance to a number of rare species, especially three listed under the Endangered Species Act—the San Joaquin kit fox, giant kangaroo rat, and the blunt-nosed leopard lizard.

The controversy sparked nationwide interest, receiving considerable press coverage. Most emphasized the irony angle: green vs. green, environmentalists opposing renewable energy. Pro-industry groups and their ilk took the opportunity to take a swipe at the environmental movement, brandishing its followers as unreasonable, unrealistic, and impossible to placate. Even within environmental circles, opinions were divided. Officially, the Sierra Club denounced the project due to its abysmal location, yet some members favored getting that plant built regardless, as if solarizing Panoche would reverse the melting of the ice caps.

Meanwhile, locals organized a grassroots group, Save Panoche Valley, to fight the facility, while Solargen hired a consulting firm to prepare an environmental impact report, as required by law. They were also trying to drum up support for the plant, courting elected officials as well as the general public, holding an open house and saying all the right things. Some were downright amusing: to counter that Panoche Valley is a well-known birding destination, Solargen claimed the solar plant itself could become a tourist attraction. Controversy ensued when it was revealed that Solargen intended to purchase solar panels manufactured in China. This became an issue because Solargen spent so much time telling anyone who would listen how committed they were to providing local jobs. Yet even that commitment didn't stand up to scrutiny. The bulk of those jobs would be temporary, during construction. Once the facility was up and running, the number of employees might plummet to as few as ten. Solargen also downplayed the effects of the panels on wildlife, claiming that once the panels were installed, whatever wildlife was displaced during construction would return as if nothing had changed.

Solargen seemed anxious to get the permit approved and begin construction. Some speculated this was because, in order to be eligible for federal stimulus funding, the project had to break ground before the close of 2010. That didn't happen. Project opponents clung to the hope of rumors that Solargen was on shaky ground financially, and was struggling to find investors. Maybe, having missed the federal stimulus deadline and under financial strain, Solargen would dry up and blow away like a tumbleweed. That didn't happen either. Instead, Solargen was purchased by Duke Energy, a well-entrenched company with much deeper pockets, and they had no intention of abandoning their new investment. The two sides went to court. Save Panoche Valley sued, along with the local chapters of the Audubon Society and the Sierra Club, claiming that the county had illegally cancelled Williamson Act contracts in the course of approving the project, and that the environmental impact report for the project was flawed and inadequate. The case was heard at a lower court in 2011, and Save Panoche

Valley lost. They appealed. The case reached the Sixth District Court of Appeals in June 2013. The three-person judicial panel also ruled against Save Panoche Valley.

Given that verdict, perhaps the best hope for stopping the project lies with two agencies, the California Department of Fish and Wildlife and the US Fish and Wildlife Service, which must grant their blessings in order for construction to begin. Without permits from both state and federal wildlife agencies, the project cannot proceed. Both agencies have ample reason to deny the permit, namely because the site is atrocious—Solargen couldn't have picked a worse location if they tried, in terms of the number of sensitive and endangered species present. Forget for the moment the dozens of other special-status species that could be impacted by the project and concentrate on the three that carry the most legal weight, listed under both the state and federal Endangered Species Acts: the San Joaquin kit fox, giant kangaroo rat, and blunt-nosed leopard lizard. According to the environmental impact report, if the project was built, impacts to all three would be unavoidable and unmitigable. That's not the opinion of an advocacy group, outside agency, or some tree-hugging alarmists-—that's the opinion of the wildlife biologists hired by Solargen. The Panoche region has been singled out in the United States Fish and Wildlife Service's recovery plan as a core area for all three species. For the giant kangaroo rat and blunt-nosed leopard lizard, the Panoche region may represent the limit of their distribution in the north range. For the kit fox, the Panoche area likewise constitutes the most northerly core population. The Panoche populations for all three are important on at least three counts: the genetic variability they provide, their ability to sustain the species if other populations die off, and the potential for growth and range expansion as recovery proceeds. And while I'll concede that, no, construction of the solar facility will not in and of itself cause the imminent extinction of any species, it will make the long-term prospects for each that much more tenuous and recovery that much more difficult. I know of no wildlife biologist worth his or her salt that would argue otherwise. Any who would must have, like Robert Johnson, sold their soul to the devil at the junction of two country roads, not in the Mississippi Delta but at the junction of Panoche Road and Little Panoche Road.

I'd like to believe both wildlife agencies will emphatically reject the permit request, drop-kick it into the trash and never let it see the light of day. They certainly have the grounds to do so, and they have the science on their side. But I'm not holding my breath. Rather, I fear they will ultimately issue those permits, reaching some heinous compromise. They might insist the project be scaled back and cover less acreage. Or, they might approve it if adequate mitigation was purchased. The concept of mitigation is good in theory and is written into some of our best environmental laws. Basically, if someone wants to develop an environmentally valuable area, they are required to compensate by buying (or purchasing conservation easements for) another similar property agreed upon in advance. The properties thus purchased are to be protected in perpetuity and often are larger than the developed property. It sounds great: developers get their projects and atone for the loss of habitat by funding the protection of other lands. But in practice, mitigation rarely lives up to its lofty goals. Often, the agreed-upon mitigation lands turn out to be much less environmentally valuable than the lands impacted by the project. In 2009, Solargen offered to purchase some nearby habitat as mitigation for the project, but the lands they offered were of little use to the listed species. They had to go back to the drawing board. In the final environmental impact report, they proposed something considerably more substantial: two ranches covering twenty-three thousand acres in the southern part of Panoche Valley. One of those, the Silver Creek Ranch, has been highly coveted by both state and federal wildlife agencies as a conservation property.

In the eyes of some, that should be enough to compensate for the loss of five thousand acres in Panoche Valley. But not to me and not, I hope, to the California Department of Fish and Wildlife and the US Fish and Wildlife Service. Here's why: because the Panoche Valley is too important to be compromised, even if you can permanently protect over half the valley in one fell swoop. Let's say you keep $100,000 stashed in a suitcase in your attic. Your brother-in-law arrives, takes thirty thousand for himself, and places the rest in a bank account under your name, to permanently protect it from fire, thievery, or what have you. I don't know how you'd feel, but rather than feeling seventy-thousand was secure, I'd feel like I just lost thirty grand. As far as Panoche Valley is concerned, the entire area should be protected and off-limits to the impacts of energy development, clean or otherwise. Solargen/Duke can go somewhere else.

If not Panoche Valley, where else can the project go? Panoche Valley is hardly the only sizable parcel of flat, sun-drenched land in central California. To the east lies the San Joaquin Valley, chock-full of such places. One area in particular stands out: the Westlands CREZ. Comprising thirty-three thousand acres straddling the border of Fresno and Kings Counties, the area provides habitat for no endangered species. Westlands CREZ was taken out of agricultural production for its own good. Decades ago, when canals and aqueducts delivered water from the rivers of Northern California to the parched lands of the west side of the San Joaquin Valley, it enabled people to grow crops where they otherwise could not. The Westlands Water District was formed to allocate and administer that water. But there was a price to pay for turning the desert green. The west side of the San Joaquin Valley has an unforgiving geology, an impenetrable layer of clay just below the surface. Repeated irrigation increases the concentration of salts and minerals in the soil because the hard clay layer won't permit them to leach down deeper. Over time the soil becomes saltier, and, in some cases, toxic, if minerals such as selenium are present. Thousands of acres have been taken out of production due to this, including the Westlands CREZ. In case you're wondering, CREZ stands for Competitive Renewable Energy Zone.

If the Westlands CREZ and the solar project seem like a match made in heaven, well, so did Rock Hudson and Doris Day. Solargen/Duke claim to have looked into the area as a potential site but found it inferior to Panoche. For one thing, Westlands lacks transmission towers. Most importantly, the two parties could not agree on a price for the land. Supposedly, the property was going for between $15,000 and $25,000 per acre, which seems like an awful lot for deteriorated, out of commission farm land miles from any suburban or industrial development. I don't know how much Solargen agreed to pay for land in Panoche Valley, but it was probably considerably lower.

The recent judicial ruling maintained that, despite its environmental pluses, the Westlands CREZ was not a reasonable alternative. Besides the higher cost of land and lack of transmission towers, the judges ruled against the site because Solargen/Duke would have to go through the permit process again, incur additional expenses, and have no guarantee of being approved by Fresno and Kings Counties. The judges also stated that, because San Benito County, the permitting agency, would derive no benefit from a plant built in another county, the Westlands site was not a viable alternative. So, while the Westlands CREZ may be both a logical and an environmentally responsible site for a massive solar project, the chances of this project relocating there are, unfortunately, remote.

After reviewing the intricacies of the Panoche solar case, I find myself stepping back and taking in a bigger picture. As I do, one simple question begs asking: Why can't we take the time to do it right? We have a long history of botched land use decisions, acting quickly and rashly when we ought to have been slower and prudent. As a result, we clear-cut forests, suppressed fires we ought to have left burning, insisted on farming poor soils, siphoned water out of rivers to slake the thirst of people living in deserts, erected dams in national parks, allowed development in flood-prone areas and fire zones, and promoted sprawl. You'd think that with over a century of hindsight, we would have learned a lesson or two about planning in advance, especially when it comes to renewable energy. I'm not insisting we rethink solar power, as many have suggested, and explore rooftop solar and a decentralized power system (much as I'd love to see that). No, I can tolerate a behemoth, centralized, corporate-structured system. Why, it's the American Way. We just need to do it better. It's not 1950 anymore. We recycle everything these days, except land. To allow an industrial-size energy project—a renewable energy project, no less—to be built atop crucial wildlife habitat when hundreds of thousands of acres of abused agricultural land sit nearby gives new meaning to the term irresponsible.

There's plenty of culpability to go around, starting with the San Benito County Board of Supervisors. At this point, after years of head-scratchingly poor decisions covering a wealth of issues, bashing the board is too easy, like striking a piñata without wearing a blindfold. But the board deserves it because it continues to sell its natural heritage down the river for fanciful promises of jobs and revenue. In fairness, however, San Benito County's supervisors are little different than those elsewhere. They're the result of a dysfunctional system that pits cities against cities, counties against counties, and states against states in an atmosphere where there's little incentive to cooperate on regional issues.

The recent judicial opinion also deserves criticism. The judges repeatedly invoked the best interests of the public in their ruling against Save Panoche Valley, maintaining that clean energy, job creation, and the economic benefits of the plant take precedence over preserving Panoche Valley as wildlife habitat. Fair enough. Yet they accepted Solargen's glowing estimates of the amount of money the project would pour into local coffers and the number of jobs it would create at face value, while subjecting the arguments of Save Panoche Valley to intense scrutiny. The judges were also quick to dismiss the Westlands CREZ as a viable alternative site. Yes, it's sixty miles away from San Benito County, the land is more expensive and the project would have to go back to square one. So be it. Better that than reward a poor decision, as they ultimately did, simply because Solargen spent a lot of time and money on it. Solargen must have known, going in, that the Panoche Valley site was going to be highly controversial and would face stiff opposition and litigation. Yet they chose to pursue it anyway. For that, they deserve no reprieve.

Further admonishment goes to the environmentalists who would write off Panoche Valley in the name of green energy. As one so succinctly put it, "You can't save every lizard." That statement reveals the misunderstanding that so many have about the plight of rare species and the struggle to keep development out of prime habitat. Left with as little as 1 percent of its original habitat intact, it's less a question of saving every lizard than saving any lizards. We've already ransacked 99 percent of the territory they once had; the blunt-nosed leopard lizard has sacrificed enough for our often mercurial visions of progress. So, no, you can't save every individual lizard, but you sure as hell can save the species, and because you can, you should. After all, there's nothing green about habitat destruction.

Finally, there is Solargen/Duke, who have stared at the sun so long they see green everywhere. Consider this quote that appeared on their website: "We invest in large environmental mitigation projects to set aside land for permanent sanctuary from development." How noble. I think I'll give it a try: "I give eight thousand dollars annually to support a wide variety of local causes, from education to law enforcement, libraries, and parks." Makes me sound like a regular Saint Joseph. But if I told you the truth—that I was doing so simply by paying my property taxes—my halo would suddenly seem a little rusty. Solargen's lofty claim of funding land preservation is no act of altruism, or even an act of goodwill—it's mandated by environmental laws, and they can't build without doing so. A more accurate statement would read like this: "Environmental laws force us to atone for the damage we do by requiring that we protect other lands from developments such as ours."

Another gem: "Environmental sensitivity is at the core of Solargen Energy's values. Our solar projects are designed to have minimal environmental impact."

This from a company doing all that it can to construct their project on five thousand acres of vital habitat for three endangered species. This from a company that rejected the Westlands site—a renewable energy zone, for heaven's sake—in order to build on some of the most important endangered species habitat in the entire region. This from a company that continued to lobby for constructing their plant in Panoche Valley even after the biologists they hired to prepare an environmental impact report stated that the effects of construction on the three endangered species would be unavoidable and unmitigable. If environmental sensitivity is at the core of their values, I shudder to think what they'd propose if it was on the periphery.

We're both looking at the same thing, Solargen/Duke and I, yet I'm not sharing their vision. They're seeing green, but I'm seeing red.

Where Have All The Foxes Gone?

Hope Versus Logic on the Peripheral Range of the San Joaquin Kit Fox

THE BIOLOGY DEPARTMENT at San Jose State University is situated in Duncan Hall, a concrete multistory edifice near the southeast corner of campus. The building has all the charm of a Motel 6, its stairwells dark and musty, its lengthy hallways nearly windowless. Besides furnishing classroom space, Duncan Hall houses the department's specimen collection, and because it does, I can overlook the lack of ambiance. On the fifth floor, there's a room known to biology teachers and students as the Head Room. Its walls are adorned with the mounted heads of big-game mammals from around the world—caribou from North America, wild sheep from Europe, and antelope from Africa, all donated by a generous patron. Tucked inside the cabinets below is an equally impressive collection of mammal specimens from California—stuffed skins of bats, shrews, and rodents; all kinds of skulls; and hides of numerous fur bearers. In my hand I'm holding what I consider the crown jewel of the collection, not only for what it is, the pelt of a San Joaquin kit fox, but for where it was collected—Hollister. It was taken in 1966, on a ranch just east of town. As far as I know, it is the only one ever taken from the Santa Clara Valley, the one, the only, and in all likelihood the last, for it seems as if, today in 2013, the San Joaquin kit fox no longer exists there.

Kit foxes are inhabitants of arid lands throughout the Southwest, adapted to life in a harsh land of heat and little water. Their discovery came rather late; C.

Hart Merriam offered the first taxonomic description of the species in 1888. In 1902, Merriam recognized the San Joaquin kit fox (*Vulpes macrotis mutica*) as one of three subspecies, the other two being the long-eared kit fox (*Vulpes macrotis macrotis*) and the desert kit fox (*Vulpes macrotis arsipus*). Unfortunately, the long-eared kit fox was not long for this world; it inhabited coastal plains south of Los Angeles, and habitat loss drove it to extinction by 1903. Today, the desert kit fox persists from the Mojave Desert of California south into Mexico, east into West Texas, and north into the Great Basin of southeastern Oregon and southern Idaho. The San Joaquin kit fox has a much more restricted range, a California endemic found only in the San Joaquin Valley and outlying areas.

Long ago, they must have been common, especially in the southwest portion of the valley, the San Joaquin Desert. There's an account of a trapper harvesting one hundred in a week along a twenty-mile by two-mile area in western Fresno County in 1919, yet by 1930, the era of abundance was over. Joseph Grinnell, the eminent zoologist, was the first to attempt to document the range of the San Joaquin kit fox in his 1937 volume *Fur-Bearing Mammals of California*. Tellingly, he included both a current and historical range map, an acknowledgment, perhaps the first, that the range of the fox was shrinking and its numbers waning.

While Grinnell's historical map had the fox ranging from the southern end of the San Joaquin Valley north to Tracy and La Grange, his contemporary map, circa 1930, showed a range reduction, with the fox disappearing north of Los Banos. He attributed the demise to a host of factors. One was habitat loss, for between 1900 and 1930 much of the northern range was converted to row crops and orchards. Fur trapping took its toll, as did varmint hunting and poisoning. By the 1930s, the fox was in decline, but no one took notice. No one knew how many remained, and for the next thirty years, no one bothered to find out.

That changed in 1967, when the San Joaquin kit fox became one of the first species protected under the Endangered Species Act. That drew attention to the long-neglected fox, ushering in an era of studies and surveys that continues today. In the 1970s, the California Department of Fish and Game decided to reevaluate the range of the San Joaquin kit fox, and when they did, the results were unexpected. Kit foxes were turning up in places they hadn't been seen in years: the outskirts of Tracy, eastern Merced County, and eastern Alameda and

Contra Costa Counties, locales written off by Grinnell nearly forty years earlier. Even more surprising were reports of kit foxes west of the San Joaquin Valley, beyond the historical range: Camp Roberts and Fort Hunter Liggett in Monterey County, the margins of the Salinas Valley and the low-lying lands surrounding Pinnacles National Monument, in the southern Santa Clara Valley near Hollister, and even in the hills southeast of San Jose.

What accounted for this resurgence? How could a species recently recognized as endangered be expanding its range without any efforts undertaken on its behalf, at a time when habitat loss continued to hammer away at the fox? If anything, fox range and numbers should have continued to shrink.

Some contested the validity of the sightings. Those reported outside the historical range, in habitats such as oak savannah that were never associated with kit foxes, were suspect. They argued that such reports were cases of misidentification, in which gray foxes or juvenile coyotes were mistaken for kit foxes. Identifying a small canine in the fleeting glare of a headlight can be challenging, for young coyotes bear a striking resemblance to kit foxes. Yet misidentifications can't explain away all those reports, for kit foxes were captured, collared, and studied in both eastern Alameda County and Camp Roberts in Monterey County.

So it appeared as if kit foxes had, improbably enough, expanded their range. One researcher theorized that as valley floor habitat diminished, displaced foxes moved to the foothills, scattering north and west where they had never been seen before. Others cited a combination of factors explaining the fox's resurgence. A widespread increase in grazing was believed to have created the low vegetation favorable to kit foxes, opening up new lands and adding quality habitat. Meanwhile, an intense predator control program made enough of a dent in the coyote population to allow kit foxes to increase. This seems to be the most widely accepted theory. Me, I'm partial to another possibility, albeit one with no supporting evidence at all: maybe they were present all along, surviving in low numbers in marginal habitats on the outskirts of their range.

The research that began in the 1960s provided information about the San Joaquin kit fox that can help us better conserve it. We know they have low population densities, so viable populations require large tracts of land. Ideally, those lands should be connected through travel corridors, for young foxes disperse from their natal dens, striking out on their own during their first year. Independence exacts a heavy toll; less than a quarter of those dispersing foxes survive. Even those that do lead short lives—rarely do kit foxes live to the age of five.

Kit foxes are also prone to fluctuations that parallel the up-and-down numbers of the small rodents they prey on. Those rodent populations, in turn, are heavily influenced by rainfall. Dry years mean less plant growth and less food, resulting in less breeding and fewer kangaroo rats. Excessive rainfall, however, produces a similar result, because dense vegetation reduces the quality of habitat and a drop in population follows. As their prey goes, so go the foxes, who struggle in both wet and dry years.

Kit foxes are not scattered evenly throughout the lands they occupy. Shrub habitats and areas where grasses grow even modestly high may not contain foxes. Likewise, they steer clear of steep slopes, occupying level ground instead.

Rather than call a single den home, kit foxes rely on multiple dens throughout their territory, sometimes numbering in the dozens. This dependency on numerous dens restricts them to areas of loose, dry soil. Kit foxes are rare or absent from rocky locations, areas of heavy soil, and places where the water table is high. Dens are usually not dug by the foxes themselves but by rodents. Foxes later appropriate those burrows and modify them to suit their needs.

Research on mortality unearthed one factor that went unnoticed when the fox was listed under the Endangered Species Act. Predation is the leading cause of death for kit foxes, and while a number of species are known to kill them—bobcats, golden eagles, badgers, dogs—one in particular, coyotes, was responsible for over half of all kit fox deaths among studied populations. Coyotes kill kit foxes not for food but to reduce competition. Kit foxes respond by using dens with entrances too small for coyotes to enter, using a number of dens scattered across their territory, avoiding tall grasses and shrubs that limit their ability to detect coyotes, and avoiding slopes in favor of open, level terrain.

Unfortunately, the encouraging range expansions noted in the 1970s have not stood the test of time, for the fox has declined in or disappeared entirely from all of those regions. The number of sightings, so robust in the 1970s, 1980s, and 1990s, had dwindled to a trickle by 2000. Sightings in the Salinas Valley peaked in the 1970s and dropped off later; those near Hollister continued into the 1990s but have stopped. What appeared to be a promising population in eastern Contra Costa and Alameda Counties is apparently no more; the meager handful of reports from 2000 on are probably dispersing stragglers from the south. The situation at Camp Roberts serves as the starkest example. Straddling the boundary between Monterey and San Luis Obispo Counties, the military reservation is a mosaic of grasslands and oak savannah, bearing little resemblance to classic kit fox habitat. Kit foxes were first detected there in the 1960s. The population increased and became the subject of several studies. However, a rapid decline ensued in the 1990s, and the last reported sighting took place in 2003. They are now gone. What happened?

There may be multiple factors explaining the disappearance of the San Joaquin kit fox from the periphery of its range, and the causes may vary from location to location. In Contra Costa County, a ground squirrel eradication program in the 1980s robbed the fox not only of its primary food item but its major source for den sites. The area contains few kangaroo rats, the primary food source throughout most of the foxes' range, and some wondered if kit foxes could exist at all in areas where kangaroo rats were absent or uncommon. But kit foxes will pursue other prey, and in the north, they subsisted largely on ground squirrels. The northern range also features coarser clay soils, making foxes all the more reliant on other species to provide den sites for them. Ground squirrels are nothing if not adept burrowers; their decline led not just to a loss of food but also the loss of shelter from predators. It also echoed ghosts of the past, for widespread rodent control throughout the state, featuring now-banned poisons such as Compound 1080, surely hastened their demise, as foxes lost their prey base, their den sites, and suffered secondary poisoning after eating poisoned rodents.

Rodent control wasn't a factor in the disappearance of kit foxes from Camp Roberts, where the shocking population collapse in the 1990s coincided with a rabies outbreak. Until then, disease had never been implicated in kit fox declines.

Predation surely played a role, but the issue may be more complex than one of coyotes banishing kit foxes from outlying regions. Coyotes were present in all the areas where kit fox range extensions were documented during the 1970s. How did kit foxes manage to colonize new territories in the first place given the presence of coyotes? Some answer by claiming that coyote abundance is a recent phenomenon. According to them, decades of predator control campaigns kept coyote populations suppressed enough to allow kit foxes to increase and extend their range. That a formidable number of coyotes were killed in the region is irrefutable; what I question is how effective those programs truly were. Coyotes are notoriously difficult to eradicate, especially across a large landscape, for when populations decline, females often compensate by producing larger litters. Long-time residents claim that coyotes were less common in the past than they are today. If that's true, is that due to control efforts or widespread land-use changes that have made the countryside more hospitable to coyotes? Specifically, did the spread of farmland and increase in water sources result in more coyotes today than in the past?

The introduction of red foxes further complicated the equation. Red foxes are not native to the lowlands of California; they were released in the Sacramento Valley just before 1900. Today they are widespread. Red foxes here rely heavily on altered landscapes, especially in providing water. Canals, irrigation ditches, and stock ponds have allowed them to thrive in a land that, in its natural, arid condition, would be hostile toward them. Where land conversion went, so went red foxes. Larger and more prolific, red foxes may act as formidable kit fox predators, killing them in acts of interspecific aggression much as coyotes do. This dynamic may be even more intense because red foxes compete not only for many of the same foods as kit foxes but also for den sites. Being smaller than coyotes, red foxes are able to access kit fox dens, so the sanctuaries that kit foxes have long used as protection from coyotes may not help them evade red foxes. Red foxes were first reported in the northern range and at Camp Roberts in the 1970s; they probably arrived in Hollister and the southern Santa Clara Valley at that time as well. This closely coincides with the era in which kit fox distribution was at its height. It's tempting to wonder if the subsequent decline and range contraction of the kit fox has a red fox paw print all over it.

Fortunately, red foxes have yet to colonize the arid natural lands in the heart of kit fox range, and if such areas are left unmodified, they may never. Another bit of encouragement comes from the fact that coyotes kill red foxes with as much gusto as they do kit foxes, so coyotes may yet redeem themselves by keeping red foxes in check. The ultimate effect of having two such intense predators might be that kit fox populations are kept chronically suppressed in the core of their range, preventing them from dispersing and expanding.

A final factor at play in the kit fox saga is the one that is unfortunately as relevant today as it was a hundred years ago, and that is habitat loss. By 1958 it was estimated that the San Joaquin Valley still contained 50 percent of the natural communities it once had. By 1979 that estimate was down to a sobering 7 percent. That number has continued to fall. For a time it was thought that habitat conversion might not be as alarming as some feared. Maybe kit foxes were able to persist in pistachio orchards and melon fields after all. However, subsequent studies revealed that kit foxes merely passed through such areas when moving between natural landscapes. Lacking den sites and prey, such altered landscapes conferred little benefit to them. Even oil fields, which pockmark the southwestern corner of the valley like the face of the moon, turn out to be less favorable habitat than was once believed. While foxes persist there, they do so at reduced densities than foxes on surrounding natural lands. Habitat loss has been chipping away at the San Joaquin kit fox for over a century, and the result of that, besides a massive reduction in the size of kit fox range and overall population, has been extensive habitat fragmentation. As populations become isolated, they are increasingly vulnerable to disappearing one by one, through a variety of factors: inbreeding and the loss of genetic variation, disease outbreaks, food scarcity, and random catastrophes. Habitat fragmentation has chipped away inexorably at a multitude of species, and the San Joaquin kit fox is no exception. In the northern range, considerable effort was spent to preserve kit fox habitat, but by the time those habitats were set aside, the foxes were gone. More troubling has been the loss of foxes from protected areas closer to the heart of their range. Kit foxes, once present on the San Luis National Wildlife Refuge outside Los Banos, have not been detected there in over a decade. On Pixley National Wildlife Refuge, a once extant kit fox population is now gone as well, despite several thousand acres of fully protected habitat. At Pixley, the refuge has become increasingly isolated, the surrounding lands converted to dairy farms and other forms of intensive agriculture. Unless movement corridors can be secured between those areas and intact populations, kit foxes may never return.

Today, the San Joaquin kit fox exists primarily within three core populations. One is in the natural lands of southwestern Kern County, west of Bakersfield. Another is the Carrizo Plain, farther west beyond the Temblor Range. Together, those areas comprise the bulk of what's left of the San Joaquin kit fox population. The third is found one hundred miles north, in the Ciervo-Panoche region. Though that area is similar in size to the other two, it harbors fewer foxes because much of the land there consists of steep terrain inhospitable to kit foxes. Resident foxes persist on flat lands west of Highway 5 and a handful of inter-mountain valleys west of the foothills.

Over the years, the three core areas have allowed kit foxes to establish satellite populations, formed when dispersing foxes successfully colonize new territories. The Camp Roberts population was thought to be just such a satellite, a result of foxes moving in from the Carrizo Plain forty miles east. Likewise, the northern range population of Contra Costa and Alameda Counties was presumably a satellite of the core population in the Ciervo-Panoche region. In order for the core/satellite equation to succeed, the core population must be stable enough to permit excess animals to disperse to other areas. A core can exist without satellites, but the reverse is not true; without a core population, satellites won't become established. Movement corridors are also vital, allowing foxes to move back and forth between core populations and satellites. Between Ciervo-Panoche and the northern range, that corridor is jeopardized west of Los Banos, where habitat alteration threatens to sever the already tenuous connection between the two areas. Already hampered by Highway 5, Highway 152, the O'Neill Forebay of San Luis Reservoir, the Delta-Mendota Canal, and the California aqueduct, migrating foxes must also deal with encroaching orchards and suburban development. In some spots, the corridor seems so narrow that it's hard to see how it exists at all. That doesn't bode well for the future.

There is one place, one bizarrely anomalous place, where kit foxes are bucking the odds and thriving. There, they occur in densities exceeding those in any other location, live longer, and prosper in a way that no other kit fox population does. That place is Bakersfield. There, in vacant lots, school grounds, and golf courses, a sizable population of kit foxes has taken to a highly unnatural environment. Safe from coyotes and able to exploit all kinds of novel food items—pet food, house mice, and garbage—the foxes are doing quite well, despite the threat of becoming road-kill and other risks of city life. The CSU campus harbors dozens of foxes despite a total area of just one square mile. Recently, I took a walk through the campus at dusk. Foxes trotted indifferently like stray cats across the grass while students made their way between classes, each oblivious to the other. Dens dug in the grass were cordoned off, probably to alert the groundskeepers to let them be. In the twilight, I watched a litter of pups cavorting about around a natal den in a small patch of dusty earth and low-lying weeds between the buildings and a parking lot.

I'm not quite sure what to make of the urban foxes of Bakersfield. One the one hand, it's encouraging to know that foxes are doing well there, that they can not only persist but thrive in a landscape that has been completely transformed. It's even been suggested that the Bakersfield foxes could someday serve as a source population if the day ever comes when reintroduction becomes part of the recovery strategy. That's a hopeful thought. Maybe the good folk of Bakersfield will cultivate a proprietary attitude and adopt the kit fox as their own and support its recovery.

On the other hand, the ability of the kit fox to prosper within the heart of Bakersfield—at least for now—might lead people to believe that all is well with the kit fox when it most certainly is not. It may be hard to convince people how imperiled the fox truly is when they see them scrounging at a dumpster behind the Circle K. Likewise, it may prove difficult to get across the importance of preserving natural lands and habitat corridors to people who see foxes denning behind the bleachers at a little league diamond. After all, if those foxes can live in a vacant lot, why can't they live in a solar farm or almond orchard? Hell, why can't they live in other cities?

The answer is that Bakersfield sits beside a core population, from which it has received an influx of foxes over the years. In that, it may not be unique, for smaller towns such as Taft and Coalinga are also situated near core populations and may have foxes residing in their midst. However, in cities removed from core populations, such as Salinas, Tracy, Antioch, and Hollister, there are no urban foxes.

At present it appears that the San Joaquin kit fox has been extirpated throughout the periphery of its range, with only occasional dispersers wandering where once populations existed. The contracted range proposed by Grinnell in the 1930s has become today's reality. Worse, this reduced range, although nearly a million acres in size, is fragmented, and fragmented populations are vulnerable to a laundry list of threats that larger, connected populations are buffered from. Isolation from core populations may explain the puzzling disappearance of kit foxes from otherwise quality habitat. Yet even core populations are not secure. The Ciervo-Panoche population is the smallest of the three and a hundred miles from the others. Though movement between all three core areas is still possible, future land use decisions could sever those and other connections. In the past, the region has weathered plans to construct a behemoth storage reservoir in Los Banos Valley just north of the Ciervo-Panoche area. Currently, a coalition of environmental groups is fighting plans for a sprawling solar energy project in the heart of the Panoche Valley. Meanwhile, both the west Kern County and Carrizo Plain core populations—the last, best hope for the San Joaquin kit fox—are deemed to be vulnerable to extirpation in as little as ten years in a worst-case scenario. Such a scenario could include climate change, for years of abnormally high or low precipitation could decimate prey populations and cause the kit fox population to crash along with them.

Over forty years have passed since the San Joaquin kit fox was listed as an endangered species, and as 2013 comes to a close, the best that can be said about the recovery effort is that the fox is not extinct. If that sounds like damning with faint praise, so be it. The US Fish and Wildlife Service, tasked with overseeing the fate of endangered species, managed to slow the decline of the kit fox but not advance it toward recovery. This is troubling because the fox has been earmarked as an umbrella species, one whose recovery would enhance that of many listed species sharing similar habitat. So, even if kit fox recovery proves expensive, doing so could be a bargain if other listed species improve along with it. Unfortunately, the service lacks the budget, if not the political will, to truly commit to kit fox recovery.

Driving through cities such as Tracy, Merced, and Los Banos, I'm reminded that those areas were all once kit fox habitat, and while such habitat loss is a shame, it doesn't register deeply with me, perhaps because it's so difficult to imagine those places as natural landscapes anymore. An endless parade of mega-retail chains and a soul-withering scourge of charmless stucco housing tracts have rendered me numb. However, when I stand atop North Chalone Peak and gaze south, over thousands of acres of dry, rolling hills with hardly a building in sight, that's when it hits me. The habitat is there, but the foxes are not, and that's a tragedy much worse than their disappearance from Visalia.

Sometimes I think I live too much in the past, spending too much time and emotion dwelling on things that cannot be changed. It manifests itself acutely when I consider the plight of vanishing animals. I'll scour records, searching locations where those animals were once seen. Then I'll go there. Why, I'm not sure. Maybe, like a visitor to a memorial, I'm paying my respects. In the case of the California grizzly, that makes sense. But for the San Joaquin kit fox, it's something else. Rather than seeking some somber closure, my pilgrimages represent something different—that somehow, in the face of all logic, foxes still persist where they haven't been seen for years. A shard of hope.

Hope—it can possess us, dominate our lives. Hope is a dangerous thing. That's what Red told Andy in *The Shawshank Redemption*. But Andy disagreed. Hope, he countered, was a good thing, maybe the best of things. And when you worry over the fates of rare animals, hope may be the only thing.

According to the specimen tag, the kit fox in Duncan Hall was taken on the Vaca Roja Ranch just east of town. I drove out there at dusk the other night, toward the end of Mansfield Road. The scientist within berated me for this folly. Surely they are gone, and even if they were still miraculously present, my chances of seeing one were lottery-winning thin. Not a wise expenditure of time. I told my inner scientist to shut the fuck up. Excitement welled up inside as I passed the last home lining the road and reached the end. The Vaca Roja Ranch no longer exists; it has changed hands and names over the years. But maybe that was all that changed, for as I stared off to the south and east, I saw a spacious plain followed by a series of rippling hills. In my mind's eye, where hope dwells, I see kit foxes emerging from their dens at dusk, chasing kangaroo rats in the moonlight, giving a wide berth to badgers and ever watchful of coyotes. The land took on a new aura and became wild and beautiful again. Without the foxes, why, it's just another pasture.

Wild Onions For Rebecca

Flowers, Friendship, and the Passing of Time

THE HILLSIDE SOUTH of the house is, for most of the year, a straw-colored grassland. Come winter, rains send fresh shoots upward through the downed wraiths of the dried grasses, a velvet-soft green cloak I appreciate less for its texture or color than for what it portends: the wildflowers of spring. They arrive in the same manner as rain, the first sprinkles being milkmaids (*Cardamine californica*) just after the holidays, then California buttercups (*Ranunculus californicus*) and lowland shooting stars (*Dodecatheon clevelandii*), which appear around Valentine's Day, followed by drops of California violets (*Viola pedunculata*). By March a shower of white popcorn flowers (*Plagiobothrys nothofulvus*) ensues, and by the end of the month, a downpour of color transforms that otherwise ordinary slope into a scene of soul-satisfying beauty. The dark hues of common brodiaea (*Dichelostemma capitatum*), purple sanicle (*Sanicula bipinnatifida*), and miniature lupine (*Lupinus bicolor*) stand as counterpoint to the bright yellow violets and orange California poppies (*Eschscholtzia californica*), while all are enhanced when bird's-eye gilia (*Gilia tricolor*) erupts across the hillside. I've tried taking pictures, but photographs just can't capture it all. You have to be there.

I've tried to cajole friends to see that hillside in its splendor, to no avail, for not only are schedules demanding, but the window of opportunity is mercilessly brief, perhaps a ten-day span when the full spectrum of color paints that slope. So far, I've been the only person taking in the message of that hillside, and what the flowers say to me has much to do with time, friendship, and loss.

Her name was Rebecca, and of the small number of neighbors I've had, she was the one with whom I shared the most in common. In a community where everyone rides ATVs, pickups, or on horseback, Rebecca was the only other person I saw on foot, walking the road for exercise or, more likely, for the sheer enjoyment of being outdoors. With their children off to college, she and her husband left the suburbs for a homestead-size property where they intended to retire. They built a sepia-toned Southwestern-style home, one of those rare houses that managed to feel both grand and welcoming. During my first visit, I noticed a bird feeder hanging from the limbs of an oak, where a black-headed grosbeak had descended to furtively pluck sunflower seeds.

Rebecca asked, "Do you know what kind of bird that is? I just started seeing them a couple of weeks ago, but I never seem to get a good look at them."

Thus, a friendship was born. Thereafter, whenever we'd run into each other, we'd lapse into conversation. We started off talking about wildlife, but gravitated toward flowers when we discovered we each amassed a scrapbook of wildflower photos from our properties. We compared pictures, using Barry Breckling's *Spring Wildflowers of Henry W. Coe State Park* as our guidebook. I'll admit to a little envy here: her property is three times the size of mine, and it had a stream. Yet there were flowers on my property that she'd never seen, two in particular: *Fritillaria agrestis*, a dainty, drooping lily whose blossoms appear briefly at the beginning of March, and peninsula onions (*Allium peninsulare*), a magenta flower that bloomed in April.

It may come as a surprise to learn that not only are there wild onions, but that they produce highly attractive flowers. To think of an onion as something to chop and add to an omelet is to shortchange it; when we think of onions, we're visualizing the bulb, an underground stem surrounded by fleshy, modified leaves functioning as storage vessels. Thousands of years of cultivation have given us the large commercial strains we slice and place on hamburgers. The bulbs of wild onions are considerably smaller but edible nonetheless.

Elsewhere, wild onions are considered a nuisance, relegated to the lowly status of lawn weed. Here they are not. While California boasts fifty or so species of wild onions, I have found just two on my property, scattered in modest stands. Tempted as I may be, I just can't bring myself to harvest even one, for long ago I swore off picking wildflowers. Why, I'm not exactly sure. Perhaps it's because they fade so fast when housed in a vase. Could be I'm afraid that plucking even one would diminish the population. Maybe I just think a flower is more attractive out in a field than propped up on a kitchen counter. Still, those onions aroused my curiosity. How big are the bulbs? How tasty? I imagined myself preparing a batter and frying them. According to Barry's field guide, the ancient Egyptians were similarly enchanted by onions, but they saw in them something more profound than onion rings. To them, the bulb's circular patterns symbolized eternal life.

With the fritillaria blooming in March and the peninsula onions in April, viewing both on the same day wasn't possible. We planned several outings to see those flowers, but March flew by, and with it the opportunity to see the fritillaria. We finally made it out in early April, too soon, though, to see the onions. Still, we made the most of the occasion and saw what flowers we could. We drifted in and out of conversation. At one point, she confided that she had survived a bout with cancer just prior to moving up to the pass.

We planned to return in a week or two, in time for the peninsula onions, yet that hike never materialized. In May I was exploring the creek on Rebecca's property when I came across a pretty, pale-blossomed flower I had never seen before along the banks of the stream. They were onions, in fact, not peninsula onions but clay onions (*Allium unifolium*). I called her; she came down to have a look. I never saw her again.

Summer came suddenly, withering the wildflowers of spring. With the onset of winter, it occurred to me that I had neither seen nor spoken to Rebecca for quite some time, but I had been busy, returning to school. The following spring found me outdoors, but Rebecca was nowhere to be seen. I left phone messages but got no reply. One July afternoon, I was picking up the mail when a neighbor informed me that Rebecca was not expected to last the week. Her cancer had returned with a vengeance and would not be denied. I remember feeling that awful sensation in the pit of my stomach that wells in the wake of unexpected tragedy. I stumbled home, silently asking existential questions for which there are no answers—no satisfying answers, at least. And I'm not quite sure why, but it troubled me that Rebecca never got the chance to see the fritillaria or peninsula onions.

Services were held on a sweltering Saturday, when the only flowers to be found were those adorning memorial bouquets. I would have gladly violated my own rule if I could only have found a peninsula onion to pick in her memory, but they had long since faded.

The following spring I was traveling east on Pacheco Pass, on my way across the Central Valley. Near San Luis Reservoir, a ridge of treeless hills stands east of the highway, rising five hundred feet. As I rounded a bend, a flash of color entered my peripheral vision; glancing up I saw a gorgeous display of wildflowers, one that could represent the month of April in a glossy calendar. Near the top, two dense bands of purple were interspersed by a broad swath of California poppies. With a clear sky and green grass in the background, it was an irresistible blend of four colors converging in one place and time. I had a decision to make. I had my camera. Do I photograph that hillside now, when it may never present itself so incredibly again, or do I return later, when I have no demands on my time? Shooting it now would involve some time-consuming complications: I was on the wrong side of a four-lane highway. I would have to turn around and find a place to pull over. Then I would need to scale the fence and climb the hill. I decided not to. I had somewhere to go, and I didn't want to show up late. I opted to return on the weekend.

Saturday arrived, and I was ready. I had everything planned: I would shoot the hillside in the morning light, then hike to the top and view those flowers up close. I would descend in late afternoon to catch the flowers in the fading light. I was ready. I drove down that highway. I rounded that bend. I looked up at that hillside—but the flowers were gone.

Meet Joe Sparks

The Human Animal in All Its Primal Glory

THERE ARE PEOPLE of character, and then there are simply characters. This is a story of a man who has landed decidedly in the latter camp. Ladies and gentlemen, meet Joe Sparks.

Joe Sparks, I must confess, is not his real name; it is his nickname, bestowed upon him years ago by yours truly. Bearded, burly, and hirsute, Sparks could pass as a lumberjack, construction worker, or hillbilly, depending on the garb. He is a man of many vices, yet not without virtues, the most obvious being a boundless sense of humor. Bawdy, ribald, and thoroughly unpretentious, for Sparks there is no movie too asinine, no joke too tasteless, no cow too sacred to be sacrificed on the altar of humor. Not only unabashedly politically incorrect, Sparks possesses a sixth sense, an uncanny ability to locate and push the buttons of those around him, which he does with great relish. Not that all his humor is provocative. Shortly after seeing one of the Austin Powers movies, he spoke in a Scottish accent for several months, enthralled by the Fat Bastard character. He and I have been known to converse for hours on end in pirate-speak, using the term "scalawag" with greater frequency than anyone this side of the eighteenth century and, in the process, confusing the hell out of several coworkers for whom English is a second language. Together we've had some memorable adventures.

It was Memorial Day weekend during the first year of the pond study in Coe Park, and there were three ponds I planned to survey. Earlier in the week, Sparks asked if I had any weekend plans. When I told him I would be surveying, he asked to tag along. I usually try to talk people out of accompanying me on my survey jaunts; there's a lot of walking, a lot of wading (for me), and a long day in the field. Joe Sparks was one of the few people I knew who might not mind such an excursion.

We drove to the southern section of the park, and left the car at Dowdy Ranch. Morning fog draped the hills, and while waiting for it to dissipate, we hiked to the top of Burra Burra Peak. As the fog lifted, we dropped down to the first of the ponds. I entered the water with my dip net, while Sparks alternately snoozed, snapped photographs of the countryside, or peered into the distance with binoculars. This same scenario was repeated at the second pond. The last pond proved problematic, for it was not depicted on the official park map. As a result, I was forced to rely on my backup map, a 1987 version that was fast becoming obsolete. Unfortunately, it provided scant detail regarding trails, roads, peaks, and contour lines, and its scale was woefully small. Relying on that map to find pond P-19 would be an adventure.

We bushwhacked through drying grasses and scattered brush, following game trails. Unfortunately, the canyon below was cloaked in dense vegetation that hid whatever body of water might lie there. I led us down the ravine, praying the pond would reveal itself. It didn't. We doubled back and tried the next ravine. The morning fog was by now a distant memory, for it was past noon and the sun was shining in full ninety-degree force. I'm not one for hiking in heat, but if there is one person even less inclined, it's Sparks, who by that time was sweating profusely. I knew it was only a matter of time before there would be hell to pay.

"I can't believe it," Sparks began, "nature boy got us lost in his own backyard!"

"We're not lost," I tersely replied.

"The man who tells direction from moss growing on trees, by which side of the hill squirrels dig their holes, has gotten us lost. Boy, you really screwed the pooch this time. They'll probably find our bleached bones sometime after Labor Day."

"We are not lost. In fact, I know exactly where we are."

"Right. That's why we've been walking in circles for the past half hour. You just can't admit a mistake, can you? Vanity, thy name is Joseph. Why can't you just admit that you have no fucking clue where this pond is?"

"That depends on what your definition of *is* is," I responded in my best Clintonian drawl. "The pond is in the Pacheco Creek drainage about half a mile west of the creek. I'm just not one hundred percent certain which ravine it's located in."

I thought I had acquitted myself rather nicely, but Sparks was having none of it.

"I can't believe I skipped the Adrienne Barbeau Film Festival for this!" he sputtered.

At that precise moment, an involuntary shudder surged down my spine as I envisioned a dimly lit theater in some cash-strapped Central Valley town full of forty-something-year-old men ogling scenes from the director's cut of *Swamp Thing*, pervishly fixated on the buxom costar of *Maude*. Before additional details of that vision sank in, I spotted the mystery pond in the distance. I resisted the urge to gloat, for just beyond lie Kaiser-Aetna Road, the very road we drove in on. The sight of this only gave Sparks more to rant about, as he cackled loud and long about how we should've stuck to the road in the first place.

After surveying, Sparks remained in a foul mood, lying prostrate on the side of the road in the shade of an oak. I told him I'd get the truck, pick him up, then head into town for some pizza. Upon my return, Sparks was a new man. Something had revitalized him—the promise of pizza or perhaps teenage memories of Ms. Barbeau, San Jose's own. I arrived to find him line dancing alone, warbling "Sympathy for the Devil," replete with backing vocals. After I herded him into the car, we proceeded toward Gilroy, an hour away. I turned on a CD, *Surfacing*, by Canadian songstress Sarah McLachlan.

"Sweet Sarah," Sparks opined. "You'd have to travel far and wide to find a woman like that."

"Damn right," I replied. "She's got it all: creativity, social consciousness, beauty, not to mention a voice that would arouse the envy of the saints. I can't *believe* she was teased in high school. I would *never* tease Sarah."

Sparks looked at me slightly askance but said nothing. The song "Building a Mystery" was playing, and its most provocative line pulsed through the speakers: "*You're a beautiful...a beautiful, fucked-up man...*"

"She even *swears* like an angel!" I gushed.

"You know, she could've been thinking about *me* when she wrote that," Sparks bragged.

"*You??* Please! You're just fucked up. I think if you listen to the song in its entirety, even you would agree that *I* would serve as a more apropos subject of that song."

"You? You're neither fucked up nor beautiful!"

"That's not the point! You've got to absorb the *gestalt* of the song. She's describing a complex man, a human paradox, an enigma wrapped in a riddle slathered in intrigue, topped with a certain *je ne sais quoi...*"

"Right! You're about as mysterious as a grilled cheese sandwich!"

"Oh, I beg to differ, mister! Think about it: by day I'm a warehouse worker, but at night I'm a budding conservation biologist. During the week, I'm a mild-mannered laborer, stacking cases of bottled water, but on weekends I'm surveying for endangered species with an official government-issued permit."

"You mean you've got that alter ego action going."

"Bingo! You are learning well, grasshopper!"

"So what you're saying is, you go *way* beyond Thomas Crown. You're like Batman or Jethro, when he couldn't decide between becoming a brain surgeon or a soda jerk!"

For the next ten minutes, we engaged in an unmemorable argument over which of us would best serve as Sarah McLachlan's muse and live-in lover. Then we lapsed into silence. After several minutes, Sparks changed the subject.

"You seein' anybody?"

"Nope."

"Don't tell me you're still hung up on that actress." He was of course referring to Sean Young, the versatile siren who graced the silver screen in *Blade Runner* and also figured prominently in *Stripes* and *No Way Out.*

"Her name is Sean Young, and I am *not* hung up on her."

"Yeah, Sean Young, the psycho!"

"Bite your vile tongue! Where do you get off uttering such slanderous blasphemy?"

"I heard it on Howard Stern. He had James Woods on, who used to date her, until he broke it off. After he dumped her, she began stalking him. He had to get a restraining order! What a wacko!"

"Well, there you go—Howard Stern. Now there's a source of accurate information, a modern-day Walter Cronkite. And James Woods! I have a hard time believing they were ever a couple to begin with—talk about beauty and the beast—let alone that he dropped her. Actor, my ass! He's like Denis Leary and Tommy Lee Jones, playing the same character over and over. His specialty is slimeballs: drug dealers, Nazis, that segregationist murderer Byron de la Beckwith. None of those roles are much of a stretch for him. He even looks like a Nazi! The hell with Werner Klemperer; he should've played Colonel Klink on *Hogan's Heroes* or Fearless Leader in *Rocky and Bullwinkle*. And he's not just ugly on the outside. He's ugly on the inside, too. What kind of man kisses and tells, opening his big mouth to a nationwide audience? I would *never* kiss and tell on Sean."

Sparks looked at me askance before replying. "Well, it's good to know she's in your rear view mirror. I'm gonna tell you something right here and now that someone should've told you a long time ago: forget all those famous women—Kate [Winslet], Salma [Hayek], Ashley [Judd], Mira [Sorvino], Monica [Bellucci]—none of them will ever look twice at you. Ever! What *you* need is a mountain woman, a lady who's not afraid of snakes, who'll follow you up hills and down canyons, who drinks, chews tobacco, can cook a screamin' pot of chili, eat it all in one sitting, then let one rip afterward, a woman who can suck the leather off a saddle horn…"

His description of a dream woman for me started with potential but plummeted in a hurry. In fact, the longer it went on, the more it disturbingly seemed to describe him rather than any woman I'd ever met, though I can't vouch for the saddle horn comment.

"Don't you worry about me, Sparks. There's a method to my madness. My credo is this: never become involved with a rising star. Too much narcissism. Let them date actors, rock stars, and athletes and get it out of their system. Let them become jaded to the Hollywood scene and figure out there's more to life. That's where I jump in. Better to catch a falling star or an angel with clipped wings, which is why I've set my sights on Winona!"

"Wynonna Judd, the singer?"

"No."

"Winona LaDuke, the activist?"

"No."

"Who, then? I don't know no other Winonas!"

"Yes, you do…Winona Ryder, the…

"The klepto! Yeah, now I see your MO! Fallen stars is right! You went from a psycho to a klepto!"

Sparks was referring to allegations that the lovely Ms. Ryder had recently attempted to leave a swank department store without paying for an item or three. I hastened to restore Winona's good name.

"Those are unfounded rumors and innuendo! Whatever happened to innocent until proven guilty? I would *never* convict Winona, even in the dubious court of public opinion, without hearing her side of the story."

Once again, Sparks looked at me askance.

"Never mind that; what I want to know is, how the hell are you ever going to meet Winona Ryder?"

"I've got it all worked out. Some hanging judge with political aspirations will sentence her to community service at a location far removed from any ritzy shopping mall. They'll distance her from the temptations of trendy LA and try to scare her straight at a more remote location. I expect to see her picking up trash along Pacheco Pass Highway any day now."

"I thought you said she was innocent?"

"You know how it is with celebrity justice—it's either the penthouse or the outhouse. Most of 'em get off scot-free, while a lesser number are made examples of."

"And that would be Winona's fate?"

"Precisely. I imagine I'll soon see her in Day-Glo orange, daintily mopping her brow along the side of the road as I retrieve the mail. A mildly flirtatious conversation ensues; a dinner invitation is proffered; I envision a repast involving my own home-made chicken pot pie, asparagus, and peaches from Sweet Home Ranch, with Gizdich Ranch olallieberry pie for dessert. Afterward, we'll adjourn to separate rooms, where we'll each analyze *American Pie* verse by verse, emerging later to compare results. We'll cap that off with a spirited discussion of the habitat requirements for the silvery legless lizard!"

"I see you're a great believer in spontaneity. Why should she date a self-absorbed bore like Johnny Depp when you can sweep her off her feet with lizards and old pop songs?"

"What?" My concentration had shifted as I turned into the parking lot of the pizza parlor.

"I said good luck with that one."

With that, we went in and ordered a giant pepperoni. Several years have elapsed since then, and I have to admit I've pretty much abandoned any hope of coming across Winona Ryder. They must have sentenced her to work along Hecker Pass instead. Oh well. Thank God for Janeane Garofalo!

Several years ago, Sparks and I decided to take an abbreviated fishing trip to the east slope of the Sierras. I had long been familiar with the West Walker River, where my father had taken me fishing when I was a boy. As an adult, I returned every couple of years or so. In truth, neither Sparks nor I were dedicated anglers; fishing became secondary to venturing out onto one of the most scenic landscapes in the country.

Our trip would be brief—a weekend outing. We left early Saturday morning, and arrived at our destination shortly after noon. Our plan was to fish Saturday afternoon, camp Saturday night, fish Sunday morning, and head home Sunday afternoon.

Instead of choosing a site in any one of several forest service campgrounds nearby, I decided to camp in solitude on national forest land at a spot called Little Walker cow camp, a dilapidated outpost that consisted of little more than a forlorn, abandoned cabin and some corrals that had seen better days. A humble dirt road blazed through a sea of sagebrush led us to this impromptu campsite in a meadow above the gurgling banks of the Little Walker River. We decided to fish first and set up camp later.

Although it was mid-September and the aspens were cloaking the distant slopes in stunning shades of yellow, summer was far from a memory, for the afternoon temperature approached ninety degrees. Before setting out, I put on some sunblock. This simple act was sufficient to arouse the ire of Sparks.

"I can't believe you, of all people, bought into that scam!"

"What scam?"

"That sunscreen bullshit."

"What have you got against sunblock?"

"The skin is a living organ, man! It wasn't meant to be slathered in make-up, gels, or lotions, especially that crap! Check out the label. Think of all those chemicals entering your body through your pores."

This he explained between drags on a cigarette.

"All right, so maybe you don't get skin cancer, but God knows what those chemicals will do to you. What'll you do ten years from now when you grow a third nipple and your balls glow in the dark?"

"Maybe I'll get a job with the circus and hike at night without a flashlight! Woo-hoo! Hey, I just want to avoid a sunburn."

"That's your problem right there, mister. It's your attitude. You gotta pay to play, buster. No pain, no gain. You gotta get that sunburn out of the way, get your skin used to the sun. After that, you build up tolerance. Look at me: I may burn today, but by tomorrow afternoon, I'll be bronze, like a Greek god!"

As if to prove his point, Sparks defiantly removed his long-sleeved shirt and ventured out in a tank top. With that, we made our way toward the river, each heading in a different direction. We agreed to meet back at the car in time to set up camp before heading to Bridgeport for dinner. We weren't about to depend on catching our supper. For my part, I had long ago become a catch and release angler. As for Sparks, I had a suspicion he spent as much time dozing as he did fishing. I spent the afternoon taking in the scenery, including birds rarely seen in the Diablo Range. Yellow-headed blackbirds cackled near a small wetland, a snipe flushed in front of my feet along the grassy banks of the river, and a pair of nighthawks cavorted over a plateau of sagebrush in the clear light of the afternoon.

Upon my return, I was surprised to see no trace of Sparks. I had been gone several hours, and neither of us had eaten all day. It wasn't like Sparks to be late for a meal. Above the melody of running water, I heard the unmistakable rumblings of a snore. Following the sound to its source, I hesitantly entered the long-neglected cabin. The front door had long since disappeared, and the windows no longer held glass. The makeshift kitchen counter was stained in unsanitary hues of brown and yellow, while rodent droppings—I presumed those of woodrats—were piled high in corners and in the open compartments of a defunct refrigerator. In the corner of the room lie the remains of what was once a bed. It was absent of sheets, with a mattress pee-stained and ravaged by rodents, and springs perforating through here and there. On top of this rested our hero, the only person I know who would willingly recline on such a surface.

"What the hell are you doing there? Are you *trying* to contract hantavirus?"

"Just gettin' me some shut-eye."

He was indeed a sight for sore eyes. His hair was contorted in a manner for which the English language has no adequate adjectives; our bronzed Greek god was definitely a work in progress, presently as pink as a boiled crustacean.

"By the way, which Greek god are you? You look like Hades. C'mon, let's set up camp."

That would not take very long, for we had packed lightly, as befitted a one-night trip. Evidently, some of us were packed lighter than others, for Sparks simply unfurled a sleeping bag on the ground before ambling in my direction. I was setting up my tent when he approached.

"A tent? What a puss! Real men sleep under the stars! What else did you bring?"

He began rummaging through the small set of items I brought until he spied the small metal spade next to a roll of toilet paper.

"What the hell is that?" he asked condescendingly.

"It's the li'l partner."

"Little partner? Isn't that what the skipper used to call Gilligan? Y'know, I think the old skipper had a little sugar in his tank—why else would he keep that useless imbecile around?"

"First of all, it's not little partner. It's *li'l* partner. Also, the skipper referred to Gilligan as little buddy."

I was mildly irritated that Sparks had dredged up memories of what was perhaps the most inane program in the annals of television and more disturbed still that my mind recollected such brain-corroding trivia.

"What's it for?"

"Digging," I replied tersely, hoping futilely to change the subject.

"I gather that. What kind of hole could you possibly dig with that sorry excuse of a shovel?"

"A cathole."

"A cathole? What in the name of Jesus H. Christ is a cathole?"

"A cathole is what a cat digs in order to bury its droppings."

"Why do *you* need to dig a cathole?"

It had been a long day; perhaps the sun had gotten to Sparks and left him unusually slow on the uptake.

"Haven't you ever heard of that book *How to Shit in the Woods*?"

"Yeah, but I didn't read it. I'm waiting for the movie to come out."

"When you answer the call of nature, you're supposed to select a site at least a hundred yards from a stream, lake, or spring, dig a hole at least half a foot deep, and use that as a latrine, covering it completely when you're finished."

Sparks stared at me briefly as if I had just declared myself eligible for the NBA draft before bursting into a long, loud fit of laughter. In between guffaws, he proclaimed, "I've heard it all...I've fucking heard it all! That's your problem right there! You have rules for everything, even taking a dump! You're like those religious fanatics. No wonder you're such a mopey, miserable bastard, what with your little partners, catholes, one hundred yards...I'll bet you even have your own breeding season, say, between April and June, but only on evenings with a waxing crescent moon!"

I knew the l'il partner would not be well received. After another round of one-man laughter subsided, we piled into the car and headed south toward the small town of Bridgeport, twenty miles away. Just south of town stood a little restaurant on the side of the highway where we planned to indulge ourselves. We arrived early, and the restaurant had only a handful of patrons inside. A cordial waitress handed us each a menu.

"Look, they even have Caesar salad..." Before I could even complete the sentence, I realized I had made a horrible blunder. I desperately wished I could retrieve the six words I had just uttered, but it was too late. Years ago, the warped mind of Joe Sparks had flexed its creativity by noticing the similarity in pronunciation between the name of that most famous of Roman emperors and the words "seize her." For a decade, we worked side by side in a grocery warehouse, handling packaged salads daily, and every time he spotted a case of Caesar salad he would utter his homespun mantra as faithfully as if he were Poe's raven. It was one thing to do this in the relative privacy of the workplace; it was quite another to do so in public. Unfortunately, that behavior had become hard-wired in his brain, for my untimely mention of the word Caesar had triggered a Pavlovian response with which I was all too familiar.

"Caesar!" he began in a low, sinister whisper, while sporting a wicked smile and rolling his hands over and over in anticipatory glee. "*Seize*-er," he continued, emphasizing the word "seize" by drawing it out. "*Seize her!*" he implored at a fever pitch, his whisper louder and ever sharper. I braced myself for the embarrassing denouement. "*Seizeherenormousboobs!*" My only hope for salvation lie in that Sparks rasped that penultimate statement in such rapid-fire succession, and so blurred the words, that the atrociously juvenile comment went undetected. There we were, with beet-red faces, his due to sunburn, mine to shame. Thankfully, it appeared as if no one had noticed the impromptu performance. The waitress returned and took our orders. I had the good sense to order a house salad with my meal.

After we finished off a hearty dinner, the sun was sinking on the horizon as we headed back. Unfortunately, I would not long enjoy the scenery due to acute discomfort of a most personal nature. Out of nowhere, a civil war had erupted in my digestive tract, and it was not long before I found myself in the kind of agony you wouldn't wish on your worst enemy, or even Dick Cheney. Worse still, to endure this in the presence of Sparks, who could perceive misery like a shark detects a drop of blood in the ocean, would seem a bitter fate. I was fervently hoping that Sparks, a borderline narcoleptic, would continue napping all the way back to camp. Beads of sweat formed on my forehead; I gripped the steering wheel like a man suspended from the ledge of a skyscraper. The pain was intense; I was holding up well until I uttered a barely audible groan. Unfortunately, that was enough to rouse Sparks out of his brief slumber, and he seemed to know exactly what was going on.

"Oh, the pain, the pain!" he warbled, not in empathy or concern but in wicked humor, imitating Dr. Zachary Smith, the prissy, treacherous stowaway on *Lost in Space*. I drove ever faster, trying my best to ignore him as he uttered disparaging remarks about the li'l partner. Finally, we arrived back at camp, but I was far from out of the woods. Had I been alone, I could simply have walked a short distance in order to accomplish the task at hand. In the company of Sparks, however, I wanted to cover a lot of ground in order to do what I had to. I hobbled nearly a quarter mile before I felt I was far enough away. My next task was to find a patch of friable soil. I prayed that this ground, on the edge of the Great Basin, would not consist of the clay soils so prevalent in the Diablo Range, impervious to the shovel unless wet. Thankfully, the ground was suitable for digging, yet excavating an adequate hole was still no walk in the park. In delirium, I cursed the li'l partner, and at that moment, I believe I would've given up my credit card for an honest-to-goodness shovel. About that time I came to the terrifying realization that I could not control myself indefinitely, and at some point, my body would do what it had to. Should this occur in my case, without a change of clothing, I was poised to suffer the worst humiliation since the downfall of Pee-Wee Herman. To my eternal gratitude, that scenario never unfolded. Without going into further detail, the crisis passed without incident. Like Frank Sinatra, I did it my way and returned to camp a new man.

The next morning dawned cold and clear. During the night, the temperature had dropped below freezing, and just before dawn, I awoke to spot Sparks's snoring head protruding from his sleeping bag. He looked like a scuzzy Santa Claus. His beard was covered with frost and festooned with leftover crumbs from last night's garlic bread. I relished the notion of waking him up, and if I had had a trumpet, I'd have done my damnedest to blow reveille.

"Rise and shine. Up and at 'em. Daylight's burning. Today's the first day of the rest of your miserable life..."

His eyes slowly opened, and he tilted his head sideways in quizzical fashion as if he were a puppy watching his owner take a leak for the first time. We eventually broke camp and drove to our next destination, the West Walker River.

We pulled off Highway 108 onto a dirt road heading toward the river. As we had the day before, we went our separate ways, agreeing to meet back at the car at noon. Upon my return, I was greeted by the sight of Joe Sparks. Besides wearing a goofy grin, he had that look in his eye. He was up to something.

"What's up?" I asked.

"I ran into a little trouble," he volunteered sheepishly. With Sparks, that could mean just about anything. I surveyed the scene, looking for the long arm of the law. To my relief, we were alone.

"What *kind* of trouble?"

"The kind of trouble you were in last night."

"You had to go to the bathroom?"

"I had to take a dump!" This he proclaimed in a pitiful Scottish accent.

"But…the li'l partner…you…you didn't use the li'l partner!" I stammered.

"Relax, Al Gore. I stayed away from the river. I went up in the sagebrush!"

"In the sagebrush! I *knew* bringing you here was a mistake! For this I'm sure to be excommunicated from the Sierra Club, the Nature Conservancy, the Audubon Society, and God knows who else. I'll be blacklisted!"

Then I realized there were no trees within miles of where we stood, and those closest were pines. The nearest broad-leaved trees were the aspens miles distant and uphill. Without the toilet paper lying next to the li'l partner in the car, he was faced with quite the conundrum.

"What did you use for toilet paper?" At that very moment, I noticed for the first time that his socks were missing. "Hey, what happened to your—"

It was one of those rare moments in life when asking a second question immediately revealed the answer to the first. Before I could even finish the question, his body language told me all I needed to know, as a diabolical ear-to-ear grin spread slowly across his face like an eclipse.

"No! No! Tell me you didn't!"

He merely stood there with an ass crack of a smile.

"What's the matter with you? Why do you go to such great lengths just to be a contrarian? All you had to do was return to the car, grab the li'l partner and the toilet paper, and everything would've been fine. Now look what you've done! That little coprolite you left behind, not to mention your soiled socks, will take ages to break down in this dry, high-desert ecosystem. Why, *you'll* be dead and gone long before they disappear. Some people leave behind works of art, others are remembered for their philanthropy, and then there's you! Do you realize that little souvenir you just deposited will in all likelihood represent your most lasting legacy to your tenure on this planet, your sole accomplishment to stand the test of time, your gift to future generations? Tell me, how does that make you feel?"

I had just delivered my equivalent of the Gettysburg Address, my very own I Have a Dream speech, and I allowed myself to believe that I had finally pierced the incorrigible conscience of Joe Sparks. He certainly looked repentant. Until he spoke.

"Arr, Avast, ye scurvy scalawag! Methinks it be time to set sail, find a tavern with a saucy serving wench, and knock the froth off a couple o' cold ones! Arr!"

Sigh. There are people with character, and then there are characters. Ladies and gentlemen, meet Joe Sparks.

The Man Who Walked Off
The Edge Of The Earth

Ishi and the Era of Solitude, One Hundred Years Later

It's a summer afternoon in 2011, and I'm watching from the porch as my son's car recedes down the hillside, around the bend, and out of sight. My eyes linger at the spot where the taillights disappear, as if doing so could somehow make the car reverse course and return. He was the first visitor I've had this year. The last was in October.

It wasn't supposed to be this way; when I settled in six years ago, I thought I'd have a steady stream of guests. I told friends to drop by whenever they were down this way or give me a call when they had some free time, simple but unspecific invitations. I had few takers. Maybe Pacheco Pass really is that far out of the way, or perhaps people are busy. I was at first too preoccupied to give it much thought, busying myself with one project after another. But during lulls between activities, I found myself behaving differently. I started watching TV during dinner because it suddenly seemed strange and incomplete to eat in silence. I began checking e-mails every day instead of a couple of times a week, and when my phone calls and e-mails weren't returned promptly, I wondered if I had done something wrong. Most of all, it became harder to say good-bye. As these blue, lonesome thoughts swirled around my head that afternoon, I thought of a man who, one hundred years earlier, endured a bout of solitude the likes of which you and I will never know, let alone comprehend.

Early in the morning of August 29, 1911, a man perhaps fifty years of age sat huddled in the corral of a slaughterhouse just outside of Oroville. Several days earlier, for reasons known only to him, he had abruptly left the only land he had ever known—the foothills of Mount Lassen—and wandered into the lowlands forty miles south. As dawn approached, barking dogs betrayed his presence, and soon he was discovered by men working nearby. Clad only in a makeshift canvas poncho, he neither spoke nor understood a word of English. They took him to be some kind of wild man and called the sheriff.

When the sheriff arrived, he could see the man was Native American. He hauled him away peacefully and placed him in a cell in the county jail, not for any offense but for his own well-being. News of the incident traveled quickly, and people began pouring in from miles around to take a look at the wild man of Oroville.

Representatives from two local tribes, Maidu and Wintun, were summoned, and both tried to speak with him but met with no success—he did not respond to their questions, and when he spoke, they found his utterances unintelligible. Yet Maidu and Wintun were not the only tribes in the region, for there was a third, smaller tribe that in its heyday never exceeded a population of several thousand. This was the Yana, who dwelled in the foothills east of the Sacramento Valley. The Yana were further divided into four regional groups: Northern, Central, Southern, and the Yahi, each with its own customs, territory, and dialect.

Newspaper coverage spread quickly and caught the eyes of two anthropology professors, Alfred Kroeber and Thomas Waterman, at the University of California, Berkeley. Waterman was especially intrigued; three years earlier, a party of surveyors had stumbled across a tiny band of natives in a remote canyon to the north, an area from which the Yana were thought to have vanished decades earlier. He suspected the man held captive in Oroville was not only Yana, but possibly Yahi, the southernmost band of Yana. Professor Kroeber sent a telegram to the Butte County sheriff two days later, asking that the captive be transferred to his custody. The sheriff replied promptly, granting that request, so later that day Professor Waterman took a train to Oroville, packing a list of vocabularies from the Northern and Central Yana dialects.

Waterman arrived to find the man besieged by onlookers trying futilely to communicate with him. Waterman entered the cell, sat beside the man, and slowly began reciting words from the Yana vocabularies. It was not until some time had passed that Waterman uttered the word *Suwini*, the term for yellow pine, and a spark of recognition followed. Both men repeated the word over and over, and soon, more words followed. The Northern and Central Yana vocabularies were different from those of the Yahi, but not to the point of being unrecognizable, and Waterman's hunch that the man was Yahi proved correct. Meanwhile, a man of Yana ancestry was recruited to serve as an interpreter once the captive was transferred to the custody of Professor Kroeber. With that, Waterman, the native, and the interpreter boarded a train for San Francisco. They arrived late in the evening, only to confront one of many differences between the Yahi and American cultures. Until that point the man had been referred to in the press as "wild man," "stone age man," or "the last wild Indian," all vague, impersonal monikers. They wanted to know his name. Professor Kroeber explained that among the Yahi, names were private, personal entities and were neither revealed nor uttered publicly. They found that hard to believe, so to silence the throng, Kroeber replied that his name was Ishi, a Yahi word simply meaning "man." Thus, from that day forward, the world knew him as Ishi, and although he responded to that name, he never applied it to himself.

Ishi was housed at the UC Museum in San Francisco, a residence he readily adapted to. Transforming a middle-aged hunter/gatherer into a citizen of an urban industrial society was an acculturation process rife with challenges, yet Ishi was determined to fit into his new world while still retaining the values and customs he grew up with. And although he wanted to fit in, he never behaved like a fawning lackey or a downtrodden member of a subjugated race. He was different; he knew it, but he neither felt nor acted inferior. He was also sociable and curious about the new world he entered and eager to impart knowledge about his culture.

Ishi's contribution to our understanding of Yahi culture was unique, the kind of linguistic and ethnographic information no one else could have provided. True, he was measured, analyzed, and studied like a test subject. For a time he was even put on display at the museum, appearing along with Dr. Kroeber on Sunday afternoons. This was conducted not as a publicity stunt or money-making scheme but as a way to satisfy the growing curiosity of the public. Those responsible for his welfare could have seen him first and foremost as a source of data, an informational bonanza, or even worse, a source of profit. But that's not how it was. Ishi developed a sincere friendship with Kroeber, Waterman, and a handful of others that were part of his everyday life. He may have come into their lives as a one-of-a-kind scientific opportunity, but he left as a friend. His time in their company was far too brief; Ishi contracted tuberculosis in 1915 and died in the spring of 1916, not five years after wandering down from his ancestral homeland.

The details of Ishi's life are wonderfully chronicled in *Ishi in Two Worlds*, by Theodora Kroeber, wife of Alfred Kroeber, and her account provides a compelling portrait of the man. Ishi's story is incredible, all the more so in light of the life he led before mysteriously wandering down to Oroville. I'm not referring to the prodigious knowledge and skill set required to live entirely off the land. No, what most interests me is the poignancy surrounding his existence: he was born into a small group that diminished with each passing year, until the day finally came when he was the only person left in it. The Yana had inhabited the Lassen Foothills for perhaps three thousand years. Unlike tribes along the coast, the Yana were not subjugated by the Spanish during the Mission Era but remained intact and isolated until the Gold Rush. As settlers populated the region, conflicts and hostilities arose. Tribes inhabiting the floor of the Sacramento Valley, such as the Maidu and Wintun, were subdued in short order. The Yana, dwelling in the rugged terrain to the east, did not go down without a fight, and of the four Yana tribes, Ishi's people, the Yahi, or Mill Creeks, as the settlers called them, were the fiercest of all.

Conflicts between the settlers and the Yahi date back to 1849, initially involving livestock. The Yahi did not understand the concept of livestock as property or, for that matter, the existence of domesticated animals. In their world, all animals were wild. In 1850, settlers twice launched attacks on the Yahi in retribution for stock killing. One in spring killed seventeen Yahi, while one in December resulted in a village being burned to the ground. In 1853, spurred by ongoing stock losses, settlers shot or hanged twenty-five Yahi. The Yahi responded by seeking revenge in equally brutal fashion. Meanwhile, the neighboring Yana tribes were dwindling, with many sold into slavery (legal in California until 1861) or prostitution. Disease also took its toll, and loss of territory was inevitable with the arrival of evermore settlers.

As the 1850s came to a close, the Yahi had enjoyed considerable success conducting guerrilla warfare, and settlers began clamoring for the removal of all natives. In response, the federal government established several reservations in the region, but the effort was poorly planned and attempts to relocate natives were futile and tragic. With little faith or trust in the federal government to begin with, settlers formed vigilante groups led by mountain men and Indian fighters. It was into this hostile environment, a time of raiding, warfare, and terror, that Ishi was born.

An 1863 skirmish brought the attention of the United States Army, which promptly botched an attempt to round up all natives in the region and send them to a reservation in Round Valley. In 1864, vigilantes responded to the murder of two white women by nearly clearing the region of all Yana, except the intractable Yahi. At the beginning of 1864, the Northern, Central, and Southern Yana had a combined population of about two thousand. By the end of the year, that number was down to fifty, and none were left living on the land. Only the Yahi remained. But all that had taken a heavy toll on the Yahi. They had lost much of their territory and were driven to areas inaccessible to settlers. As a result, they relied on raiding, both of livestock and food in cabins. Raiding was serious business; raiders risked their lives if caught, and raiding resulted in a continuation of the vicious cycle of retaliation.

The 1865 murder of a white couple led to vigilante retribution. Vigilantes discovered one of the few remaining Yahi villages and invaded before dawn on August 16, killing indiscriminately, in what came to be known as the Three Knolls Massacre. Ishi and his mother were among the few to escape. In 1867, another murder prompted a vigilante reprisal in which thirty-three Yahi were tracked to a cave and killed. The final massacre took place in 1870, and this event did not even have murder as its catalyst. Four cowboys rounding up stock on Lower Mill Creek discovered a broken arrow beside a freshly killed steer. The next day, they used dogs to follow a trail and surprised a band of thirty Yahi at a cave on Upper Mill Creek. All were shot. One of the men felt a twinge of discomfort because his rifle tore up the children too much. Rather than cease firing, he switched to a revolver.

Many settlers believed the Kingsley Cave Massacre put an end to the Mill Creeks, as they called the Yahi. But they were wrong. The bodies of the victims were removed from the cave and cremated by the few remaining Yahi who were not present that fateful morning. This was hinted at later by Ishi, who was understandably reluctant to discuss the incident. He was about ten years old at the time.

Even before the Kingsley Cave tragedy, the Yahi had ceased seeking revenge and raided purely as a means of survival. A year or so after Kingsley Cave, another cattle rustling incident prompted a party of four led by a man named Segraves to track down the stock thieves. They tracked for miles before coming to a village that, though deserted, showed evidence of recently butchered stock. Pressing on, they came upon a small band of Yahi. Segraves did not believe in killing women or children, so after killing one man, they abducted three women. Two weeks later, a group of twelve Yahi, seven women and five men, traveled to the settler's cabin. The leader spoke to Segraves, and his male cohorts each presented him with a bow. Though Segraves understood nothing of what was said, he believed the bows were offered in exchange for the three hostages. He tried to explain that the captives were not housed at his property but were held at a neighboring ranch, which he led them to. His neighbor was not home, but his hired hands were. When one of the workers inexplicably threw a rope over a tree (he claimed he was attempting to weigh himself), the Yahi thought they were about to be hanged and fled. No one knows what became of the three captive women. Thus began what Theodora Kroeber called the era of concealment.

By 1872 the Yahi were down to a single band of about fifteen individuals, including ten-year-old Ishi. Those survivors adopted a lifestyle that enabled them to disappear without a trace, fugitives in their own land. All raiding stopped; they fished, hunted, and gathered food in silence. They lived in camouflaged huts hidden within the vegetation of Upper Mill Creek. Their storage shelters were disguised as shrubs. When walking, they avoided leaving tracks, covered up prints they left behind, and walked through the waters of creeks rather than along the banks. They were careful not to fashion trails, going so far as to travel underneath chaparral and brush like quail, rather than carve a path through. They kept fires small and destroyed evidence of them immediately after. For twelve years, the Yahi lived like this, and they were highly successful. Soon after 1872, they were presumed to have died out. But by 1884, circumstances had changed, and the thorough concealment the Yahi had so assiduously designed was getting harder and harder to maintain. Most of their hunters had died, and even gathering was getting riskier, for the ever-expanding white population was pushing farther into the hills. Out of desperation, the Yahi took to raiding again, knowing that death and retaliation might be the consequences. For the next ten years, they raided when they had to. Once they were caught in the act, but the owner of the cabin was a generous man who not only let them be but allowed them to keep what they had taken. Fortunately, none of those raids resulted in violence.

In 1894, the raiding stopped for good. Twenty-two years after the era of concealment, the group had seen no births, only deaths, and they were down to just five individuals. Those five were Ishi, his mother, an older man who may have been his uncle, a woman who was either his sister or cousin, and a young man unrelated to him. Further encroachment by settlers along Mill Creek had made even that area increasingly risky, so they decided to move to the most inaccessible area remaining in their territory, in Deer Creek Canyon, a spot they knew as *Wowunupo Mu Tetna*, Grizzly Bear's Hiding Place. This final retreat sat five hundred feet above Deer Creek, along a small shelf in a dense thicket of trees just below the rim of the canyon. Here they constructed two tiny villages. Their once spacious territory had been reduced to two small tracts along Deer Creek, each about three miles long. Though not far from a homestead, it was nearly inaccessible and all but invisible to the outside world. It was there in 1894 that the Yahi made their last stand. Shortly after that, the young man in the group died, leaving only four. Over time the two elders became less and less active, leaving Ishi and his sister to do most of the food gathering. Here they managed to live undetected, until things fell apart in 1908.

The Oro Light and Power Company planned to construct a hydroelectric dam upstream of the village on Deer Creek and sent a survey party to assess the area. On November 9, two surveyors walking along Deer Creek surprised Ishi while he was fishing. He gestured at them to leave, which they did in a mixture of excitement and disbelief. Back at camp, their story was met with skepticism, but that vanished two days later when the survey party began clearing a line along the canyon and stumbled onto the village. Ishi was not present; his sister and uncle took flight and were never seen again. Ishi's mother lay on the ground, covered in hides, helpless and immobile. She appeared to be paralyzed. The men tried to talk to her but to no avail. They discussed taking her with them but decided against it. Unfortunately, they helped themselves to as many possessions as they could carry, perhaps not realizing that those souvenirs—bows and arrows, snares, tool kits—were essential items to the Yahi. The men returned the next day, only to find the old woman gone and the village deserted.

The discovery of the village made the papers, and the news reached Professor Waterman in Berkeley. Waterman was keenly interested, so much so that he explored the area for a month in the fall of 1909, hoping to locate survivors. He found no one, just the abandoned village. It is left to Ishi to reveal the fates of the others following the discovery of the village. Of his sister and uncle, he never saw them again and was convinced they both died while trying to escape, perhaps drowning in Deer Creek. As for his mother, he was the one who removed her from the village after the survey party blundered and plundered through. She died soon after, and it was with great reluctance that he mentioned her fate.

For the past thirty-six years, Ishi had lived with a small and ever-dwindling number of people, living like fugitives in the era of concealment. With the passing of his mother, Ishi would enter the era of solitude. From the time of her death in November 1908 until his sojourn to the corral outside Oroville on August 29, 1911, he was completely and utterly alone, alone in a way none of us will ever face or can even imagine. He was not merely the last of his family; he was the last of his tribe, culture, and language. He had reason to believe that he was the last Native American as well, for it is doubtful that the Yahi had had contact with any other tribes since Ishi's boyhood in the 1860s. True, Ishi knew he was not the last person on Earth; he could see the comings and goings of settlers in the distance, but that had to be of cold consolation to him, for a lifetime of intermittent experience with whites led him to believe that they were a cruel and murderous race.

Here's a question: if you could sit down and talk for a while with one historic figure, who would it be? Christ? Da Vinci? Einstein? Lincoln? Mozart? Darwin? A tough choice, but given the opportunity, I might just choose Ishi. Sure, I'd like to know how to construct a durable shelter without modern tools and which plants to seek out to soothe a sore throat, but such questions can be answered by a multitude of natives. No, the questions I'd like to ask Ishi are two personal ones that only he can answer. The first is, how? How did he make it as the sole survivor, day after day, night after night, for almost three years once his tiny tribe had been discovered? What toll does loneliness extract from the psyche and soul? What happens to the human spirit when the future offers nothing but more isolation? What's it like going to sleep at night alone and waking that way the following day? What must it be like to never hear your language again or to never speak to anyone, evermore? As much as I'd like to hear his answers, I'm not sure I'd be comfortable asking such pointed questions any more than he'd be eager to answer them. At any rate, nowhere did I find any reference to or discussion of the time Ishi spent alone. Theodora Kroeber wrote that speaking of past tragedies left Ishi depressed. Perhaps some insights are not worth pursuing.

The second question is, why? Why, after having endured almost three years of absolute isolation, did Ishi so uncharacteristically walk away from the only land and life he had ever known and risk death traveling to the lowlands and the realm of whites, a group that had only brought misery to his people? Unlike the question of how, the question of why has received a fair amount of attention but not by Ishi. If he ever confided that to anyone, I am unaware of it. So it has been left to others to speculate why Ishi took the drastic step of ending both the era of concealment and the era of solitude with one fateful journey. Some say he did it because he was starving, and a photo taken of him on the day of his capture shows a gaunt, emaciated man. Others suggested that he was despondent, that he undertook his perilous quest because he no longer cared whether or not he lived or died. That same photo reveals a man with hair singed short, a customary practice for one in mourning. So, hunger and despair, both plausible reasons. But I hold my own belief about why Ishi suddenly walked away from his world, a belief formed after reading the words of Theodora Kroeber following Ishi's entry into white civilization. She noted that despite his fear of crowds, he much preferred companionship over solitude. He made friends easily and always had a smile for anyone who spoke to him. He loved to joke, tease, and be teased, and to talk, despite the language barrier. Most of all, he loved to give things, objects he made himself, to his friends. Representatives from the Bureau of Indian Affairs reminded Ishi on several occasions that he had a say in his future. He was not obligated to remain at the museum beholden to the professors; he could have moved to a reservation where he could be among other Native Americans. They also informed him that he was free to simply return to his ancestral home along Deer Creek, where he need not live like a refugee anymore. Yet he emphatically chose to stay with the professors, among his newfound friends, despite the wide cultural gap.'

Finally, Theodora Kroeber offers this nugget of insight into Ishi's personality that carries the weight of an anvil: "For whatever personal or custom-ingrained reasons, there attached to parting a significance best not accorded a recognition in words."

So Ishi, it seems, also had trouble saying good-bye.

Maybe he wandered down out of hunger; perhaps he did so because he lost the will to live. I'm not buying either of those. I think Ishi was just lonely.

July 2008

Home Range

When Badgers Indicate Quality of Life

I STILL HAVE the first field guide I was ever given: *A Field Guide to the Mammals* by Burt and Grossenheider, which I received on my seventh birthday. I was a bit young for that book—the scientific names seemed unnecessary and unpronounceable, I had no clue what a gestation period was, and the section on dental formulae was so far over my head it may as well have been written in Sanskrit. Yet I loved that book anyway. Now it's dog-eared, and its yellowed pages emit the stuffy odor that only an old book can. To my young mind, that book represented something beyond technical knowledge: it was a revelation as hallowed as any historic or religious document, for it had range maps. I may have struggled with the text, but those maps were something visual. They represented divine knowledge, for they revealed where the wild things are.

I grew to love field guides. My favorites are those of mammals, reptiles and amphibians, and birds. Besides range maps, field guides also provide information on diet, breeding, and habitat use. A comprehensive field guide might also contain insight into home range.

The concept of home range doesn't apply to all species. Home range, as I use the term, is comprised of the area in which an animal spends its adult life. It may not defend this territory, and it may share the area with others of its kind. Species whose social structure consists of herds or colonies are thus exempt from this interpretation of home range. Further, this concept of home range applies only to species that are nonmigratory. Home range may fluctuate within a species, with males often assuming larger ranges than females. Areas of superb habitat may allow members of a species to have smaller home ranges if food is abundant. In such locations, a bobcat might have a home range as small as one square mile; in less hospitable habitat, that territory may exceed forty square miles. In general, carnivores require larger home ranges than herbivores, and predators need more real estate than prey. A second rule of thumb: the larger the animal, the larger the home range.

Yet there are exceptions. Wolverines are creatures of modest size. However, they possess one of the most extensive home ranges of any animal in the North America. Wolverines, of course, do not inhabit the Diablo Range, but badgers do, and they provide another example of an animal inhabiting a disproportionately large home range.

Whisky Flat, where I make my home, is not flat like a valley. It's more like a trough between two ridges, a series of small rises sprinkled with oaks. One of my first journeys into the flat took place on a winter afternoon in 1992. As I walked along a dirt road, I noticed a pair of coyotes atop a rise a quarter mile beyond. They were walking away, descending into an arroyo. As soon as they vanished from sight, I skirted the hillside, hoping to intercept the pair from the other side of the ravine. As I reached the crest of the hill, I peered downward, where they stood seventy-five yards away. Cautiously, I made my way downslope, taking advantage of a cluster of gooseberry bushes and buckeyes. At the bottom of the canyon, there was no cover to conceal me, so I stood still and watched through binoculars. They were poised in front of a ground squirrel burrow. Both had their backs to me. The smaller one was digging at the burrow entrance, while the larger stood ten feet behind. Yet the smaller animal was not the second coyote, but rather a badger, the first I'd seen in the Diablo Range. I had read accounts of such coyote/badger interactions, but never thought I would have the luck to witness one. Suddenly, a warning bark reverberated through the canyon, uttered by another coyote on the opposite slope. The first coyote bolted, leaving only the badger, thoroughly engrossed in its toilings, behind. After the coyotes left, I approached the badger, moving ever closer, quietly and slowly, waiting for the badger to react. After ten minutes of stalking, I stood ten feet behind the badger, which was still digging away. Then, abruptly, it abandoned the effort and began ambling down the canyon, following a game trail. I followed behind. If it knew I was there, it didn't show it. It continued on at a leisurely pace for two hundred yards, at which point the canyon becomes steeper and wooded. Approaching another burrow, the badger stopped and began digging. I stood right behind the badger as it dug. By now I was fascinated—was the badger truly oblivious to my presence, or was it merely ignoring me? I cleared my throat to speak (what do you say to a badger?), and as I did so, it wheeled around and bared a set of small but sharp white teeth, emitting a growl that I did not think possible from a fifteen-pound animal. I backed away and let it dig in peace.

Two years later, I was walking across the flat on a sunny March afternoon, just east of that same canyon. I noticed a squat, brown shape making its way through the green grass and saw that it was a badger—maybe even the same animal from the earlier encounter. This time, I had my camera, but the badger noticed me and loped off toward a rock outcrop, where it entered a fissure. I followed, climbing to the top of the outcrop, intending to wait the badger out. Half an hour later, the badger emerged, and I was able to take some memorable photographs of an animal I'd only encountered twice in my life.

Sometime between those two sightings I bought a parcel of land in the flat. Perhaps not coincidentally, it included the area of the first badger encounter. At that point in life, I was in the throes of some existential angst that I can best sum up like this: I needed to live in the country. I wasn't just fed up with the everyday grind, the hordes of people, and the overcrowded roads in an ever-increasing urban and suburban landscape. I was beyond frustrated with the ceaseless drone of engines, white noise, and the general din that pervades the soundscape. And while I'll own up to a heady share of asocial tendencies, it was more than just wanting to get away from it all that drove me toward the hills. My exodus went beyond wanting to drop out of the rat race. After all, I wasn't merely getting away from something—I was being pulled somewhere. I wanted to live in the *real* real world, where the wild things are.

In that light, I had no idea how truly out of step I was. I got an inkling of this whenever someone assured me that the property was a "good investment." An investment? I found the idea of regarding land in such terms as offensive as marrying for money. I was also struck by the number of people who truly believed that my land lie in the middle of nowhere, when to me it was as close to town as I could tolerate.

I needed to live where natural processes still predominate, where wild things come and go of their own accord. Aldo Leopold said there are those who can live without wild things and those who cannot. It's important to me to know that I can look out my window and watch a bobcat saunter by or look up in the sky and see a golden eagle overhead. I may never glimpse a mountain lion from my house or watch a condor glide past while riding a thermal. Yet just knowing that such things are possible, that they can still happen here, confers to my property a value that cannot be translated into dollars. I wouldn't trade my fifty-five acres for a mansion in Los Altos, because something of incalculable value, the wild, would be missing. Badgers require a large home range. So do I.

Badgers are also solitary. Some look at isolation and misinterpret it. Solitude and loneliness, after all, are hardly the same. Given the right circumstances, the former can be exhilarating, whereas the latter can be felt acutely in the midst of a crowd. Being physically distant from others has never been difficult for me, and it pales in comparison to feeling alienated with a different set of values. It was a sobering experience to realize that many things important to me—wildlands diminishing, species disappearing—mean so little to so many others. At times I feel hopelessly out of touch, even in my home range. I've never questioned my values; rather, I wonder why more people don't feel like I do.

Maybe, in order for landscapes and species to matter to people, they must first develop a connection with them, and I'm afraid that we, as a culture, have become increasingly disassociated with such things, particularly during childhood, when so many of our strongest bonds are forged. In California this situation is compounded by the fact that so much of the state's population is transient. Californians seem to move a lot, bouncing from one community to the next as opportunities dictate. Such restlessness doesn't lend itself to making a connection to the land, and while one can develop an affinity for an area in a short time, the odds of such a bond forming are greater when people set roots down and finally call a place home. Today when people develop a sense of place, it's likely to be restricted to their neighborhood rather than any natural lands, which are receding with each passing year. I'm dismayed by the lack of familiarity people have with their surroundings—the kinds of animals that roam the canyons, the types of trees that dot the hillsides. That doesn't bode well for the future. In order for people to protect something, they must first value it, and you cannot value what you do not know.

Over a dozen years passed between the time I purchased the property and the time I settled in, and during that interlude, things had changed. I hoped to raise my sons there, but by the time I could afford to build, they were grown. I pictured us exploring our land, living a lifestyle removed from the pace of the homogenized suburbs. Yet that never transpired. I was reminded of that recently on a rainy afternoon.

I keep a box full of mementos tucked in a closet. Perhaps you have a similar repository. It's filled with letters, cards, newspaper clippings, old photographs, and the like—an attempt, I suppose, to hold on to things, a lifetime's worth of remembrances crammed inside an apple box. While ruffling through its contents, I came upon a sheet of binder paper. It held an illustration featuring the wonderfully crude art that only crayons and a six-year-old hand can produce. In the drawing, there's the sun, a few clouds, a tree, a hole in the ground, a badger, my son, and me. Everything is labeled. I'm pointing toward the badger, showing it to my son, and we're both smiling.

I stared long and hard at that drawing. I didn't remember it, although I must have seen it before. Or maybe I blocked it out, for the idyllic events in the drawing never took place. There was no shared badger sighting, not enough hikes, and too damned few smiles. That time had passed; his childhood had vanished. "The Cat's in the Cradle," writ large and in real life. It was at that moment that solitude and loneliness became one, and my home felt like merely a house instead.

The countryside had changed as well. Several houses had been erected and dotted the flat, along with gravel roads, power poles, and barbed wire. Though hardly suburbia, the flat seemed less wild. The barking of dogs competed with the yipping of coyotes; the drone of engines drowned out the sound of the wind. And it only promised to get worse. Of course, I had a share of complicity in all of this, and I can at least be grateful that my neighbors are salt-of-the-earth types. Still, shortly after arriving, I began to feel hemmed in, longing for more space. Leave it to me to feel crowded in the middle of nowhere. While talking with a neighbor, we were discussing wildlife when the topic of badgers came up. She mentioned that she had never seen one and wondered if perhaps her dogs had driven them from the area. I hadn't seen one either in over a decade. Perhaps we all drove them away.

I was also aware that the three outlying cities—Gilroy, Hollister, and Los Banos—though all about thirty miles away, were only going to get bigger, and the very real possibility that Pacheco Pass would be selected as the site through which a high-speed rail track would be constructed posed yet another threat to the land. I began to think that maybe I should find some other place to settle, but where? Certainly not in California—land prices are obscene. Maybe Oregon, Colorado, or Montana. Perhaps northern New Mexico. Those areas held their seductive charms, and while it would be exciting to learn the flora and fauna of a new region, I wasn't looking forward to being an outsider. California expatriates are about as desired in other Western states as social diseases and IRS agents. The welcome wagon would be sparse.

Such thoughts were floating through my mind late one April afternoon. I was fixing dinner, staring out the kitchen window toward the bird feeder twenty feet beyond in a field of rapidly drying grasses. From out of nowhere a squat, dark shape emerged from the tall grass and headed toward the base of the feeder. A badger, the first I had seen in a dozen years, passed by just long enough to sniff the base of the pole. Maybe it had caught the scent of the ground squirrels that feed on sunflower seeds shaken loose by the wind. I watched it as it drifted back into a sea of green and gold grass, and for the first time in a while, I felt like I was home.

Acknowledgments

A NUMBER OF people were instrumental in making this collection of essays a reality.

Barbara Dean and Maureen Gately of Island Press were most generous with their time and provided useful insight and advice regarding the publishing world.

A number of friends read sections of the book prior to publication. I appreciated their advice, opinions, and comments, and their words of encouragement were invaluable at a time when I was considering walking away from the project entirely. To Jess Auer, Cynthia Boche, Julie Boudreau, Barry Breckling, Winslow Briggs, Pete Collom, Sue DeKalb, Lee Dittmann, Shelley Francis, Daniel George, Earl Gonsolin, Teddy Goodrich, Allison Harness, Mason Hyland, Verna Jigour, Jennie Jones-Scherbinski, Neil Keung, Brian McInerney, Richard Neidhardt, Sean Parnell, Bob Patrie, Mike Powers, Dawn Roh, Dan Ryan, Don Savant, Lee Sims, David States, Donna Thomas, Peter Thomas, Libby Vincent, Alacia Welch, Rachel Wolstenholme, and Rebecca Wren, thanks for going above and beyond the call of duty and breathing life back into this book.

Over the years, I've been fortunate to have learned from a number of teachers in both classroom and field settings. To Gavin Emmons, Jesse Grantham, Adam Grimes, Dr. Jim Halfpenny, Paul Johnson, Dr. Charles Jonkel, Dr. Susan Lambrecht, Rey Morales, Mitchell Mulks, Scott Scherbinski, Dr. Jerry Smith, Dr. Pete Trenham, Professor Stephanie Trewhitt, Ralph Waldt, and Dr. Mike Westphal, thank you for your commitment to protecting the natural world and your willingness to share with me your knowledge and expertise. I hope some of it has sunk in.

I have benefited from interacting with a number of students and faculty members at both Gavilan Community College and San Jose State University, as well as volunteers and staff at Henry W. Coe State Park and Pinnacles National Park, especially the condor crew.

Tracie Cone and Anna Marie dos Remedios, former editors of *The Pinnacle*, a weekly newspaper based in Hollister, deserve recognition for their laudable efforts to alert readers to numerous environmental blunders being perpetrated in their community.

I also wish to thank several childhood friends for the companionship and shared adventures—Kimble Gause, Brock Gause, Walter Hawkins, Peter Hawkins, and Todd Saracco.

Kate Woods was instrumental in getting these words to print. During her tenure as an environmental reporter for *The Pinnacle*, she was a source of information and inspiration. Her willingness to allow me access to her family's property and the legal and scientific documents concerning San Carlos Creek allowed the essay "A Tale of Two Creeks" to be much better than it otherwise would have been. From the first essay to the last, she was unwavering in her support and enthusiasm for the book.

Finally, I thank my family: my grandparents, Joey and Florence Franco; my parents, Lee and Joy Belli; my brother, Leland; my sisters, Joylyn and Lizabeth; my aunt Kathleen Jalalian; her daughters, Joey and Valy; and my best friends, my sons Joe and Ryan.

Author Biography

Joseph Belli has hiked and explored the Diablo Range extensively since the 1970s. He holds a master of science in conservation biology and has worked as a wildlife biologist for the National Park Service. He has conducted surveys for the Bureau of Land Management and California State Parks, and has worked with California Condors, California Red-legged Frogs, and other sensitive or endangered species.

Belli's writing has appeared in *High Country News*, *The Ponderosa*, and *The Wonder of It All*, a collection of stories from National Park Service employees and volunteers. He lives on a rural property in the Diablo Range.

Made in the USA
Columbia, SC
29 October 2024